D0065626

Advance praise for Richard D. Lewis', *The Cultural Imperative: Global Trends in the 21ˢᵗ Century*

Richard Lewis' approach has been an absolutely marvelous way to get my students to appreciate how and why cultures are different, and how to benefit from this. It is great to see him now turn his practical wisdom to the *future* in such a spellbinding, readable and timely new book. A real imperative for understanding cultural trends!

—Ulla Ladau-Harjulin, Principal Lecturer FRSA
Swedish School of Economics and Business Administration
Helsinki, Finland

A very revealing and sometimes shocking vision of confrontation and/or cooperation of world cultures in the twenty-first century. A must-read in MBA programs and to be highly recommended to everyone involved with the study or practice of cross-cultural interaction and management.

—Peter N. Shikhirev, Ph.D., Director
Centre for Social and Psychological Studies
Graduate School of International Business
Academy of National Economy by the Government of Russia

Richard Lewis has developed a rich and powerful tool that serves to disseminate cultural complexities, which allows for leveraging opportunities and minimizing threats. Such issues would be paramount in any international business situation.... A global mindset is imperative for us all.

—Marta Szabo White, Ph.D., Assistant Professor
J. Mack Robinson School of Business, Georgia State University

[The] thesis of the book is the argument linking cultural dimensions of nations to national competitive advantage. Richard Lewis develops a simple yet convincing model for understanding the historical evolution of the major national cultures and their juxtaposition to the rest of the world today. The value of [*The Cultural Imperative*] is its new way of weaving a new explanation for considering the role of national cultures, language development, national aspirations and history in understanding the sources of future conflicts relating to global economic development.

—Arie Y. Lewin, Professor
Director, Center for International Business Education and Research
The Fuqua School of Business, Duke University

Richard Lewis' extensive experience and knowledge of many cultures provides rich anecdotes coupled with interesting insights and opinions. The book stimulates personal reflection on the continuing importance of culture in a globalizing economy.

—Susan Schneider, Chaired Professor of Human Resource Management
HEC University of Geneva

The Cultural Imperative

Other works by Richard D. Lewis

Books

English You Need (1958) Lisbon: Publitur

Suomen Kirja (1958) Helsinki: Berlitz

Vous-souvenez-vous (1959) Lisbon: Publitur

Reading for Adults (1968) London: Longman

Travelling Abroad (1971) Lisbon: Libraria Francisco Franco

Cambridge 2000 (1971) Lisbon: Linguasonica

The Billingers (1976) London: Riversdown Publications

Finland, Cultural Lone Wolf (1993) Helsinki: Otava

When Cultures Collide (1996) London: Nicholas Brealey

Memoirs of a Linguist: The Road from Wigan Pier (1998) Winchester: Transcreen Publications

Cross-Cultural Communication: A Visual Approach (1999) Winchester: Transcreen Publications

Humour across Frontiers (in preparation)

Multimedia

Englantia Hauskaa ja Helppoa (film series) (1961) Finnish Television

Walter and Connie (film series) (1962) London: BBC

Transcreen English (video series) (1988) Winchester: Transcreen Educational Films

Gulliver: Performing Successfully Across Cultures (1999) (CD-ROM and intranet training tool) London: Richard Lewis Communications

National Cultural Profiles and Cultural Assessment (2002) (Web-based support system) London: CultureActive

Richard D. Lewis is available as a cross-cultural trainer, consultant, speaker, and language specialist in the subjects covered in this book. He can be reached at:

Richard Lewis Communications
Riversdown House
Warnford, Hampshire SO32 3LH
United Kingdom
e-mail: info@crossculture.com
phone: +44-1962-77-1111
fax: +44-1962-77-1050
Website: www.crossculture.com

The Cultural Imperative

Global Trends in the 21st Century

Richard D. Lewis

First published by Intercultural Press. For information contact:

Intercultural Press, Inc.
PO Box 700
Yarmouth, Maine 04096 USA
Tel: 207-846-5168
Fax: 207-846-5181
www.interculturalpress.com

Nicholas Brealey Publishing
3–5 Spafield Street
London, EC1R 4QB, UK
Tel: +44-207-239-0360
Fax: +44-207-239-0370
www.nbrealey-books.com

© 2003 by Richard Lewis

Design and production interior and cover: Patty J. Topel
Cover Art: Painting titled "Cross Culture" by Richard D. Lewis

All rights reserved. No part of this publication may be reproduced in any manner whatsoever without written permission from the publisher, except in the case of brief quotations embodied in critical articles or reviews.

Printed in Finland

06   05   04   03   02   1   2   3   4   5

Library of Congress Cataloging-in-Publication Data
Lewis, Richard D.
    The cultural imperative: global trends in the 21st century/ Richard D. Lewis
        p.   cm.
    Includes bibliographical references and index.
    ISBN 1-877864-98-6
    1. Culture.   2. Cross-cultural orientation.   3. Globalization.   4. Religion and culture.   5. Cognition and culture.
I. Title.
    GN357.L49 2002
    306—dc21
                                        2002075943

To Serge Morette and Michel Tissier, two splendid Frenchmen

One ship drives east and another drives west
With the self-same winds that blow;
'Tis the set of the sails
And not the gales
That tells them the way to go.
Like the winds of the sea are the winds of fate
As we voyage along through life;
'Tis the set of the soul
That decides its goal
And not the calm or the strife.

—*World Voices*
Ella Wheeler Wilcox
New York: Hearst's International Library Company, 1916

Table of Contents

Preface   xi

Acknowledgments   xvii

Introduction: Genetic, Economic, and Cultural Determinism   xix

Chapter 1

From 2,000,000 B.C. to A.D. 2000: The Roots and Routes of Culture

From 2,000,000 B.C. to A.D. 2000: The Roots and Routes of Culture 1

Incomplete Version of History   1

Culture—Genetics or Cultural Programming?   3

Roots and Routes   7

Chapter 2

Culture and Climate

Culture and Climate 13

East Side Story   14

The Effects of Climate   16
Summary   26

Chapter 3

Culture and Religion 29

Influences on the Religion-Culture Connection   32
Islam   37
Hinduism   44
Judaism   47
Jainism   49
Sikhism   50
Buddhism   51
Shinto   53
Christianity   55
The Globalization of Religion   60

Chapter 4

Cross-Century Worldviews 65

The Categorization of Cultures   67
Intercategory Comparisons   76

Chapter 5

Cultural Spectacles 91

The English and the French   92
The Germans and the Italians   99
The Americans and the Japanese   106
Conclusion   112

Chapter 6

Cultural Black Holes 115

Cultural Black Holes, by Country   121
State-Induced Black Holes   126

Chapter 7

Cognitive Processes 129

Language and Thought   132
Collective and Individual Thought Processes   137
Logic, Logic, Logic   144
Concept of Time   147
Changes in Cognitive Habits?   149

Chapter 8

The Pacific Rim: The Fourth Cultural Ecology 157

Riverine Cultural Ecology   159
Mediterranean Cultural Ecology   160
Atlantic Cultural Ecology   161
Pacific Rim Cultural Ecology   162

Chapter 9

The China Phenomenon 167

China's Achievements   168
China's Decline from Preeminence   170
Phenomenal China   177
Enduring Chinese Cultural Traits   180
Conclusion   187

Chapter 10

Americanization versus Asianization 191

The American Era   191
The Japanese Model   192
Asianizing   193
Masculinity and the Western Intellectual Tradition   195
East and West   198
The Asian Model   204
Summary   220

Chapter 11

Culture and Globalization...223

    Globalization   224
    Information Technology and Globalization   227
    The Standardization of Culture Itself   229
    The Answer: Cultural Adaptation   236

Chapter 12

Empires—Past, Present, and Future.....................................245

    Cultural Traits as Predictors of the Future   246
    Past Empires   248
    Impending Chinese Dominance   249
    Future Alliances: Who Wants China?   251
    Most Nation-States to Survive   257

Conclusion 261

Epilogue

After September 11 271

    The Rise of Islam   272
    The Moorish Legacy in Europe   274
    The Crusades   277
    Coexistence   278
    Islam's Own Problems   282
    What the West Has to Learn   286
    Whither the West?   291

Appendix A: Cultural Categorization Characteristics   295
Appendix B: Leadership Test   299
Appendix C: National Traits   307
Appendix D: National Communication Styles   311
Glossary   313
Bibliography   319
About the Author   323
Index   325

Preface

This book is being published at a time when cross-culturalists are engaged in lively debate about the future course of humankind in the early twenty-first century. In an age of developing globalization, questions are being raised about the importance of cultural differences that will surely impede rapid progress toward standardization of rules and uniform acceptance of mutual goals. With the increasing internationalization of trade and the ubiquitous presence of the Internet, are cultural differences on the decline? Or are the roots of culture so varied that worldwide convergence can never succeed? Will considerations of gender, which is growing in importance, outweigh those of national characteristics? How can we classify cultures with any accuracy or neatness? Is it possible to cluster cultures, not only for academic convenience but to make standardized management approaches viable?

As for predicting shifts and alliances among nations, will these occur along civilizational fault lines, as Samuel Huntington prophesies, or will national traits continue to dominate? Did history really end in 1989, as Francis Fukuyama suggested? Was the disintegration of the Soviet Union—so momentous in Europe—anything more than a mere blip in the eyes of peoples possessing unbroken cultures of two thousand to five thousand years, as is the case of the Japanese, Indians, and Chinese? Are cross-cultural universals, programmed into us by evolution, in danger of being eliminated by genetic engineering? Will humanity (not the same as the human race) be destroyed by biotechnology? To what extent have the gloomy predictions of George Orwell and Aldous Huxley been realized?

Addressing some of these issues in this book, I have tended to side with writers who stress the slowness of cultural change (Zeldin, Hofstede, Diamond) and, as I state in later chapters, I remain firm in my belief that cultural core beliefs are so deeply embedded that they will resist most forms of infiltration or erosion in the present century. Cultural adherence is a proven survival technique; what solid alternatives have up to now been offered?

The classification or categorization of cultures is an intriguing subject which has tested the imagination as well as powers of observation and analysis of several gurus in the twentieth century, beginning with Edward T. Hall, Florence R. Kluckhohn, and Fred L. Strodtbeck. The lengthy study and findings of Geert Hofstede are currently being challenged by two Norwegian professors, Paul Gooderham and Odd Nordhag. They maintain that Hofstede's results are suspect not only by being outdated but because the original data was obtained from the predominantly male employees of one large multinational (IBM).

The professors' own survey was carried out among 1,335 students at eleven different European business schools. Their main conclusion was that there is a significant convergence of values across Europe and that gender differences are perhaps more important than national ones.

In my own observations and research, I note few examples of serious convergence in European (and even less so, Asian) values. Although testing more than two decades after Hofstede, Gooderham and Nordhag might have chosen a better set of respondents than MBA students aged nineteen to twenty-six. Their results were skewed by uneven Protestant/Catholic respondents as well as their young age and age group mentality.

The Norwegians' comments on the growing importance of gender difference are, in my opinion, certainly valid, and I touch on this phenomenon in the final chapters of this work. They must be aware, however, that gender difference is culturally based and varies from country to country.

My own model for categorizing cultures that I introduce you to in this book is based not only on tens of thousands of assessments carried out among sixty-three nationalities over a forty-year period but on real-time observation and interaction inside companies in which I have worked in more than a dozen countries and over a protracted period, which enables me to draw conclusions not just from what people say in surveys but also by observing their actions in the workplace.

Looking at the predictions—economic, political, scientific, and civilizational—made by Huntington, Fukuyama, Robert Samuelsson, John Naisbett, and others—I have chosen to limit my essay into futurology to pin-pointing certain trends that are culture- or history-based. I prefer to look "back to the future" to see how major civilizations have behaved for centuries rather than take a chance with the predictions of economists and political

analysts. I suspect many of their forecasts will join the collection
I offer in chapter 12.

I believe the prophets of doom will eventually be caught out.
The world did not end in the year 1000, and history, as Fukuyama
admits, soon resumed after he said it had ended. I believe nearly
all he said in his fine book *Trust: The Social Virtues and the Creation of Prosperity* (1996), but I cannot share his gloom about
the outcome of biotechnology. It will take more than chemists
and pills to kill the human soul. Neither can I subscribe to
Huntington's views on the likelihood of major conflagrations
between China, Islamic countries, Russia, and the West. I share
Zeldin's optimism about the resilience and durability of humanity, its unstoppable impact on our planet, and the vast array of
options open to us in the Information Age. I recognize the strength
of Diamond's thesis that human progress, including its cultural
aspects, has been rooted in avoidance of disease and strategies of
food production. If the world currently has two great ills, they
are AIDS and famine, not political issues.

I can only dabble in twenty-first century trends—that is haz-
ardous enough—but I share the positive outlook of Theodore
Zeldin and Jared Diamond and believe that humanity knows how
to save itself and that *culture knows the way*. World War I started
almost accidentally, and World War II was initiated by a one-off
Austrian corporal. Governments are more careful now, as has been
shown by fifty years of peace among the most lethally armed
major powers in human history. As I explain in the Epilogue, the
positive side of Islam has been underestimated. Mighty China's
bark is worse than its bite, and the West has less to fear than
pundits think. India and Japan have everything to gain from peace
and trade, and Russia is heading for the European Union (EU).
Above all, I see a shining beacon of Western versatility. Errors,

lack of unity, stupidities, double standards, yes, but the eventual cultural alliance of the United States of Europe and North America will possess an in-depth organizational and institutional richness and vibrancy that will resist any final erosion.

—R.D.L.

Acknowledgments

Just as I acknowledged the influence of Glen Fisher, David Rearwin, John Paul Fieg, Margaret Nydell, Joy Hendry, and Yale Richmond in various chapters of *When Cultures Collide*, I have again relied on their experience in some of my remarks in the present work. Since then I have been impressed by the insights of Meirion and Susie Harries in their writings about Japan, have drawn inspiration from the impeccable analysis of Harry Irwin in his book, *Communicating with Asia*, and finally have leaned heavily on Jared Diamond's awesome history of mankind in *Guns, Germs and Steel*.

Eminent culturalists such as Professor Arie Lewin of Duke University, Professor James Téboul of INSEAD, Professor Susan Schneider of the University of Geneva, and Professor Peter

Shikhirev of the Graduate School of International Business, Moscow have given me valuable advice. Marta Szabo White of Georgia State University, Ulla Ladau-Harjulin of the Swedish School of Economics, Helsinki, and Jeff Russell of the Fuqua School of Business have also been unstinting in their encouragement.

Some of my remarks about Internet culture reflect points made in an excellent lecture on the subject by Professor Leif Sjöblom of IMD.

I would also like to thank Judy Carl-Hendrick, Managing Editor, for her thoughtful and meticulous editing of the book, Toby Frank, President, for her guidance and support, and the rest of the staff at Intercultural Press.

Finally, as author, I take full responsibility for any and all errors that may have inadvertently found their way into the book.

Introduction

Genetic, Economic, and Cultural Determinism

The influence of different cultures on human behavior has been considerably downplayed since positivism substantially took over the social sciences in American universities in the 1950s. Cultural diversity (cross-cultural issues) was depicted as a "soft" subject—based on uncertain knowledge, unscientific, anecdotal, itself culture-bound. The study of culture depended on historical evidence and reasoning that might be ambiguous, era-affected, and hard to unearth.

It became fashionable, in the closed world of academia, to seek an explanation of human behavior in two more "reliable" theories: genetic determinism and economic determinism. The dictionary defines *determinism* as "the philosophical doctrine that every event, act, and decision is the inevitable consequence of antecedents, such as physical, psychological, or environmental conditions *that are independent of the human will.*"

To begin with the former, during the last decades of the twentieth century *Homo sapiens* was assumed to possess over 100,000 genes—in fact some quoted precisely a figure of 142,634. This was considered a sufficiently large number to account for the great complexity of human characteristics around the globe as opposed to the relative physiological (and psychological) simplicity of other living creatures. In other words, the complicated variety of human comportment could be explained by the richness of our genetic makeup, unmatched by any other species.

Then on February 12, 2001 (Darwin's birthday, incidentally), genetic determinism received a deadly blow. Two groups of researchers released the formal report of data for the human genome, revealing that we humans possess only around 30,000 genes, merely twice as many as the fruit fly (approximately 14,000). Furthermore, all humans, with all their evident diversity, were found to share 99.9 percent of their genes. According to this finding, all human beings should be extraordinarily alike, if genetic code determines behavior.

But we are not alike. We will see in chapter 1 that certain cultural characteristics are universal, such as love of one's children, a desire to belong to a group, the wish for acceptance or popularity, gratitude for help, anger at injustice, and a strong survival instinct. Such commonalities are, however, vastly outnumbered by hundreds of visible and invisible differences of national or regional origin, even between close neighbors such as Americans and Canadians or Norwegians and Swedes. Whence, then, the diversity?

The economic determinists—liberal and Marxist thinkers,

market economists—had an answer: man is an economic animal. According to this theory, economic change generates social change and political progress. Market economists, especially in the period from 1950 to 1980, saw economic theory as dominating the "antecedents" and "environmental conditions." Culture was hardly mentioned—it might have been considered racist or, at best, ephemeral.

When the world was decolonized in the mid-twentieth century, backwardness was considered a product of colonialism. The former colonies that possessed strong indigenous cultures buttressed by written languages and written knowledge progressed, according to the economists' theories, in a relatively satisfactory manner: the Indian subcontinent, Singapore, Malaysia, Hong Kong, and the former European and U.S. enclaves in Shanghai have all gone forward. Indonesia, Myanmar, and the Indo-Chinese trio—Vietnam, Cambodia, Laos—have development problems, but their cultures and future orientation remain intact. It has been a different story in Africa.

The Africans had their historical cultures all right, with complex codes of ritual and well-established core beliefs and values, not to mention substantial artistic sophistication. Unfortunately, Africans lacked, in almost all areas, written language and written knowledge. The sudden dismantling of the colonial system and the rapid departure of the colonizers left Africans in a cultural wasteland. Because of deficiencies in the transition mechanism, Africans had little familiarity with Western cultural and administrative strengths; failure by the West to sufficiently encourage the Africans to resuscitate their own rich (but tenuously oral) cultures left them floundering. Social and political violence and chaos ensued, economies collapsed, and educational systems and public health rapidly deteriorated and were quickly devastated. Incompetence, expedient exploitation, commerce in weapons, agricultural ruin—all run unchecked up to the present day. The absence of a strong, culturally based society is a very serious matter.

This leads us to a third recourse: cultural determinism. Lawrence Harrison and Samuel Huntington in *Culture Matters: How Values Shape Human Progress* (2001) reiterate assertions made by Edward T. Hall, Geert Hofstede, and me in my earlier work *When Cultures Collide* (2000)—namely, *culture counts most in economic development* (not the other way around).

How can theorists or earnest researchers remain blind to the ubiquitous reality of culture-bound behavior? Can one not point to a cultural development emerging from Classical Greece and Rome, the Christian religion, and the European Renaissance without being accused of denigrating other cultures? Can the momentum of 2000 years be stopped that easily? Unbroken cultures have strongly defined modern humanity in China, India, France, Spain, Japan, and elsewhere. Cultures are especially resilient at the national level. Although culture is passed on to individuals from a number of sources—parents, peers, social institutions— *governments* have a vested interest in their citizens sharing cultural values in order to reduce the potential for cultural conflicts. Government-directed social institutions, such as schools, are therefore particularly important in transmitting culture. Large numbers of young, receptive students are introduced simultaneously to the same information, values, and concepts, conveyed in the same language. History is taught thoughtfully, often being "remodeled" in a concern for the consolidation of shared values and myths. Figures such as Napoleon, George Washington, Queen Elizabeth I, and Abraham Lincoln are depicted, often in a favorable light, as part of the cultural heritage. The significance of controlled public schooling is evident when there may be societal disagreement as to how to treat certain historical events.

Controversial issues such as wars, monarchies, revolutions, and past presidents can be presented in many different lights. Such interpretations are all part of the ongoing process of defining a national identity and refining a nation's culture.

To those who contest the importance of the concept of national identity, I address the following questions:

- Why are Americans obsessed with individual advancement, popularity, material success, and (especially) money?
- Why are the Japanese and Chinese invariably obsessed with the concept of "face"?
- Do the Swiss and Germans have the same attitude about time as Mexicans do?
- Do the Chinese and Indians eat in the same manner?
- Do Australians and Germans share the same attitude toward authority?
- Do the French and Americans have the same cultural goals?
- Is partying in Sicily and Norway similar?
- Are South Americans of Spanish and Indian descent equally theatrical?
- Does eye contact among the Japanese share the same meaning as among Spaniards or Greeks?
- Is gift giving as prevalent in Sweden as it is in China?
- Do Tongans have the same work ethic as Koreans do?
- Are Poles as passive as Czechs?

A nation's culture is its *blueprint for survival* and, hopefully, success. It is an all-embracing pattern of a group's entire way of life, including a shared system of values, social meanings, and agendas passed on from generation to generation. Bold is the child who challenges the assumptions of parents, teachers, and peers! Culture incorporates such distinguishable attributes as language, attitudes, religion, artifacts, dress, beliefs, music and dance, art, sport, tools, etiquette, values, behaviors, food, and other material and nonmaterial components. Some of these attributes are subject to change, but the cultural framework generally endures. The younger generation, particularly, indulges in experimentation with different lifestyles and trends (often temporary), but a national or regional silent agenda or stability underlies such digression.

Today the process of globalization is creating more economic and political links among countries, regions, and cultures, but cross-century conflicts in Serbia, Kosovo, Chechnya, the Middle East, and Timor (and other parts of Indonesia) as well as India's and Pakistan's long-lived conflict over Kashmir show how regional cultural identities resist erosion. The concept of a global village sharing a global culture is a cozy one, and the twenty-first century, with its galloping information facilities and trade links, would seem a suitable time frame for its realization. However, cultural barriers, though frequently permeable, are formidable. In subsequent chapters I attempt to examine and quantify some of these barriers, to trace the links from past to present and future cultural development, and to give some predictions as to the direction cultural trends will take in the coming decades.

Chapter 1

From 2,000,000 B.C. to A.D. 2000: The Roots and Routes of Culture

Incomplete Version of History

Ask British people—even educated ones—what they know about British history, and the odds are that you will receive a creditable account of what has happened since 1066—the Norman invasion—and a somewhat sketchier description of life in Saxon and Viking times. The Roman invasion (55 B.C.) may well be recalled, but any knowledge of British life in Celtic times is likely to be restricted to vague references to Boadicea; woad, a blue dye; and Stonehenge. Ask about earlier periods and you will draw a blank. Yet archeologists tell us that Britain has been inhabited (by humans) for approximately 500,000 years, indicating that her people are ignorant of 99.5 percent of the islands' cultural development. Indeed the British seem to organize the study of history (certainly as it is taught in schools) according to a timetable of military activity. The benchmarks are the Roman invasion, 55 B.C.; the Saxon invasion, A.D. 350; Viking incursions, 900; the Norman Conquest, 1066; the Thirty Years War, 1618–1648; the Crimean War, 1853–1856; the Boer War, 1899–1902; the First World War, 1914–18; and the Second World War, 1939–45. This is not to say that Britons have not made outstanding contributions to human cultural development in the fields of aesthetics, invention, societal organization, and technology, but these contributions do not serve as benchmarks in the same way.

If we consider the cultural awareness of other Anglo-Saxon peoples, we find that historical chronology has served to limit their knowledge to even briefer recollections. American history has been well documented since the arrival of the *Mayflower*, but little is generally known about the Aztec and Inca empires and hundreds of other Native American tribes from their arrival in North America about 12,000 B.C. up to the beginning of the second millennium. Similarly, the 40,000- to 50,000-year dreamtime of the Australian Aborigines is only vaguely recalled by modern Aborigines and white Australian scholars.

Westerners devote most of their attention to historical events that have occurred since the birth of Christ, even though the emergence of writing in the Fertile Crescent (Sumeria) in 3000 B.C. provides us with an overview of happenings in Mesopotamia and Egypt for the three millennia before the Christian era. Furthermore, most Western world history books confine themselves largely to European history and take up the history of other peoples only in terms of their contacts with or colonization by Western Europeans.

It would come as a surprise to many Westerners to learn that for the greatest part of recorded history, the most populous, influential, and technically advanced country has been China. Animals and plants were domesticated in Britain around 3500 B.C., but this accomplishment was contemporaneous with similar developments in the Andes and in Amazonia and had been preceded in China and the Fertile Crescent by about 4000 years! In other words 99.9 percent of the five-million-year history of the human species is missing, or at least gets only the most minuscule attention by modern historians.

What does this mean for the cross-culturalist who seeks the roots of culture from their earliest origins? One might say that the most recent events in a country's history are the ones that will be most significant in terms of influencing the culture. This, however, is only true to a degree. While Japan's traumatic defeat in 1945 did much to change modern Japanese attitudes toward war and peace, the significant roots of Japanese cultural behavior go back at least two thousand years and in the case of China, at least five thousand years.

Culture—Genetics or Cultural Programming?

In fact the real roots of culture—for all of us—are much older than that. The supposed emergence of early humans in Africa more than five million years ago gets pushed back each decade by the astonishing revelations of scientists and archeologists. We know a lot about the social behavior of the men and women of two million years ago, and the traits and characteristics that have been passed on to us genetically constitute a pattern of inheritance separate from our subsequent cultural evolution (see diagram on page 4). These genetically inherited characteristics are not national or regional, nor are they taught by any authority. They are universal traits that every nationality or cultural group

Rival Patterns of Inheritance

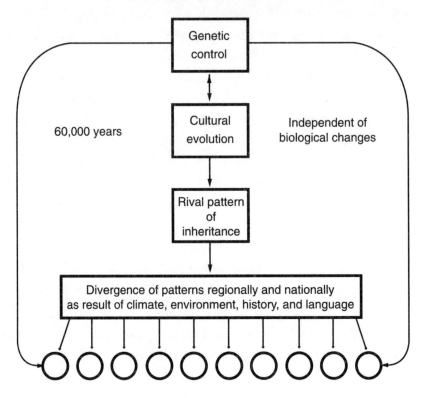

shares in common. They are qualities that have been bequeathed to us by our hunter-gatherer ancestors.

What were the traits of our nomad forebears? To begin with, they lived and worked (hunted) in groups, learning the benefits of cooperation and solidarity. They were grateful for help and favors and were angry about injustice. They wanted to be liked; friendship and family support were important, and they loved their young. The roles of the sexes were different. The survival instinct was strong in the face of dangers from wild beasts. Maintaining their way of life necessitated not only cooperation and collusion but also the ability to communicate quickly and sometimes to deceive. Because weapons and tools were vital, these

early nomads acquired inventiveness and a do-it-yourself mentality. They were resourceful, shared strategies, and together
solved major problems; for example, they learned to cope with
the cold, control fire, and ultimately go to sea. Their keen inventiveness was allied to a sense of aestheticism; we have examples
of their art over the last 50,000 years in magnificent Australian
Aboriginal paintings and glorious murals in Lascaux and Altamira.

Cultural Diversity Development Calendar

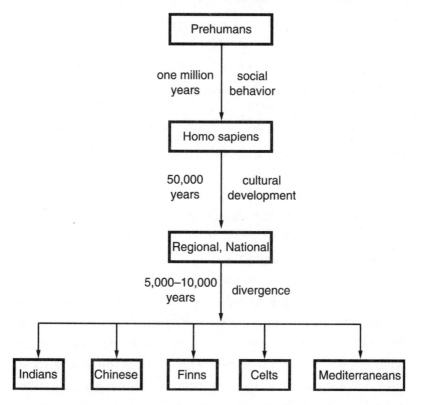

What, then, has come down to us? It is a fact that all people
living today love their children, want to be liked, are grateful for
favors, are angry at injustice, will cooperate or deceive in order to
survive, and have a desire to procreate. The majority want to "be-

long" to one kind of group or another, and most people claim family as their first loyalty. Artistic sense still unites all cultural groups.

What is comforting about genetically inherited traits is that they are, almost exclusively, positive. They can unite people who differ dramatically in terms of conscious cultural evolution. The suspicious, unsmiling Russian, uneasy with the initial flashing (Hollywood) smile of the American businessperson, is quickly won over by the exchange of their young children's photographs. Greeks and Turks are united in their admiration of Ephesus. The Chinese, Japanese, and Koreans, not always the best of pals, share art. And the school bully who hits a smaller boy provokes anger in Britons, Mexicans, and Tongans alike.

The current divisions and antipathies deriving from differing *national* versions of cultural programming lead to dissension, rejection, hostility, and often war. The enduring altercations between Greeks and Turks, Jews and Arabs, the English and the Irish, and the Japanese and Koreans are well documented and have not been satisfactorily resolved at the turn of the century. What we know from early history and can surmise from our knowledge of prehistory is that many modern types of prejudices did not exist then, or at least were far less damaging to our early ancestors. They probably killed others to survive, but their behavior does not seem to have been caused by some kind of cultural or traditional hatred or programmed antipathy. Tribal wars were often symbolic and frequently only demanded one killing per side. Sacrifices for this symbolic role were often volunteers. Fanaticism and suicidal stance in war came only with organized religion. Collusion between politicians and priests produced the manic fervor that caused the Crusades to continue for over a century. Early humans would have thought the whole affair somewhat ridiculous.

The universal traits we all possess lead some people to the conclusion that "all people are really the same." This is, of course, quite untrue, as anyone who sees Finns and Italians socializing or Americans and Japanese negotiating will readily perceive. Nevertheless, all human beings probably have a common origin, and it is indeed a remarkable phenomenon, or even achievement, that over a period of two million years, a plethora of innate characteristics survive to give humans a basis for mutual understanding, eventual friendship, and consequent survival. National or religious "programming" occasionally urges its adherents to exterminate their enemies. Genocide has occurred in Tasmania, Rwanda, and other places. The cultures of many Native American groups and Australian Aborigines, though not currently targeted in this manner, have precarious futures.

Why did human mental programming differ so amazingly? What led to drastically diverging values, opposing codes of behavior, and enduring prejudices and hatreds?

Roots and Routes

In order to consider these diverging cultural streams in some kind of context, we must go way back in history and prehistory. The *roots* of culture align themselves to some extent with the *routes* of culture (see diagram on page 8), that is to say, we must follow the emergence of humankind, beginning with its separation from apes and chimpanzees and leaving Africa to migrate first to the Middle East and Southeast Asia, then to Europe and other parts of Asia, and ultimately to Polynesia, Australia, and the Americas. Half a million years ago, when the first humans reached Europe, they were not *Homo sapiens*, only *Homo erectus*, but human culture had begun to develop and disperse.

Over the million or more years when early human groups departed from Africa, they took different routes, went in different directions, and moved at different speeds. Some of these migratory groups would not meet again until 1788 (Europeans and

Routes of Culture

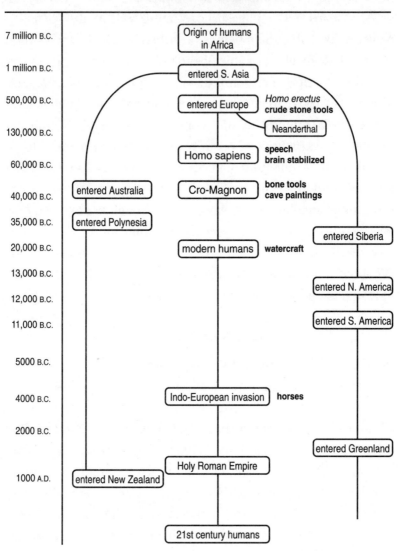

Australian Aborigines). Others would have repeated contact and influence each other culturally (North Africans, Europeans, and people in the Fertile Crescent). Perhaps the most interesting historical "rendezvous" is that of the people who headed for the Far East a million years ago, splitting from those who went west into Europe. The eastbound group(s) eventually acquired Asian characteristics and qualities. They crossed the Bering Strait in 12,000 B.C. and finally met up with their European cousins as Blackfeet, Cherokee, Sioux, Incas, and Aztecs in the sixteenth century A.D.!

Another interesting aspect of cultural development is the relationship between having had "an early start" and present power or dominance. This is a complex matter. Our origins in Africa do not seem to have bequeathed any significant advantages to African cultural life. The head start gained by the Fertile Crescent, especially in agriculture and settled living, was lost. Europe is still far from being unified, and the United States has been a cohesive force for only one hundred years at the most. China stands out as the only major country with impressive cultural, linguistic, political, religious, and philosophic unity, unbroken for five thousand years. There are some geographic reasons for this. In general, however, cultures have waxed and waned, affected by a complex interplay of influences from the four basic roots: geographic environment and climate, religion, language, and historical happenings. The particular routes followed by different groups were also of major significance, inasmuch as great varieties of climate, overland and maritime challenges, ethnic contacts, soil fertility, abundance of game, and ultimate choice of settlement dictated the final destinies of each band, tribe, or nation.

In the next two chapters as well as in other, later chapters, I will examine in depth the influence of climate and environment, religion, and language in cultural development. (See the diagram on pages 10–11, which outlines those influences and prefigures

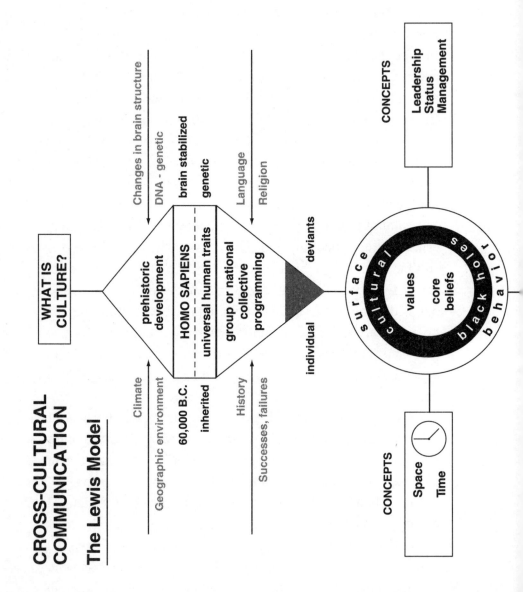

CROSS-CULTURAL
COMMUNICATION

The Lewis Model

WHAT IS
CULTURE?

Changes in brain structure

DNA - genetic

brain stabilized

genetic

Language

Religion

Climate

Geographic environment

60,000 B.C.

inherited

History

Successes, failures

prehistoric
development

HOMO SAPIENS

universal human traits

group or national
collective
programming

individual

deviants

surface

cultural

black holes

behaviour

values

core
beliefs

CONCEPTS

Leadership
Status
Management

CONCEPTS

Space
Time

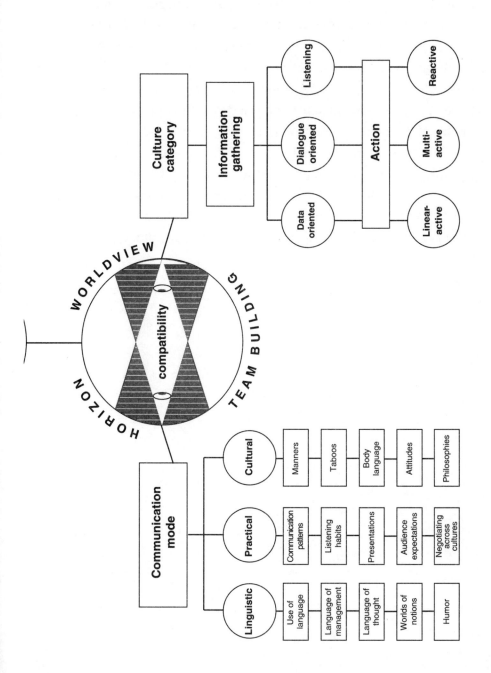

many of the topics to be discussed later.) At the beginning of the twenty-first century, we have a minimum of two hundred different cultures, and we speak four hundred to five hundred different languages, with thousands of diverging, entrenched values and core beliefs! The first years of the twenty-first century seem to herald an age of globalization and standardization of values and modes of behavior, especially in the area of international business. This would indeed be a source of gratification to our less polemical ancestors, the honest and uncomplicated hunter-gatherers of two million years ago. Are cultures really aligning themselves? Will national prejudices disappear? Will the twenty-first century be the end, not of history, but of irrelevant cultural diversity?

Read on.

Chapter 2

Culture and Climate

Culture has been succinctly defined as the collective programming of the mind that distinguishes one category of people from another. This is largely true, especially when we examine the societal norms imposed within national or ethnic frameworks. Parents program their children, teachers their students, society its citizens. We cannot, often do not wish to, escape the passing on of the accumulated wisdom or lore of previous generations, which, after all, seems to have assured the continued existence of our culture or nation.

Yet, culture's programming itself, the very curriculum of rules, precepts, and taboos it prescribes, is essentially culture-bound; it has age-old origins we are not always able to locate or readily perceive. We can, however, enumerate some of them. Painting with a broad brush, we might say that the cultural roots of the organization of society are language, religion, history, geography and environment, and climate. Is it possible that the last factor, climate, may be the most influential? Read further.

It is often said that of the three most important events in our lives—birth, marriage, and death—we have a choice about only one. If we look at the factors that influence our culture and the way we live, we can make a parallel observation: we have some choice as to religion, we make part of our own history, we can certainly change our environment (Japan, the United States, and Singapore are good examples), and we can even tinker with our geography (Holland), but when it comes to climate, human influence is, so far at least, minimal.

East Side Story

In a chapter on the influence of climate on human culture, it makes sense to begin by spotlighting its most dramatic, indeed cataclysmic, phase—the engendering of the species itself.

Yves Coppens, Chair of Paleoanthropology and Prehistory at the College of France in Paris, wrote papers for the scientific community as early as 1975 in which he provided convincing evidence for a clear correlation between the evolution of climate and the evolution of the hominids. Human beings' roots lie in the animals. We are at the tip of one of the branches of an immense tree of life that has been growing and diversifying for over four billion years. From an evolutionary point of view, locating the time and place that our branch separated from the rest of the tree is of great importance.

The great majority of scientists in a variety of fields today concede that our birthplace was Africa. Whether one believes in the genesis theory, implying that all humans are descended from one original group in one geographic area, or the alternative theory of polygenesis, which suggests parallel evolution in different areas, the emergence of the genus *Homo* certainly took place on the African continent.

Eight million years ago a tectonic crisis occurred in Africa that entailed two distinct movements: dramatic sinking, producing the Rift Valley, and rising of the western rim, which gave birth to a line of peaks.

The valley and the mountain barrier obviously disturbed the circulation patterns of the air. To the west, thanks to the Atlantic, precipitation was plentiful. The east side remained drier. The west kept its humid forests, the east evolved into open savannah. The common ancestors of the Hominidae families were also divided by the Rift Valley. The larger western group pursued their adaptation to life in a humid, arboreal milieu and became our closest cousins, the chimpanzees. The smaller contingent in the east began to adapt to their new life in an open, drier environment.

The species in the east evolved into the human predecessor we call the australopithecines. These beings were still more ensconced in tree-filled habitats than are the more recent species, those called robust. Two and a half million years ago a drastic change in climate (a cooling of the whole earth) left East Africa dry. The robust australopithecines emerged as a product of aridity. Grasslands afforded lengthening horizons of visibility, which encouraged an upright stance. This in turn enabled hominids to be warned of the approach of animals, and it facilitated hunting them. They progressed from a vegetarian to a meat-eating diet. The brain enlarged, bringing with it an opportunistic diet, a higher degree of reflection, a new curiosity. The continuing dessication of East Africa allowed hominine progress, which led (through catching meat) to greater mobility and a sense of adventure. For the first time in history, humanity spread out from its origins and in less than three million years conquered five more continents—the entire planet—and has begun the exploration of other planets in the solar system. Coppens calls his model "East Side Story."

Climate and climatic change continue to affect human development and culture. We cannot predict with certainty the eventual or ultimate effects of global warming, the melting of the ice caps, the rise of the oceans, the wild fluctuations of wind and ocean currents. Climate continues to control us more than we control it.

The Effects of Climate

In what ways are our lives influenced—or even dominated—by climatological conditions? Which characteristics of a people are most likely the products of climate, temperature, and weather? Are some countries more affected than others? Can we combat or rise above the restrictions imposed upon us by natural forces of this kind?

Some of these questions are easier to answer than others. To begin with, one can surmise that some countries suffer fewer climatological problems than others. Let us take France as an example. The French, apart from those who, in the northwest corner, live dangerously near England, enjoy what is certainly the most equable climate in Europe. The temperate nature of French weather, especially south of Paris, allows its inhabitants a relatively easy coexistence with nature. The temperature is generally pleasant; grain crops, fruit, vegetables, and grapes grow easily; pasture and clean water are abundant; and the delights of the Riviera speak for themselves. The French suffer few or no impediments of climatological origin. One would expect, therefore, that the dominant features of French culture would be a result of other factors (e.g., history) rather than adaptation to climate. It would be tempting to conclude that equable weather would make the French easygoing and laid-back (which they are not), but it

might on the other hand contribute to their calm feeling of superiority over others (which they do possess). Other temperate zones
around the world are Madeira and the Canaries, Costa Rica, Guatemala, Ecuador, northern California and some other parts of the
United States, many islands in the Northern Pacific, some areas
around the Black Sea, and the highlands of the Caucasus region.

It is obvious that in such diverse countries as Finland, Russia,
Chad, the Congo, Canada, Afghanistan, and Indonesia, climate
will dominate, perhaps even define, customs, habits, viabilities,
culture itself. Russia with its months-long frozen steppes, Finland with its long winter nights and its inhabitants' mighty heat-
ing bills, Saudi Arabia with its desert heat, and Singapore with its
intense humidity are all hampered for a considerable part of the
year by the severity of their weather. How do their inhabitants
react?

Climate and Work

In our modern world, with the globalization of the economy, the
first question you might ask is this: How does climate affect the
way people work? People living in cold climates have a ready
answer. *We* work; Mexicans, Sicilians, Africans, and Arabs *don't*
(they lie in the shade of tropical trees). There is of course some
truth in this (the Mexican peasant would be mad if he lay in the
hot sun), but there are hidden cultural aspects here as well (see
my remarks on communication patterns below). We can, though,
make the generalization that low temperatures are conducive to
vigorous physical activity. You don't sit around, play chess, or
paint landscapes in minus twenty degrees centigrade. Cold
weather gets you on the move, makes physical work almost a
pleasure. Farmers, laborers, dockhands, construction workers,
mail deliverers, meter readers, errand boys, football players, and
athletes of all kinds do well in cold weather. There are some

grounds, too, for believing that low temperatures enable people to think clearly. Brits, Nordics, Germans, Dutch, Belgians, and Canadians would agree with this (of course), as would others who ponder in air-conditioned offices. When Northern Europeans find themselves in sweltering temperatures, they find physical work oppressive, and they don't make "cool" decisions easily. Perhaps therefore we should forgive the Andalucíans and the Congolese for their apparent indolence. But are there any compensating factors? To answer this question we have to touch on the subject of communication.

Climate and Communication

After inquiring about the work ethic, it is only natural, in our telecommunications age, that we be curious about the influence of climate on communication patterns. Here we are left in little doubt as to the direct effect of sunshine, heat, and cold on the way people greet and talk to each other. Let us begin with Europe, in the very north. Finns, Swedes, and Norwegians, meeting friends and acquaintances on the street in winter, indulge in only brief interaction. The greeting (*hei*) is short in itself, the information exchanged (usually as to where one is heading) often compressed into a 20-second burst at temperatures around freezing, 10 seconds at −10 degrees centigrade, and snapped en passant at twenty below. It does not make sense to dally longer. A broad American smile at twenty below in a Helsinki easterly makes your front teeth ache. Winter visitors to Stockholm or Oslo are fed directions in 5 to 10 seconds flat—20 after Easter—if they need the emergency ward of a hospital or wish to report a double murder to the police.

With the Nordics this culture of outdoor succinctness (called "winter behavior" by the Finns and the Swedes) carries over to their indoor communication habits, where economy of expression and the ability to summarize are prized. The Scandinavian languages, with their abundance of monosyllabic and bisyllabic words, lend themselves to this mode of speech. Finnish is more flowery, but Finnish males make up for this by remaining silent. The women are another matter. This cold weather taciturnity is by no means confined to Scandinavia and Finland. We observe it in Maine, Montana, and Wyoming, in Lancashire and Yorkshire, in Murmansk and Arkhangelsk, in Japan's Hokkaido.

Returning to the European scene, the influence of sunshine and heat on people's speech habits is clearly discernible around the Mediterranean. *Le Midi de la France*, Italy south of Genoa, Sicily, Greece, and half of Spain enjoy the kind of weather that tempts people out of doors. Greeks, Neapolitans, Sicilians, and Andalucíans spend a large part of their lives on the street—at their front gate; in roadside cafés, open-air taverns, and restaurants; on the waterfront; by the seashore; in the village square. In these locations, conversation is not hurried, brief, or succinct. Words cost nothing, say the Italians, why not splurge? In these countries conversation is an art, a social enjoyment, a never-ending continuum. It is also more than that; it is an information-gathering and -sharing mechanism, a valuable vehicle of communication for both social and business purposes.

Gossip—a word with nasty connotations in Nordic ears—is an essential component of the social structure in Mediterranean and other hot-weather cultures. This is visible nightly in the custom of the Spanish *paseo,* where men and women march around town squares in opposite directions, shouting greetings, compliments, insults, and newsy tidbits to each other as they cross each other. The Italian *chiacchiera*, conducted by women on doorsteps and by men in cafés, is a kind of binding social glue that aligns people's opinions and increases trust between them.

Nordics, Brits, the Dutch, and North Germans are unable to benefit from unhurried, outdoor networking customs. The climate does not allow it. They lean, instead, on their facts, figures, and computers. Sunshine encourages outdoor dalliance, voluble discussion, unhurried examination of all aspects of a question or issue. Much probing goes on, many avenues of persuasion are explored, fervent desires are pressed time and time again. The Nordic takes no for an answer and whisks herself off. The southern Latin, with the appropriate body language, pleads, cajoles, demonstrates his wit, and entertains. Out-of-doors conversations are conducive to body language. Sweeping Italian gestures would cause the banging of elbows against walls in narrow Japanese offices or the knocking of glass vases off Swedish desks.

Sunshine, slowing down people's progression from one location to the next, allows Italians, Spaniards, and Greeks to develop open, smiling, exterior appearances in contrast to the pinched faces of cold Nordics or suspicious Germans or Brits, who are unused to unlimited loquaciousness. Of the European Latins only the Portuguese modify this social exuberance. Talkative enough in general, the Portuguese have their regular downswings of melancholy when they talk morosely of their *saudades* (nostalgic longings) or of the meaning of death or other problems they might have. This lack of verbal alignment with other Latins is said to derive from their cold Atlantic coastline. No part of Portugal touches the Mediterranean, though they enjoy a lot of sun in the south.

Between these northern and southern extremes of Europe, climate affects communication habits in different ways. Germany has a variety of climates from south to north—Bavarians are more outgoing than Prussians. In Poland the biting winters cool Slavic temperament, and excitable Italians from Milan and Turin have a keener work ethic than Romans and talk less, but not much. In Britain the situation is rather special. It is often said that while other countries have climates, Britain really has *weather*, not only a lot of it but definitely the *changeable* kind. This is just as well for Britons; otherwise they might never talk to each other (like people in trains reading newspapers). The weather is the perfect entrée for contact with another Briton, for Brits are never bored by the subject.

On my first day in Australia—it was a sunny one—I met an Australian on the village street and said, "Good morning, nice day, isn't it?" He looked at me as if I were mad or maybe trying to seduce him. When he realized I was normal, he looked up briefly at the Aussie sun and replied, "Oh, yeah, mite, yeah." Brits are the equal of many Latins when it comes to smalltalk, but it would not be so if they didn't have this weather crutch.

Elsewhere around the globe, climate conditions communication and behavior. Australians, with their five sunny big cities (Melbourne is the exception), are open, friendly, smiling, and talkative. Their New Zealand neighbors with their British-type changeable climate are more guarded and conservative. Much of the United States lies in zones where there is a lot of hot weather, which is reflected in their extroversion. Constant sunshine in southern California causes the residents to be loquacious, extroverted, and leisure- and sports-minded. Hot weather Africans talk interminably on the street, often holding hands while they speak. In Asia courtesy and modesty curtail extroversion, but the heat in Indonesia, the Philippines, and other Southeastern Asian nations causes words to flow faster than in Japan, Korea, Manchuria, or Mongolia. In South America, Brazilians, Argentinians, and other people inhabiting the coastal plains are verbal and communicative in the extreme; the Indians of the cooler highlands are more reserved and speak more softly.

Eye contact—another component of communication—is also affected by climate. Latins, Greeks, and Arabs maintain almost constant eye contact with their interlocutor. Arabs often take off their sunglasses to heighten the effect. Nordics and Brits, used to

cold winds whipping their faces, often speak outdoors with nar-
rowed eyes and frequently avoid prolonged eye contact during
indoor conversations. Tactile behavior is also influenced by climate. Latins, Greeks, Arabs, and Africans often touch each other
while they talk. They like the feel of human flesh; gripping a bare
arm is a way of showing your partner that you trust him or her.
This friendly gesture is less easily attainable through thick Norwegian furs or British macs and duffle coats.

Other Climate-Linked Cultural Attributes

Humor in the Rain. Something else I have heard from time to
time is that constantly changing weather imparts a sense of humor to the people who have to put up with it, especially when it
rains a lot. On reflection I believe there is some truth in this. The
British are renowned the world over for their sense of humor,
though it is of course British humor. The Irish are also a humorous lot (it is seldom dry for long there) and so are the inhabitants
of Bergen, Norway, where it rains 290 days a year. Latins are
supposed to be less humorous than the British, but they have *wit.*
Wit is word-based (*jeu de mots,* double entendres, aphorisms,
etc.), whereas humor is situation-based. Mediterranean people,
using tens of thousands of words, create many opportunities for
wit. Nordics, with their briefer exchanges, must strike home faster
with cunning shafts of incongruity or tongue-in-cheek seriousness. Britons, with their rained-out cricket matches, postponed
Wimbledon encounters, ruined garden parties, burst pipes in winter, dodgy bank holiday excursions, foggy weddings, hailstones
at Sunday school processions, and howling gales at scout camp
need that precious commodity—a sense of humor born of disappointment, frustration, disbelief, adaptation, patience, semitoler-
ance, and ultimate resignation—to fall back on.

Dress and Use of Color. The way people dress depends on

climate for obvious reasons. Less obvious is how it also affects mentality. Brits, Nordics, and North Germans are interested in the protective aspects of clothes (warmth, durability) for many months of the year. Inhabitants of Southern Europe and much of South America, free from these preoccupations, think more about appearance and style. It is not accidental that French and Italian fashions tend to achieve preeminence around the world. A feeling for color, too, is climate-dependent. Brits and Nordics visiting Greece, Turkey, Sicily, Malta, or even Portugal are struck by the vivid and attractive colors of the fishing boats. Why don't they (the northerners) paint their boats like that? The Greek, who uses light and dark blues, turquoises, and pinks to decorate his white house, obviously draws his inspiration from the azure sky, the blue-green sea, the pink sunsets. The Portuguese with their vivid orange, green, and blue boats imitate their sunny environment. It is the same with Mexican shawls, Guatemalan rugs, Indonesian dancers, Bolivian ponchos, and Maori or Tahitian tribal dress. Swiss, Finnish, and Swedish houses are usually grey, reflecting cloudy skies and cold temperatures most of the year. In contrast, in the Swedish archipelago, visited by boats only in the sunny summer months, houses are painted bright blue, orange, green, and yellow. The fuss that the Nordic countries make over the Midsummer festival reflects the longing for sunshine, so long denied. The three Baltic states celebrate Midsummer with equal fervor.

Food and Drink. It is only natural that climate dictates what people should eat and drink. Mediterranean peoples draw on their local natural resources and eat a lot of fish and seafood, fruits, and certain vegetables (eggplants, zucchinis, tomatoes, spinach, asparagus) cooked in olive oil and washed down with wine. Nordics eat much more meat with thick sauces or gravies to combat the cold. Like the Scots, they eat a lot of porridge and used to match the Scots' consumption of whisky with vodka, schnapps, and various distilled concoctions. Carbohydrates, potatoes, and bread were consumed in sizeable quantities in northern climates, though dietitians' advice has caused changes in their eating habits in recent years. In the sprawling huge geographical expanses of Asia and the Americas, eating and drinking habits vary enormously on account of the multiplicity of climates and seasons. The biggest wine consumers of the world are in those areas where vines grow best.

Sunshine and Suicide. Some links between climate and cultural behavior are rather dubious, but the "suicide league" countries (see chart on page 25) indicate a clear connection between the suicide rate and lack of sunshine.

Regional Diversity. In some countries regional variations of climate produce diverse modes of behavior. Spain is a good example: rained-on Basques and Galicians are far more industrious than sun-soaked Andalucíans; extremes of climate in the barren Castilian plateau produced a breed of haughty rulers who excelled in political dominance, as warriors, and ultimately as conquistadores. There are parallels in other countries—we are reminded of Genghis Khan and Tamerlane in Mongolia, and so on. Also in China, the area north of the Yangtze is clearly distinct from the area to its south. The Chinese in the colder north have traditionally dominated China in political and military terms. The south—the warm, rice-growing area—has met with more success in agriculture and commerce.

Natural Disasters and Culture. In some parts of the world severe extremities of climate give rise to regularly recurring natural disasters of great magnitude. Examples are the perennial droughts of Somalia, Eritrea, parts of Ethiopia, and Saharan and sub-Saharan Africa; the permafrost of northern Siberia and the life-threatening cold of the Arctic regions; and the frequent cata-

The Suicide League

Suicide rates per 100,000			
1990-95	All	Men	Women
Hungary	38.6	58.0	20.7
Finland	29.8	48.9	11.3
Switzerland	22.7	34.3	11.6
Belgium	22.7	32.0	13.8
Austria	22.6	34.6	11.6
Denmark	22.4	30.0	15.1
France	20.1	29.6	11.1
Sweden	18.6	26.8	10.6
Germany	17.5	24.9	10.7
Japan	16.1	20.6	11.8
Norway	15.5	23.3	8.0
Poland	13.9	23.9	4.4
USA	12.2	19.9	4.8
Netherlands	9.7	12.3	7.2
Portugal	9.6	14.9	4.6
Ireland	9.5	14.4	4.7
Britain	7.9	12.4	3.6
Spain	7.7	11.6	3.9
Italy	7.5	11.2	4.1
Greece	3.5	5.5	1.5

Source: World Health Organization

strophic flooding in India, Bangladesh, and Egypt. One would expect the inhabitants of these areas to be decisive about seeking habitation elsewhere. They rarely do. Climatological hardships seem to engender a fatalistic attitude among those who have to bear them.

Climate and Affinities. What about cultural affinities among people who experience similar or diverse climatological conditions? Because climate is only one factor in cultural conditioning, diversity of behavior in inhabitants of hot (or cold) zones will naturally be evident. Yet people living in very different climates will have fewer commonalities with each other. To go to real extremes, what do the Inuit and the African Bushman have in common? Assuming they had a common language, what would they talk about? Food? Sex? Weather? Could they agree about anything? A London spring would be chilly for the Bushman, hot for the Inuit. Neither would be likely to appreciate the qualities or appearance of each other's wife or husband. Each has a completely separate experience of habits, foods, philosophies, landscapes, and animals. One has no concept of ice, snow, or even cold itself; the other does not know sand, scorched earth, tropical foliage, or blistering heat. The Inuit would not be tempted by snake flambé; give him a bit of tasty blubber anytime.

If this personal encounter is far-fetched, the same principle operates to a lesser degree between different Europeans. Sicilians and Finns don't have a lot to talk about, once the first rapture of exoticism of a new landscape has subsided. Italians in Finland fail to share the Finns' enthusiasm for sauna, vodka, milk, fishing through the ice, and long, cozy silences. Finns in Palermo are bewildered by the endless smalltalk—meaningless to them—as well as by the arbitrariness of decision making, punctuality, traffic behavior, planning of any kind, volatility of emotions, and so on.

Summary

Can cultural behavior transcend climatological impositions? Evidence suggests that it can to some degree. While intense heat tends to diminish work ethic, workaholic Americans with their Protestant work ethic succeed in functioning effectively in hot states, largely thanks to the benefits of air-conditioning. Also those nations adhering strictly to Confucian tenets—Japan, China, and Korea—generally maintain a creditable work rate in the hotter months.

It can't be denied, however, that climate seems to have a decisive and sometimes devastating effect on cultural behavior—in some instances more than others. In addition it is probably the catalyst for other cultural determinants, such as geography, environmental conditions, and historical direction. I will close this chapter with the following generalizations about the influence of climate on culture.

- Climate affects culture more in some countries than in others.
- As heat increases, industriousness decreases.
- Work ethic can occasionally transcend climate.
- Sunshine and warm temperatures engender loquaciousness, openness, cheerfulness, and exuberance.
- Cold conditions produce taciturnity, brevity of expression, and valued privacy.
- A clear link exists between lack of sunshine and suicide rates (pessimism).
- Harsh, extreme climates sometimes produce aggressive, warrior-like peoples.
- Changeable, frequently rainy weather engenders phlegmatism, tolerance, adaptation, a sense of proportion, and humor.

Chapter 3

Culture and Religion

It is often said that we fail to learn the lessons of history—and there are many examples of this—but in the very long run (and we may be talking in millennia), a people will adhere collectively to the set of norms, rules, reactions, and activities that their experience and development have shown to be most beneficial to them. Infants and youth are trained by their parents, teachers, and elders to cling to these rules, which have enabled their culture to survive.

In chapter 1 I mentioned three basic roots of culture: climate, religion, and language. Here I offer a fourth—history—which I will discuss numerous times throughout the rest of the book.

In the modern era, until September 11, 2001, we might have assumed that *religious tenets*, as guides to behavior, *were dimin-*

ishing in importance in the face of scientific discovery, the advance of technology, and the globalization of business. It is easy to look back on the Crusades as an anomalous period in medieval history whose fervor and exoticism might appear misplaced—over the top—in the twentieth century. In fact the diminution or abatement of the influence of religion on societal behavior is by no means evident. *On the contrary, events in the last half of the century tend to support the opposite argument.* The partition of the Indian subcontinent, the Gulf War, the Israeli-Palestinian conflict, the breakup of Yugoslavia, the hostilities in Bosnia and Kosovo, the killings in Ambon and other parts of Indonesia, the war in Chechnya, the troubles in Ireland, all bear witness to the continuing force and tenacity of religious beliefs. The September 2001 attacks on Manhattan and the Pentagon left us with little doubt that these would occupy front stage in our youthful new century.

Hinduism—the religion with the greatest number of adherents—dominates the daily routine of nearly a billion Indians. Islam—the world's fastest-growing religion—specifies the tenets of behavior in fifty-three countries with a total population approaching one billion. The impact of Islam, with its unfortunate (though not necessarily intentional) links with terrorist activity, is dealt with in detail in my Epilogue (pages 271–93). Buddhism, often practiced in tandem with the philosophy of Confucianism, is the key to the mental workings of more than a billion people in China, Japan, Korea, Vietnam, and other parts of Asia. The world's only superpower—the United States—clings persistently to Christianity and woe betide the American president who fails to declare his faith or forgets to go to church on Sundays! Who said God was dead?

Nietzsche did, for one. The existence or credibility of a Deity met few challenges during the first millennium (after Christ) but had an increasingly rough ride in the second. Christians, Muslims, and Hindus all confidently attested to the reality of God, but they were annoyingly different Gods. In spite of comforting similarities in the descriptions of Jehovah and Allah and in the teachings of Jesus and Muhammad, the rivalry between the two creeds led to ferocious bloodletting for centuries. There were no doubters of divine existence among the Muslim and Christian combatants of the Crusades, but the striking contradictions of piety and devoutness on the one hand and fanatical slaughter on the other led cynics and men of reason to ask themselves what kind of God would permit these inconsistencies.

Few Hindus, Muslims, or Jews question the reality of the Deity even today—certainly not in public, but Westerners have given God a battering for most of a thousand years. Darwin may not have been as outrightly condemnatory as Nietzsche, but he mauled the Old Testament with his scientific findings. The French Revolution, Marx, and the Soviet Union would all bury God in due course, and resurrection became increasingly difficult after each funeral.

The inconsistencies of the God's "behavior" were matched by the multiplicity of interpretations supplied by different sects and subsects, particularly under the Christian umbrella. The major schism may have been the split between Catholics and Protestants, but the latter went on to spawn innumerable religious denominations such as Methodists, Baptists, Unitarians, Presbyterians, Congregationalists, Lutherans, and so forth. These sects eagerly created subsects, ostensibly to interpret the word of God more "accurately," so Methodists became Wesleyan Methodists, Primitive Methodists, Independent Methodists, and in the United States, Southern Methodists. Such subdenominations did little harm—there was no bloodletting—but any unity or common vision of the Deity seemed further away than ever.

Even fierce believers were less than helpful in consolidating God's permanence, for they privatized or nationalized God when it was politically expedient. Whether you were Muslim or Christian, French or German, God was on your side when you went into battle. This put God in a difficult position: Who to help? If God helped both sides, it might add to or prolong the slaughter. Later, Mormons, Jehovah's Witnesses, and countless other sects joined the fray.

The kaleidoscopic variety of creeds on offer, in the Christian world alone, gives rise to confusion and bewilderment to a would-be believer. Yet the dilemmas posed by the different interpretations of the nature of God and God's will and the continual attacks on and outright denial of God's existence have made only a small dent in humanity's belief in a Supreme Being. Many people do not attend church or temple or mosque (though a surprising number of Americans do), but less than 15 percent of Westerners deny the possibility of a Divine Being. Humankind seems to be inherently nervous about formally severing links with the Deity. As we shall see as we read on, many other historical and intellectual pressures have contributed (and still do) to the influence of religious beliefs.

Influences on the Religion-Culture Connection

The Language Factor

As we examine the inevitable links between culture and religion, we find that a third factor is involved, and that is language. The language spoken by an individual not only restricts liberties of thought and has a pervasive influence on considerations of vision, charisma, emotion, discipline, and hierarchy, but it also has a sociological bearing on religion itself. Religions, from their earliest days, relied heavily on language—in its written form—to spread their tenets. The majority of languages have as their earliest documents religious texts. One can almost suspect that writing was developed not primarily as an auxiliary to speech but as an aid to spreading religion and a depository of religious tradition.

Akkadian cuneiform writing and Egyptian hieroglyphic inscriptions are almost exclusively devoted to sacred matters (the word *hieroglyph* means "sacred carving"). The earliest Chinese writings, from about 1500 B.C., describe the soothsayer's art and techniques. The Indian Brahmanas are religious hymns and rituals. In the Indo-European area, Avestan—the sacred ancient tongue of Persia—was associated almost exclusively with the rituals of Zoroastrianism. Etruscan, though deciphered with difficulty, describes religious matters.

Religions could not spread convincingly or quickly without a prestige language to propagate their message. In turn the success of any particular religion guaranteed (sometimes worldwide) fame to the language that carried it afar. Thus partnerships were established: Jewish and Hebrew, Islam and Arabic (once an isolated language in southern Arabia), Buddhism and Chinese, Christianity and Latin (with some help from Greek).

In some cases languages survived for centuries because they were repositories of a popular religion. The Germanic invaders who overran the Roman Empire would normally have imposed their Germanic tongue on the peoples they had conquered; their conversion to Christianity, however, meant that they adopted different forms of Latin—a language that is still taught in English grammar schools and universities. The first Germanic tongue to boast a literary form—Gothic—was introduced to the world by Bishop Wulfila in the form of a fourth-century Bible. In a sense, when one creates written forms for a spoken language, one creates a culture, which can subsequently acquire status, dignity, and literature. Numerous cultures were established by clerics and missionaries. Armenian and Georgian first appeared in biblical form in the fifth century; Bishops Cyril and Methodius invented the Cyrillic alphabet in the ninth century; a Finnish Bible appeared in 1548. Perhaps the two most influential Bibles in laying the foundation of a national culture-cum-language standard were Luther's translation in 1531 and the King James Version, which signposted the route to modern English.

Christian missionaries carried their religion to a large number of African, Asian, and Pacific tribes, not to mention the Americas. They were not the only ones, however. In many localities in Asia and Africa, the sole written form of the local tongue appeared in the Arabic script introduced by Islamic missionaries. Indians and Pakistanis, speaking basically the same language (formerly known as Hindustani), demonstrate their religious differences by calling the language Hindi (for Hindus) and writing it in the Devanagari characters of Ancient Sanskrit or in Urdu (for Moslems), which is written in flowing Arabic script.

The Political Factor

Thus culture, language, writing, and religion form a complex blueprint for belief, behavior and survival. Sometimes *one* of the four leads the way, sometimes *another* (e.g., Latin in the Roman Empire, religion in Ayatollahs' Iran). The formula may break up for political or other reasons. Kemal Ataturk, wishing to modernize Turkey after he became president in 1923, gave the Turkish language pride of place by purging it of its Arabic loanwords—many of them religious in origin—and by replacing the Arabic script with the Roman alphabet. These language-cosmetic changes heralded a Turkish cultural shift in the direction of secularism. Ataturk replaced the Islamic calendar with the Western one. He abolished the wearing of the fez, and women stopped wearing the veil. In effect Ataturk tolerated Islam as a religion but banned it as a lifestyle—a situation very different from that in modern Iran!

Ataturk's intervention in Turkish cultural life in the 1920s raises the question of the political link between culture and religion. How did modern established religions arise? Is there an element of political necessity? The writings of Jared Diamond trace the development of human social organization from bands to clans to tribes to chiefdoms to states, the number of people in each category increasing as one goes along. Small bands and many clans were inherently egalitarian; as hunter-gatherers leading a nomadic life, clan members had little opportunity to practice agriculture, acquire surplus wealth, and develop strict hierarchy to control the wealth. Tribes and chiefdoms arose in many parts of the world many centuries ago, for example, in the Fertile Crescent in 5500 B.C., in Mesoamerica in 1000 B.C., and in most parts of Polynesia, where chiefdoms still reigned in post-Columbian times.

Supernatural Beliefs and Divine Descent

Tribes had supernatural beliefs that most commoners accepted (e.g., Tlaloc brought rain to the Aztecs). If these supernatural beliefs could be institutionalized and classified to form a code, they were then transformed into what we call a religion. Elite rulers from the Aztecs to the Hawaiians to the Japanese emperors claimed divine descent in one way or another. Incan emperors were carried around in litters; Japanese emperors up to Hirohito were considered to be descended from the sun.

Early states had state religions, and if the ruler was seen as divine, this status lent considerable weight to his or her authority. If the *elites* were too indelicate or unconvincing to persuade the masses of their ability to intercede with the gods, they could always hire a separate group of kleptocrats (priests) to provide the ideological justification for monopolizing wealth and power for the public good. Religions have been very useful institutions throughout history. They served the Pharaohs, the Mesoamericans, the Arabs, and the Europeans. The masses of Russian serfs, often associated with either tsarist or Communist oppression, were in fact governed (ruthlessly) for centuries by the priests of the Russian Orthodox Church, with its rigid laws, control of riches, complete censorship, and even its secret police.

The other great advantage of an official religion is that it is able to instill fervor and patriotism among its adherents, making them willing to fight fanatically and even suicidally. Spain's slogan, *"Por Diós y España,"* is only one of many. Suicidal behavior of this kind was unknown among clans and bands of hunter-gatherers.

Raids by ambush or similar cunning occurred throughout early history and prehistory. The fanaticism that drove the Crusades and both Christian and Islamic conquests came in with state religions. During centuries of struggle, religion completely dominated cultural behavior. It remains to be seen how long this alliance will survive in the coming century and beyond.

Relativity of Religious Influence

To what extent does religion influence or dominate a culture? This obviously varies a considerable degree in a nation's history. Life in Iran changed suddenly and drastically with the departure of the Shah and the advent of the Ayatollah Khomeini. Scandinavians derive their lifestyle from many Lutheran tenets, but they are not obliged to pray five times a day as good Muslims are. British citizens do not vote for their members of Parliament (MPs) along religious lines—Protestant or Catholic—but the division assumes more importance in the Netherlands, where the rival creeds are more evenly balanced. Protestant America could elect a Catholic President—John F. Kennedy—as early as 1960; it is harder to envisage a Buddhist king in Saudi Arabia.

The impact of religion on a nation's culture also depends to some extent on whether or not it is operating from a "core country." India is the core country for Hinduism, Israel, for the Jewish faith, Russia (in former times), for the Greek Orthodox Church. In such circumstances the influence is all-embracing. China may be considered the base for Buddhism, but the religion has many varieties in China, not to mention Japan, Tibet, Thailand, Cambodia, and elsewhere. Christianity has been divided for centuries with Northern Europe and North America embracing (by and large) Protestantism, while Southern Europe and South America remain loyal to Catholicism. Islam, though one of the fiercest creeds, is problematic inasmuch as it has no clear core country. Mecca may be in Saudi Arabia, but Saudis are comparatively few in number; Turkey, with its own brand of Islam, has a population of over sixty million; and Indonesia, with a more relaxed form of Islam, is out on a far distant limb but with over two hundred million adherents. Also, the bitter rivalry between the Shiite and Sunni branches of Islam complicates the question of "Islamic authority" even further. Who can claim to lead the Muslim world?

Islam

Nevertheless, if we wish to consider the question of the impact of religion on a culture's social, political, or commercial code of conduct, it is perhaps Islam that provides the clearest example. If, for instance, we take the Gulf Arabs as a cultural group, to what extent will Islam affect their interactions with Westerners? What allowances should we make when dealing with them? Can we simply ignore religious differences, or can we put them aside and get on with things? In fact we cannot, much as we may wish to.

In the first place, the Qur'an (Koran) lays down a complete set of rules covering every aspect of human behavior. The rules are clear, and every action in life is classed as Obligatory, Recommended, Neutral, Disapproved, or Forbidden. A Muslim's whole way of life and thought are thus governed. In the obligatory section are the Five Pillars of Islam:

1. acknowledge the Oneness of God and his prophet Muhammad
2. pray five times a day
3. give alms to the poor and to the mosque
4. fast during Ramadan
5. make a pilgrimage to Mecca if at all possible

If you happen to believe in a different God or none at all, if you find interruptions for prayers disruptive, or if you strongly prefer to continue strenuous negotiating during Ramadan, you will have to hold your tongue, be patient, and adapt your behavior to impress Gulf Arabs. The following list of Arab values includes many examples of the influence of Islam:

- Belief in God (Allah)
- Extended family
- Respect for the elderly
- Conservatism
- Gender differentiation
- Limitless hospitality
- Hunger for education
- Desire for justice
- Sincerity
- Morality
- Acute sense of honor
- Integrity
- Protection of the weak
- Desire for praise
- Oratory

Cultural Contrasts with the West

- The West generally separates church and state. Most Islamic countries do not, and religion strongly influences social behavior, politics, and even business.
- In the West the individual is the basic social unit; in Muslim nations it is the family.
- The Westerner believes in cold facts; a Muslim will not let facts destroy honor.
- Westerners want to be fair but just. Muslims want to be just but flexible.
- The West believes in organizations and institutions; Muslims believe in individuals (guided by God).
- Most Western countries have succeeded in or are working on creating equality for men and women. Muslims believe the two sexes have vastly different personalities and roles.
- A Westerner must appear to behave rationally. A Muslim has to impress others with integrity.
- In the West friends are good company. In the Muslim world a friend is a person who cannot refuse your request; neither can you refuse his or hers.
- Westerners like to use official channels to further their business interests. Muslims will often use personal relationships.
- When negotiating, Westerners try to find logical conclusions, whereas Muslims use personalized or religious arguments, emotional appeals, and persistent persuasion.
- Men and women mingle freely in Western societies; in most Islamic countries they do not. Muslim sexuality is territorial; women passing through public places (male spaces) are expected to wear a veil to make themselves invisible. They are rarely seen by Westerners indoors.
- The elderly are often ignored in Western cultures; they expect and receive deference and respect in Muslim countries.

Social and Business Considerations

- One of the golden rules in Islamic countries is observing their taboos: alcohol, pork, eating with one's left hand, discussing female relatives, causing embarrassment, and the mingling of sexes in public places.

- In social situations you should always keep the Muslim concept of immediate and extended family to the forefront of your mind. Each family member may come into regular contact with as many as fifty or sixty relatives, and you may well be introduced to a dozen of them or more. If you are close to one family member, the others will automatically support you.

- The eldest male is generally the head of the family unless he is incapacitated by severe illness. You must show him great respect even if his physical and mental abilities may have diminished. You should strive to find suitable gifts for him.

- If the elder is of great age, a younger brother or cousin may assume his decision-making responsibilities (without usurping his authority). He, too, must be shown great deference.

- In Arab countries and especially in the Gulf, women are not seen socially. They eat separately from the men, often in the kitchen nearby, but are generally "invisible." The mother or wife of the host may well have cooked the meal you are eating, but it is not advisable to seek entry into the kitchen to compliment her. You may "send" compliments discreetly, through the host, but comments should be brief and reflect the magnificence of the host's hospitality.

- The only females you are likely to come into contact with in the dining room of a home in the Gulf are very young ones (three to ten years of age), who may come and play happily around their father or uncles. Treat them as you would Western children. They are rarely seen as they enter their teens and usually wear a scarf after the age of twelve or thirteen.

- Lamb is the most popular meat and is invariably delicious. Normally it (as well as everything else) is eaten with the right hand only. Don't worry if gravy runs down your arm; there will be a washbasin nearby, to which you can retire at regular intervals. If you are left-handed and know you will have some difficulty eating with your right, the correct procedure is to inform the host at the beginning of the meal. Normally, he will give you permission to eat with your left hand, but do not then use your right!

- In general Arabs are governed in their social behavior toward Westerners by the rather strict tenets of their religion, but within this framework they strive to display the utmost hospitality when receiving guests. Mutual respect and showing a genuine interest in each other's culture is the key to enjoying one's involvement in the Muslim world.

Muslims disregard facts if they interfere with honor or integrity. Subjectivity dominates discussion. Nowhere is this more evident than in business.

- Securing business depends more on establishing trust than on price or quality.

- In meetings, order of seating and other items of protocol are important to Muslims. Senior people can appear arrogant or benevolent according to mood or situation.

- Muslims are hard bargainers and regard the bargaining process as a normal part of both business and social life.

- If you do not bargain with them, they will be disappointed.

- When negotiating price, proceed slowly. To offer your counterparts one-tenth of what they propose would be an insult.

- All kinds of emotional arguments can be used and are often more effective than cold reasoning.

- When big deals or joint ventures are being negotiated, expect haggling, but the language and manners used are much more dignified.

- Honor and integrity must always be seen as taken for granted.
- Always impute the best motives.
- You may appear tough, but you must always be just.
- Show kindness (or at least consideration) to weaker opponents.
- Nobody must lose face.
- The spoken word, when solemn, has much more weight than written agreements. However, in general Muslims have great respect for the written word, especially if it has a religious connotation.
- There will usually be one person present who is the real decision maker.
- In a discussion, speak in a loud voice and emphasize your sincerity and integrity.
- Most Muslims like to stand close; don't shy away.
- Personalize all business discussions. You must show you are interested in this *person* rather than his company or any contract.
- Though the cultural gulf between Muslims and Westerners yawns wide, you have a fair chance of making a favorable impression. Muslims admire education, good reputation, and expertise.
- Muslims are looking for sincerity in your dealings with them and expect to be shown the same respect they show you. If you come across as sincere and true, you will do well.
- As a Westerner, you may be uncomfortable with flattery or professions of friendship, but Muslims love these utterances. Do not hesitate to praise their country, their arts, their morality and their integrity, and their dress and food (but *not* their women!).

Note

Westerners usually associate Islam with the Arab world, probably on account of the fact that it is oil-rich and constitutes a large cluster of countries. Arabs, however, account for only about one-fifth of the world's Muslims. The Arab lands, in alphabetical order, are Algeria, Bahrain, Chad, Egypt, Iraq, Jordan, Kuwait, Lebanon, Libya, Mauritania, Morocco, Oman, Qatar, Saudi Arabia, Sudan (partly), Syria, Tunisia, United Arab Emirates (UAE), the West Bank and Gaza (Palestine), and Yemen. These countries have a combined population of approximately 250 million. Most Muslims, however, live outside the Arab world. The Islamic countries of Indonesia, Pakistan, and Bangladesh have a combined population of over 500 million! Iran and Turkey are heading for 70 million each, and there are sizeable populations of Muslims in Malaysia, the Philippines, Central Asia, and the Sahel region of Africa. Neither must we forget that predominantly Hindu India has over 100 million Muslims! In the last part of the twentieth century the Islamic religion made astonishing inroads in the Western world, including Britain, France, and the United States, where at least seven million Muslims reside.

It should also be mentioned that Islamic rules vary in their strictures according to the area and sometimes according to government policy. In general Muslim precepts are most faithfully adhered to in nations such as Saudi Arabia, Kuwait, Qatar, and Iran. Westerners notice fewer restraints in countries such as Turkey, Morocco, Jordan, and Tunisia. Eastern Muslims tend to interpret Islamic regulations more freely, especially in Indonesia, where women normally wear Western dress, mingle with men in public (eating out, etc.), drink beer, and exercise considerable political influence.

Hinduism

Hinduism consists of the values, beliefs, credos, and practices of peoples in South Asia, namely in India, parts of Pakistan and Bangladesh, Sri Lanka, Nepal, and Sikkim. It is the most ancient surviving religion on earth, having possibly more followers than any other in Asia. *Hindu* actually means the "civilization of the Hindus," originally the inhabitants of the area along the Indus River. Hinduism denotes the Indian civilization of the last two thousand years. Interestingly, it evolved from Vedism, the religion of the ancient Indo-European, or Aryan, peoples who arrived to settle in India in the last centuries of the second millennium B.C. Hinduism has experienced different periods of prosperity and decline, but throughout it has demonstrated its capacity for absorbing and assimilating competing creeds. This is because it covers the whole of life and thus integrates a large variety of heterogeneous elements: religious, social, economic, literary, and artistic. An Indian's everyday behavior, both in social and business life, is strongly affected by Hinduism.

Hinduism is a very tolerant religion. It reveres the divine in every manifestation and does not deny the validity of other religions. A Hindu may regard other creeds as inadequate but does not judge them as wrong or objectionable. Hindus may, for instance, embrace Christianity without ceasing to be Hindus.

Hinduism is both a civilization and a conglomerate of religions. It has no founder, no hierarchy, no central authority, but it does have many thousands of gods. There is a Supreme Being who controls everything in life, but many lesser gods represent forms of natural energy—the sun, moon, water, wind, and so forth; the Indo-Europeans were nomadic people who worshipped natural elements. The ultimate reality is called Brahman. Brahman is in all things and is the Self of all living beings. Brahman also has three physical manifestations—Brahma the Creator, Vishnu the

Preserver, and Shiva the Destroyer. This trinity rules over the minor gods. They are all depicted with four arms—Brahma also has four heads, depicting wisdom. The trinity is described as "the One or Whole with three forms."

Another characteristic of Hindu belief is recognition of the Veda (or Vedic scripts), which is the world's most ancient body of religious literature. For Hindus it represents fundamental and unassailable truth. It is, however, unfamiliar to the Indian lower classes, who are largely illiterate or semiliterate. Another Hindu characteristic—the sacrosanctity of the Brahmins (a noble class possessing spiritual supremacy by birth)—is losing its significance in modern India, especially in the north. Vegetarianism and the veneration and protection of the cow are both deemed important. Only about 20 percent of the population do not abhor the eating of beef.

Other, more accepted beliefs are the doctrines of transmigration of souls and karma. Karma is a law of cause and effect, whereby every thought, word, and deed in this life will together determine the conditions of rebirth (after a stay in heaven or hell). The whole process of rebirth is called samsara. Any earthly process is viewed as cyclic. Not only is it personal, enabling an individual to, ultimately, break out of the cycle and attain nirvana (heaven), but it is also collective inasmuch as it conditions the course of world history. The Hindu code of living is termed *dharma*, where an individual must conform to social and tribal duties, to the traditional rules of conduct for his or her particular caste, family, and profession. It is a close approximation to "religious practice" in the West.

Hinduism often appears playful and good-humored to Westerners, who are used to a more solemn approach. Births, marriages, and deaths are colorful occasions in India, celebrated with fireworks displays, decorated elephants, performing monkeys, music, and plenty of food.

The structure of Indian temples, the outward form of images, and the very character of Indian art are mainly determined and circumscribed by religion. Theatre and cinema also come into the religious equation. Theatrical performances of various types and artistic levels are also events to secure blessings and happiness. An element of recreation is blended with spiritual edification. Drama is produced on festive occasions based on themes from epic and legendary history. Spectators must behave appropriately, and themes are developed according to their tastes. There must be a happy ending; evil is defeated by almost obligatory buffoons. Cinema attendance is large and long films offer audiences a bit of everything in one showing: adventure, murder, struggle, humor, love affairs, wars, mystery, song, and dance.

Hindu Considerations in Social and Business Life

- Indians make business decisions against the background of their Hindu religion. They are therefore *not free agents* in the Western sense. The more a Western partner bears this in mind, the more the Indian's behavior will make sense and the better the Westerner can react to the situation.
- Certain rituals, ceremonies, and traditions may interfere with the timing of business procedures. Indians are not always available at the times you want them.
- As Hinduism is quite tolerant of other religions or beliefs, there is not likely to be any friction if you belong to another creed. This contrasts positively with Islam, where Westerners must be careful about what they say and do.
- The belief in karma means that Indians do not mind taking acceptable risks in business. If successful, well and good. If you fail, you can always blame bad karma.
- Hindus are not, however, completely fatalistic. The individual must try to follow the "right path" among those available.

This ties in to some extent with Western choice of alternatives.

- When making decisions, a Hindu is likely to look back for good precedents to follow, whereas a Westerner goes forward with personal pragmatic alternatives and choices.
- The Hindu rule of nonviolence affects business decisions, inasmuch as brute force or domineering attitudes in business are seen as essentially negative.
- The caste system must be borne in mind when doing business at different social levels. Gandhi tried to abolish it; since 1947 the Indian government has reserved up to 30 percent of jobs in government-run institutions to groups that have been discriminated against. Yet, caste not only still exists but remains an important aspect of India's social structures.
- The Westerner must constantly bear in mind the nature of the institution of marriage in the Hindu religion.
- The Indian woman (wife) is often in an unfortunate and underprivileged position. Many die burned in kitchens under suspicious circumstances. Features of extreme Hinduism that trouble Westerners are the treatment of wives, widow burning, untouchability, female infanticide, and child marriages. Hindu reform movements have, however, done much to eliminate these excesses.

Judaism

Judaism, the oldest of the three monotheistic religions originating in the Middle East (the others are Christianity and Islam), is concentrated in Israel, but large Jewish populations exist in many European and American cities.

Judaism was developed by the ancient Hebrews in the Middle East during the third millennium B.C. Tradition holds that Judaism was founded by Abraham, who was chosen by God to receive favorable treatment in return for obedience and worship. Having entered into this covenant with God, Abraham moved to Canaan, from where centuries later his descendants migrated to Egypt and became enslaved. God accomplished the Hebrews' escape from Egypt and renewed the covenant with their leader, Moses. Through Moses, God gave the Hebrews a set of strict laws. These laws are revealed in the Torah, the core of Judaistic scripture. Apart from the Pentateuch, the other holy books are the Talmud and several commentaries. Local worship takes place in a synagogue, a building where the Torah is read in public and preserved in a replica of the Ark of the covenant. A rabbi undertakes the spiritual leadership and pastoral care of a community.

Modern Judaism is split into four large groups: Orthodox, Reform, Conservative, and Liberal Judaism. Orthodox Judaism, followed by many of the world's eighteen million Jews, asserts the supreme authority of the Torah and adheres most closely to traditions, such as the segregation of men and women in the synagogue. Reform Judaism denies the Jews' claim to be God's chosen people and is more liberal in its interpretation of certain laws and the Torah. Conservative Judaism is a compromise between Orthodox and Reform Judaism, its followers adhering to many Orthodox traditions but seeking to apply modern scholarship in interpreting the Torah. Liberal Judaism, also known as Reconstructionism, is a more extreme form of Reform Judaism, seeking to adapt Judaism to the needs of contemporary society. The religious heart of Judaism is centered in Jerusalem. When the Romans drove the Jews from this area in the Diaspora of the first century, others inhabited the land. Until the twentieth century, the region was called Palestine and was populated by Muslims. In the 1880s the Zionist movement started, whereby Jews began returning in steadily increasing numbers.

Jainism

Jainism, founded around 500 B.C. by Vardhamana Mahavira, was the first major sect to break away from Hinduism. Vardhamana was an older contemporary of the Buddha. Jainism, which has always remained an Indian religion, has so much in common with Hinduism that many Hindus regard it as a Hindu sect. Many Jains, however, are inclined to see themselves as distinct. Jains, like Hindus, believe in reincarnation but see extreme asceticism as the most direct path to the world of the spirit. Jainist monks wear loincloths and wander the streets with only a staff and a bowl for alms. Jains believe in nonviolence toward every living creature, even stepping carefully to avoid crushing insects (which tend to be numerous in many parts of India). There are about four million Jains, not so many considering India's population, but they are significantly successful in commerce and finance; in fact they regard all occupations other than commerce and banking as smacking of violence!

Jainist Considerations in Social and Business Life

- Although Jains are few in number, they are respected members of society.
- To impress Jains you should support their ideals: speak the truth, do not steal (in any sense), and avoid causing intentional injury to anyone (man or beast).
- Jains believe one should bear the burdens of life cheerfully, or at least appear to do so.
- If a Westerner is a vegetarian, is celibate, or is an ascetic, he or she stands in even greater stead (but that might be too much of a sacrifice).

Sikhism

Sikhism is the religion of an Indian group founded in the Punjab in the late fifteenth century by Guru Nanak. It is therefore a comparatively new religion, a breakaway from Hinduism. There are about twelve million Sikhs, most of whom live in the state of Punjab, although about 15 percent live in the state of Haryana and in Delhi. Some Sikhs have also settled in Malaysia, Singapore, East Africa, England, the United States, and Canada.

Sikhs have a rather special relationship with the British. In the period from 1840 to 1856 they fought each other continuously, but when the Indian Mutiny broke out in 1857, the Punjab province stayed loyal to the British, and the Sikhs took a prominent role in suppressing the mutiny. For this loyalty they were rewarded with substantial grants of land, and the proportion of Sikhs in the British army was greatly increased. The British also set up a program of reclamation of desert lands in the Punjab through an extensive system of canals, bringing unprecedented prosperity to areas where Sikhs were the most favored settlers. Further, Sikh loyalty to the British cause was evidenced in World War I, when Sikhs formed over 20 percent of the British Indian army.

Sikhs can be recognized by their well-known symbols—*kesa* (unshorn hair usually wrapped in a turban), *kachcha* (short trousers), *kangha* (ivory comb), *kara* (shell bracelet), and *kirpan* (sword). The Sikhs have great skill in all forms of mechanical matters.

Sikhism differs from other Hindu-based credos inasmuch as it rejects nonviolence as a principle, allows the killing of animals for food, and recognizes only one God. Sikh violence has been demonstrated several times in the last two centuries. Sikhism had already become a militant brotherhood in the seventeenth century under Guru Govind Singh, but in the early 1980s, one branch of Sikh extremists proclaimed a separate state called Khalistan.

The armed struggles that followed destroyed Punjab's prosperity. Extremists converted the Golden Temple—the most sacred Sikh shrine—into military headquarters, and the army action in 1984 caused much bitterness among Sikhs, resulting subsequently in the assassination of Indira Gandhi by her Sikh bodyguards.

Sikh Considerations in Social and Business Life

- Sikhs are proud and sensitive; one must therefore use care when interacting with them.
- Once their loyalty has been won, Sikhs are hardworking and reliable.
- Avoid political discussions with them.
- They ally themselves easily with Westerners, especially the British.

Buddhism

Buddhism is actually an offshoot of Hinduism and once presented it with a great threat. Founded by Siddhartha Gautama in the fifth century B.C. in northern India, Buddhism was a dynamic force for more than a thousand years. It took a big leap forward in India when it was adopted by the great Emperor Asoka in the third century B.C., as a result of which the religion was carried outward to every part of his extensive empire—Burma, Thailand, Sri Lanka, Korea, China, Vietnam, Nepal, Tibet, Central Asia, and Japan. Buddhism is still the dominant religion in most of these countries, but its power declined in India in A.D. 800, when it was reabsorbed into Hinduism in the revivalist movement started by Sankara.

Buddhism incorporates Hindu elements such as karma and reincarnation but reinterprets them in more dynamic form. Buddha did not see karma as being related to fate or predestination. Rather it was a strict causal law of dynamic action, enabling human be-

ings to better their lot by their own actions and not be bound by
the harmful rules, regulations, and general extremism of Hinduism and Jainism. Hindus rejected Buddhism as a religion of compromise.

Buddhism is a "practical" religion with no mention of supernatural beings or deities. In this sense it blends well with Confucianism (a code of ethics) but differs sharply from Islam and
Christianity. At the heart of Buddhism are the Four Noble Truths:

1. All life is sorrow.

2. Sorrow is the result of unchecked desire.

3. Cessation of desire ends sorrow.

4. One must follow the Middle Way (and avoid extremes).

The *path* to follow is eightfold:

1. right understanding

2. right purpose

3. right speech

4. right action

5. right livelihood

6. right effort

7. seek the truth

8. contemplation

Buddhist Considerations in Social and Business Life

- Observance of the four precepts means that a believer con-
  ducts his or her life in a visibly unselfish manner and respects you if you do likewise. This may cause problems for
  Westerners, many of whom are strongly individualistic (for
  example, Americans and some British), or for those who

don't hesitate to apply drastic remedies to certain business situations.

- In Buddhists' eyes one should always display moderation.
- With respect to the eightfold path, one first has to be sufficiently explicit to clear away any misunderstandings about the meaning or purpose of one's intentions. This may involve more repetition than a Westerner is used to.
- One must emphasize the sharing of mutual goals. These must be expressed in "right speech" (clarity plus courtesy) and be followed up by corresponding action (often symbolic) to set out on the right path.
- Seeking the truth implies not only honesty in business but also the flexibility to change course if circumstances alter.
- Contemplation implies giving adequate time and thought to one's procedures and those of one's associates in order to avoid mistakes by rushing things.

Shinto

Shinto is the name given to indigenous religious beliefs and practices of the Japanese people. The word means "the way of *kami*" (the way of the Divine). Shinto is more readily observed in Japanese social life and personal motivations than as a doctrine of formal rules or a philosophy; it is closely connected with the Japanese value system and ways of thinking and acting. As a basic mindset toward life, Shinto emphasizes "sincerity, a pure heart, and uprightness." Ancient Shinto was polytheistic. People found kami in nature, which ruled the seas and the mountains.

Shinto does not have a weekly religious service; instead, people visit shrines at their convenience. Shinto is less ostentatious than Hinduism or Buddhism; a simple *torii* gate stands at the entrance of the shrine. Visitors to a shrine will first approach an ablution basin, where the purification that is necessary to make communion between man and kami possible is accomplished. After they have washed their hands and rinsed their mouths, visitors usually enter the shrine to pray and make small offerings of food or money. The history of the shrine is recorded in picture scrolls and small wooden plaques around the back wall. Other articles within the shrine consist of swords and other arms, sculpture, and specimens of calligraphy.

Shinto actually preceded national and cultural consciousness; thus it has no founder. The Yayoi culture, which originated in North Kyushu in the third century A.D., contributed elements to Shinto, and by the fourth century a nation with an ancestor of the present Imperial Household as its head had probably been established.

Confucianism, introduced into Japan in the fifth century, also stimulated the development of Shinto ethical teachings. As Japan became centralized, Shinto began to develop as a national cult; myths and legends of various clans were combined and reorganized into a pan-Japanese mythology with the Imperial Household as its center. The kami of the Imperial Household became the kami of the whole nation and its people. Offerings were made by the state each year.

Buddhism was first introduced into Japan in A.D. 538, and by the eighth century many began to interpret Shinto from a Buddhist perspective. Shinto kami came to be viewed as protectors of Buddhism. The two religions blended well. Buddhist temples were built within Shinto shrine precincts from the eighth century onward. Such coexistence is visible in Japan today among the sixty million believers.

Shinto Considerations in Social and Business Life

- Believers, in their search for "purification," tend to be sincere, upright, and basically honest in their social and business dealings.

- Shintoists are tolerant of other religions; relations are not only harmonious but cooperative. This is good for international business!
- Shintoists possess an inner depth; Westerners should not mistake their sincere simplicity in many matters for naïveté.
- The Allied powers ordered the Japanese government to disestablish state Shinto at the end of World War II. State rites performed by the emperor are now regarded as the private religious practices of the Imperial Family. Westerners tend to look kindly on Shinto activities, and ancestor worship causes no discord among Latin Catholics and most Protestant Christian sects.
- Westerners experience great pleasure in the aesthetic and artistic expressions of Shintoism. The major Shinto shrines in Kyoto, Tokyo, Nikko, Nara, and so on, are places of great beauty, often amidst a serene background of magnificent trees and mountains.
- Japanese art, so much appreciated by Westerners, is largely an expression of Shinto values.
- Japanese festivals (*matsuri*) and musical events are popular among Westerners; the mood is gay at matsuri, more solemn and symbolic in Kabuki and Noh theatre. Shintoists have recently begun to compose solemn religious songs using Western music (to be used in the future along with the traditional music).

Christianity

The three major monotheistic religions—Christianity, Islam, and Judaism—started in the Middle East and, despite their differences, share many key beliefs as well as some prophets. Christianity evolved from Judaism with the teachings of Jesus, which were spread to Europe through the ministry of the Apostle Paul and other missionaries and later through the influence of the Roman Empire after the Emperor Constantine was converted in A.D. 313.

Christianity subsequently split into three major branches: Roman Catholicism, Eastern Orthodox, and Protestantism. Protestantism dominates Northern European countries and some of their former colonies; Roman Catholicism is prevalent in Southern Europe and South America; the Orthodox Church dominates Eastern Europe and the former Russian Empire of the czars.

Were one to ask a selection of Protestants—Americans, Britons, Germans, or Scandinavians—about the degree to which religion affected their lifestyle, they would probably assert that it played a less important part than Catholicism does with Catholics. They often perceive the Roman Catholic Church as a rigid, dogmatic institution, brooking no rivals and dominating the behavior of its flock through a vigilant and somewhat nosy priesthood. In reality Protestant religions often define lifestyle with more persistence than one might think, while Catholicism in practice (though not always in theory) is blessed with a certain flexibility and liberalism. It is true that the confessional demands regular penitence, which the Protestant does not have to demonstrate (or even admit to), but it also grants immediate forgiveness, which is a handy escape valve for minor sinners. The priests are human, too, and frequently offer comforting advice, often deriving from their own weaknesses. The fatherly Irish priest, so often depicted by Hollywood as sharing a whisky with a local recalcitrant, is in real life a valuable social worker and therapist.

The Catholic Church in Latin countries such as Italy, Spain, and Portugal, while frequently seen as a disciplinarian among its members, is expected to show great compassion toward its less fortunate adherents. In such countries, where the religion has little competition from Protestantism, dogma is less rigid, attitudes toward other creeds less defensive. The "sinister" aspects of the Roman

Catholic Church—brainwashing of the young, disregard for other beliefs—tend to be seen only in states where religions are roughly equal in strength (the Netherlands) or where there is a long history of bitter struggle and persecution (Ireland and some parts of England). Such inter-Christian rivalry is markedly on the wane in the early twenty-first century, particularly in the face of rising Islamic influence. World events may lead to an effective amalgamation of Christian religions—at least to the consolidation of a Council of Churches—where not only Roman Catholics and Protestants see more eye to eye, but where Jews, Eastern Orthodox Christians, and splinter groups such as Quakers achieve greater integration.

To return to the question of lifestyle, the average Protestant rarely consults with the local minister about his or her social or business life, except for occasional personal therapy. The typical English vicar retains a certain visibility and reputation in small towns and villages, but many of his flock do not attend church. Scandinavians go to church for baptisms, weddings, funerals, and sometimes for confirmation classes. Americans are more churchgoing. Yet all these Protestants lead their lives according to certain rules that, though largely unwritten, are no less mandatory if they wish to command the respect of the congregation.

The work ethic is a central tenet of Protestantism, bringing with it a code of behavior that supports the concept. This includes rising early, eating meals quickly, rushing to work, planning activities, wasting little time, being efficient and tidy, observing legalities, pursuing success, and making money as soon as possible. The Protestant is expected to

- play his or her required part in community projects and social functions,
- be a good citizen who is not a nuisance to the neighbors,
- pay debts promptly and respect the police and other authorities,

- pay taxes regularly and support charities,
- be frank and direct, and
- generally tell the truth—scientific truth, that is—without the ambivalence so often heard among non-Protestants.

The rewards for this good behavior include a fine house (with land and a well-kept garden), one or two handsome cars, good local schools for (two) children, and membership in local sports clubs and other associations that provide a rich social "middle" between family and state. The family plays a less dominant role than in Catholic countries, though children are well taken care of, adequately educated, and encouraged to envisage early entrepreneurism, which will in turn lead to their perpetuating the Protestant work-equals-success ethic and their continuing prosperity.

Such a lifestyle, though not formally prescribed by the Church, derives from the drive for independence and self-reliance of early Protestants who divorced themselves from the established sources of power and "made it on their own." This way of life is particularly evident in the United States, where the pioneering attitudes of the early settlers, the frontier spirit, and the hardships involved in conquering a continental wilderness produced a competitive, driving individual the likes of whom the world had never seen.

The global competitiveness of Protestants in the area of commerce is both astonishing and well documented. *The Economist* and the International Institute for Management Development in Lausanne both publish annual surveys of the comparative global competitiveness of more than two hundred countries. Rankings reflect the ability of a country to achieve sustained high rates of GDP growth per capita. They are based on approximately 250 criteria covering such items as the openness of the economy, the role of government, the development of financial markets, the quality of infrastructure, technology, business management, and judicial and political institutions. In the 2002 rankings (headed by the United States, Finland, Singapore, Luxembourg, and the Netherlands), 17 of the top 22 countries had large Protestant majorities. One must assume therefore that there is a good case for Protestant values being conducive to successful commercial practices. Among Catholic countries only Ireland made the top 20. Spain ranked 23; France, 25; Brazil, 31; and Italy, 32.

As far as the Eastern Orthodox churches are concerned, a lot of ground has been lost in their battles with the Communist Party, particularly in Russia. In the Balkans, too, the Church took a battering, and many buildings were lost due to direct attack or lack of funds. The congregations, however, have remained surprisingly resilient. Under Tito, Yugoslavian monasteries hung on to their riches, and followers attended services in spite of Communist disdain. The Orthodox Church sets great store by lavish ceremonies, especially at Easter, and the priests and bishops continue to enjoy considerable prestige. Particularly in the countryside, in Bulgaria, Serbia and inside Russia itself, once-splendid architecture has been remarkably preserved and refurbished. As religious freedom is now guaranteed all the way from St. Petersburg to Sofia, it remains to be seen what influence will be retained by this once powerful Church.

Christian Considerations in Social and Business Life

While Westerners clearly see the impact of Eastern religions (e.g., Islam, Buddhism, Hinduism) on everyday social and business behavior, it may not occur to them that different branches of Christianity exert varying influences on comportment. The following list contrasts views of society held by Protestants and Roman Catholics.

Protestant
- honesty, truth, transparency
- justice, rule of law, discipline
- freedom of speech and of worship
- equality for women
- democratic institutions
- high taxes, social welfare
- work ethic (work=success=money)
- entrepreneurism, egalitarianism
- punctuality, neatness, cleanliness
- tidy public spaces, civil order
- early Puritanical precepts gradually liberalizing and splitting into many sects and credos

Catholic
- the existence of only one true Church
- strict dogma and ritual
- hierarchical society
- strong leaders, great power distance
- powerful families, clans, and cliques
- nepotism in business
- use of key people rather than officialdom
- close personal relationships
- respect for family and elders
- relaxed attitude toward time
- liberal view of sin (sin can be absolved through confession)
- philosophical view of truth
- compassion in business

The Globalization of Religion

This chapter began by noting that the advancements made by science, especially in the twentieth century, might have been expected to undermine or at least diminish in importance the influence of religion on human social and political behavior. Yet this has not happened. Religion seems to mold human attitudes and subsequent courses of action in a more decisive manner than ever. The diverse religious concepts discussed above indicate widely diverging mindsets regarding morality, restraints, and "right living." Although commonalities are clearly discernible in Islam, Christianity, Buddhism, and so on, any movement toward globalization of beliefs, in the twenty-first century at least, is a very tall order indeed, particularly in times when extremism runs rampant.

But what about world peace? How should we best attempt reconciliation not only of political and economic goals but also of humanity's destiny on the planet we all share? Is religion going to be the panacea or, perpetually, an obstacle to these lofty but surely desirable aspirations?

Mrs. Gro Harlem Brundtland, former prime minister of Norway, used the word *obstacle* when referring to family planning in her opening address to the United Nations' International Conference on Population and Development in Cairo in 1994.

> *Traditional religions and cultural obstacles can be overcome by economic and social development with the focus on enhancement of human resources. For example Buddhist Thailand, Moslem Indonesia, and Catholic Italy demonstrate that relatively sharp reductions in fertility can be achieved in an amazingly short time.*

Mrs. Brundtland, as a Western woman leading a government with an equal number of female and male ministers, was warming to her theme admirably, but culturally she was treading on very thin ice. The idea that religious aspects of life can be separated from such secular notions as politics and economics is entirely alien to a large number of cultures, especially in Africa, the Middle East, and Asia. In Buddhist, Taoist, Shintoist, Confucian, and particularly Hindu and Islamic cultures, religion is integrated with and permeates the whole way of life. Mrs. Brundtland, in spite of her good intentions, was roundly attacked and castigated for her remarks. Strong criticisms of points in the draft agenda for the conference concerning family planning and the decriminalization of abortions led to the Vatican's seeking and finding support for its restricted views in several Muslim countries!

If the notion that religious obstacles should be overcome through social and economic development sounds very much like evolutionism, Pierre Teilhard de Chardin went much further in his book *L'Energie Humaine* in which he attempted to equate evolution with religion. Discussing the pursuit of science, he stated that humanity is not seeking another god of infinite power but rather an understanding of its own evolution. As humanity develops, ethics have to follow suit. Teilhard de Chardin stressed that one of the great deficiencies of the old religions was that they adhered to dogmas that fossilized human thought. What was good two thousand years ago may be inadequate or even degrading in the twenty-first century. Ethics may have to change. Teilhard de Chardin discussed not only familiar arguments in favor of population reduction and depopulation considerations but also went out on a cultural limb with suggestions that scientific methods should be used to control sickness and counterrevolution. He went so far as to suggest selection methods for developing a superior human type to bypass the current "genetic roulette" system. While the earth was unbounded at the time of the creation of the major religions, today's situation is quite different. Teilhard de Chardin focuses on the sanctity-of-life ethics versus the quality-of-life ethics.

The noted Catholic theologian Hans Küng is considerably more optimistic about raising ethical standards within a religious context. One of the great ironies of our time is that while globalization ties people together economically, it also internationalizes problems: organized crime, drug trade, ethnic and religious warfare, and ecological pollution, to name a few. Globalization frightens people almost as much as it seduces them. Küng, however, sees the existence of an "inner moral standard" that is not associated with any particular religion or philosophy but is shared by most of them. Muslim, Christian, Hindu, and Shinto concepts of decency are not so dissimilar. "A necessary minimum of shared ethical values and basic attitudes" (probably already existing) could be specified by religious and secular leaders.

Some progress has already been made in this respect. In 1993 at the Parliament of the World's Religions, representatives from more than 120 religions adopted a "Declaration toward a Global Ethic." In 1997 former heads of state drafted a "Universal Declaration of Human Responsibilities" and gave copies to all heads of state as well as to the United Nations and UNESCO. United Nations Secretary General Kofi Annan formed an advisory committee consisting of Küng, Richard von Weizsäcker, and Nobel Laureate Amartya Sen to help him prepare for UN Year 2001, which focused on the dialogue among civilizations. Küng asked politicians to come up with a plan similar to the Marshall Plan, which created an international order after World War II.

As a theologian, Küng has limited hopes for globalized ethics unless religious leaders begin to lead in what is their particular domain: *"There won't be peace among nations without peace among religions."* A healthy dose of charisma is needed, among leading figures, whether they are statesmen, women, religious luminaries, or monarchs. Empress Michiko of Japan made an illuminating remark in her recent booklet "Building Bridges," where she detected the beginnings of positive juvenile globalization in the phenomenon of universally read, worldwide children's books. If we can all believe in *Alice in Wonderland....*

Chapter 4

Cross-Century Worldviews

At the end of chapter 1 we contemplated the staggering diversity of the world's languages, core beliefs, entrenched views, and cultural behavior. Our hunter-gatherer forebears probably had simpler goals and philosophies. Recorded history over the last five millennia indicates that the more civilizations come into contact, the more they seem to clash. The two world wars have been daunting both in scope and complexity.

If we regard the wars in Korea, Vietnam, Iran, Iraq, Kuwait, Yugoslavia, and Afghanistan as local conflagrations, we could claim the world has enjoyed relative peace since 1945. This peace is indeed very relative because many lives have been lost and untold billions of dollars have been spent on armaments in this period, but at least the major powers—the United States, Russia,

Britain, France, Germany, and China—have so far avoided any depth of involvement in hostilities that would have necessitated nuclear strikes and subsequent global chaos. Japan—still non-nuclear—has kept its head down.

In this same period, politico-economic associations such as the EU, NAFTA, ASEAN and MERCOSUR have been formed with the objective of facilitating interregional and world trade via an increase in international cooperation and understanding. At the beginning of the twenty-first century, we consider ourselves rational, knowledgeable, and possessing a high degree of technology and scientific insight. In theory we should have attained a level of comprehension and perception that would enable us as citizens of the world to settle for a quasi-universal worldview and consign cultural dissension to the dustbin of history.

Unfortunately, we have not yet come so far. We can bear witness to real progress in certain areas. France and Germany seem to have put an end to their traditional hostility; they trade with each other vigorously. In spite of frequent niggling, the United States and Japan have set up bilateral trade of a magnitude the world has never seen. Chinese and Korean goods are ubiquitous in both Europe and the U.S., and the success stories of Singapore, Hong Kong, and Taiwan have shown that vigorous exports pave the way to prosperity.

When trade and employment flourish, cultural problems take a back seat. In times of recessions—and these occur with annoying regularity—friction develops between states with opposing philosophies. Lack of understanding leads to breakdowns of communication, application of sanctions, and threats of isolationist policies. These crises may be exacerbated by political motives, but often cultural differences are the root of the problem. Countries belonging to the same cultural category, for instance, Nordics on the one hand or Italians and Spaniards on the other, rarely fail to sort out their differences in terms of trade and cooperation.

At cross-century we have a situation where there are many nation-states and different cultures but where enduring misunderstandings arise principally when there is a clash of *category* rather than *nationality*. For example, Germany and the Netherlands experience national friction, but they understand and cooperate with each other well because they are both *linear-active* (see later in this chapter for a definition). Friction between Korea and Japan occasionally borders on hatred, but their common *reactive* nature leads to blossoming bilateral trade.

Let us examine for a moment the number and variety of cultures as they now stand and consider how classification and adaptation might guide us toward better understanding.

The Categorization of Cultures

There are over two hundred recognized countries or nation-states in the world; the number of cultures is considerably greater on account of strong regional variations. For instance, marked differences in values and behavior are observable in the north and south of such countries as Italy, France, and Germany, while other states are formed of groups with clearly different historical or ethnic backgrounds (the United Kingdom with its Celtic and Saxon components, Fiji's Polynesians and Indians, and Russia's numerous subcultures such as Tatar, Finnic, Chechen, etc.)

In a world of rapidly globalizing business, electronic proximity, and political-economic associations, the ability to interact successfully with foreign partners in the spheres of commercial activity, diplomatic intercourse, and scientific interchange is seen as increasingly essential and desirable. Cross-cultural training followed by international experience goes a long way toward facilitating better relationships and reducing misunderstanding. Ideally, the trainee acquires deepening insight into the target (partner's) culture and adopts a *cultural stance* toward the partner/colleague, designed (through adaptation) to fit suitably with the attitudes of the other.

The question then arises as to how many adaptations or stances are required for international interaction. Not even the most informed and adaptable executive or professional could envisage assuming two hundred different personalities! Even handling the fifteen different national types on EU committees and working groups has proved a daunting task for European delegates, not to mention the chairpersons.

Such chameleon-like behavior is out of the question, but the question of adaptation remains nevertheless important. The reticent, factual Finn must grope toward a modus operandi with the loquacious, emotional Italian. Americans will turn over many more billions in trade if they learn to communicate effectively with the Japanese and Chinese.

Assuming a suitable cultural stance would be quickly simplified if there were fewer cultural types to familiarize oneself with, is it possible to boil down 200 to 250 sets of behavior to 50 or 20 or 10 or even half a dozen? Cross-culturalists have grappled with this problem over several decades. Some have looked at geographical divisions (north, south, east, and west) but what is "eastern" culture? And is it really unified? People can be classified according to their religion (Muslim, Christian, Hindu) or race (Caucasian, Asian, African, Polynesian, Indian, Eskimo, Arab), but such nomenclature contains many inconsistencies—Christian Norwegians and Lebanese, Caucasian Scots and Georgians, Muslim Moroccans and Indonesians, and so on. Other classification attempts such as professional, corporate, or regional have too many subcategories to be useful. Generational culture is important but ever-changing. Political classification (left, right, centrist) has many (changeable) hues, too.

Writers such as Geert Hofstede have sought dimensions to cover all cultures. His four dimensions included power distance, collectivism/individualism, femininity/masculinity, and uncertainty avoidance. Later he added a fifth dimension, long-term/short-term orientation. Edward T. Hall classified groups as monochronic or polychronic, high or low context, and past- or future-oriented. Fons Trompenaars' dimensions were different still: universalist/particularist, individualist/collectivist, specific/diffuse, achievement-/ascription-oriented and neutral/emotional or affective. The German sociologist Ferdinand Tönnies identified gemeinschaft and gesellschaft cultures. Florence Kluckhohn's five categories were in the form of solutions to problems: time, person-nature, human nature, form of activity, and relation to one's cultural compatriots. Samuel Huntington drew fault lines between civilizations—West European, Islam, Hindu, Orthodox, Japanese, Sinic, and African.

The need for a convincing categorization is obvious. It enables us to

1. predict behavior,

2. clarify why people do what they do,

3. avoid giving offense,

4. search for some kind of unity,

5. standardize policies, and

6. perceive neatness and *Ordnung* (order).

My own research and experience has led me to believe in a three-category classification of cultures: linear-active, multi-active, and reactive.* My extensive exposure to Asians inclined me to think that European and American cross-culturalists had failed to cat-

---

* For a chart distinguishing linear-active, multi-active, and reactive cultural attributes, see Appendix A, pages 295–97.

egorize them succinctly. Japanese are not polychronic (like Italians), but neither are they monochronic (like Germans). While Koreans are clearly particularist, the Chinese are much less so, but neither are they universalist. Japan is high context, but Indonesians and Vietnamese border on low context. Short-term and long-term orientation varies enormously between Korea and the Philippines on the one hand and Japan and China on the other.

Most Asians (with the notable exception of the Indians and Pakistanis) classify as reactive inasmuch as they will veer toward linear- or multi-activity within the framework of their reaction to their interlocutor. Thus Japanese stress their qualities of punctuality, factuality, and planning when dealing with Germans but adopt a more flexible, people-oriented approach when confronted with multi-active Spaniards or Latin Americans.

The linear-active, multi-active, and reactive categorization cuts across racial, religious, philosophical, and class divides. Protestant Scandinavians, Catholic Swiss, black and white Americans, Semitic Israelis, and rich and poor Australians are all linear as a whole. Multi-actives can be Latins, Slavs, or Africans. Chinese, Koreans, and Vietnamese are classical Confucian reactives, but quiet Finns also have many reactive characteristics, and Swedes and the British often react thoughtfully and unhurriedly to proposals from more aggressive cultures.

The diagram on page 75 summarizes the essential characteristics of each group and indicates different degrees of difficulty typically encountered when they interact with each other.

Linear-Actives

Linear-active people tend to be task-oriented, highly organized planners who complete action chains by doing one thing at a time, preferably in accordance with a linear agenda. They prefer straightforward and direct discussion, depending on facts and figures they obtain from reliable, often printed or computer-based sources. Speech is for information exchange, and conversationalists take turns talking and listening. Truthful rather than diplomatic, linear-actives do not fear confrontation, adhering to logic rather than emotions. They partly conceal feelings and value a certain amount of privacy. Results are key, as is moving forward quickly and compromising when necessary to achieve a deal.

Linear-actives believe that good products make their own way and sometimes fail to see that sales are based on relationships in many parts of the world. They normally use official channels to pursue their aims and are usually not inclined to use connections, take shortcuts, or influence opinions through presents or undercover payments. Normally law-abiding, linear-actives have faith in rules and regulations to guide their conduct.

They honor written contracts and do not unduly delay payment for goods or services received. When doing business, they are keen on punctual performance, quality, and reliable delivery dates. Mañana behavior and overloquacity are frowned upon. They are process oriented, brief on the telephone, and respond quickly to written communication. Status is gained through achievement, bosses are often low-key, and money is important. Rationalism and science dominate thinking more than religion does.

Multi-Actives

Multi-actives are emotional, loquacious, and impulsive people; they attach great importance to family, feelings, relationships, and people in general. They set great store by compassion and human warmth. They like to do many things at the same time and are poor followers of agendas. Conversation is roundabout and animated as everyone tries to speak and listen at the same time. Not surprisingly, interruptions are frequent, pauses in conversation few. Multi-actives are uncomfortable with silence and can seldom tolerate it.

In business, relationships and connections are seen as more important than products. The former pave the way for the sale of the latter. Relationships are best when they are face-to-face; they cannot be maintained over a protracted period simply by written correspondence or phone calls, although the former has less effect with multi-actives than the latter. They much prefer to obtain their information directly from people and trade in rumor and gossip. Multi-actives show less respect than linear-actives do for official announcements, rules, or regulations. Although they have limited respect for authority in general, they nevertheless accept their place in their own social or company hierarchy. Strong bosses are admired and are also expected to protect their employees.

Multi-actives are often late with delivery dates and paying for services or goods received. Less interested in schedules or deadlines than linear-actives are, multi-actives often move only when they are ready. Therefore, procrastination is common, punctuality infrequent. Multi-actives' concepts of time and discourse are decidedly nonlinear, and they fail to understand the importance that timetables have for linear-active people.

Multi-actives are flexible and frequently change their plans, which in themselves are not as detailed as those of linear-actives. Improvisation and handling chaos are strong points.

Multi-actives borrow and lend property rather freely. They are gregarious and inquisitive, valuing privacy less than company. Often epicurean, they adhere less to strict Protestant values than linear-actives do. In business, they use charisma, rhetoric, manipulation, and negotiated truth. They are diplomatic and tactful and often circumvent laws and officialdom to take "shortcuts." They entertain lavishly and give presents or undercover payments to secure deals and contracts.

Reactives

Reactives, or listeners, rarely initiate action or discussion, preferring to first listen to and establish the other's position, then react to it and formulate their own opinion.

Reactives listen before they leap, concentrating on what the speaker is saying and refusing to let their minds wander (difficult for Latins). Rarely, if ever, do they interrupt a speaker during a discourse/speech/presentation. When the speaker is finished, they do not reply immediately but rather leave a decent period of silence after the speaker has stopped in order to show respect for the weight of the remarks, which must be considered unhurriedly and with due deference.

Even when representatives of a reactive culture begin their reply, they are unlikely to voice any strong opinion immediately. A more probable tactic is to ask further questions on what has been said in order to clarify the speaker's intent and aspirations. The Japanese, particularly, go over each point in detail many times to make sure there are no misunderstandings. The Chinese take their time to assemble a variety of strategies to avoid discord with the initial proposal.

Reactives are introverts, distrustful of a surfeit of words and consequently are adept at nonverbal communication, which is achieved by subtle body language. Reactions are worlds apart from the excitable gestures of Latins and Africans.

In reactive cultures the preferred mode of communication is monologue-pause-reflection-monologue. If possible, one lets the other side deliver his or her monologue first. In linear-active and multi-active cultures, the communication mode is a dialogue. The person speaking may be interrupted by frequent comments, even questions, which signify polite interest in what is being said. As soon as the speaker pauses, someone else takes his or her turn immediately. Many Westerners have an extremely weak tolerance for silence.

Reactives not only tolerate silence well but regard it as a very meaningful, almost refined, part of discourse. The opinions of the other party are not to be taken lightly, or dismissed with a snappy or flippant retort. Clever, well-formulated arguments require—deserve—lengthy silent consideration. The American, having delivered a sales pitch, leans forward and says, "Well, what do you think?" If a reactive is asked for an opinion, he or she begins to think—in silence.

The reactive "reply-monologue" is context-centered and will presume a considerable amount of knowledge on the part of the listener (who, after all, probably spoke first). Because the listener is presumed to be knowledgeable, Japanese, Chinese, or Finnish interlocutors will often be satisfied with expressing their thoughts in half-utterances, indicating that the listener can fill in the rest. It is a kind of compliment.

Reactives not only rely on utterances and partial statements to further the conversation, but they also indulge in other habits that confuse the linear-active or multi-active. They use, for instance, a "roundabout" style, with impersonal verbs (one is leaving) or the passive voice (one of the machines seems to have been tampered with), either to deflect blame or with the general aim of politeness.

As reactive cultures tend to use names less frequently than multi-active or linear-active ones do, the impersonal, vague nature of the discussion is further accentuated. Lack of eye contact, so typical of the reactive, does not help the situation. A Finn or a Japanese, embarrassed by another's stare, seeks eye contact only at the beginning of the discussion or when he wishes to signal the interlocutor to take up her turn in the conversation.

Smalltalk does not come easily to reactives. While the Japanese and Chinese trot out well-tried formalisms to indicate courtesy, they tend to regard questions such as "Well, how goes it?" as a literal request for information and may take the opportunity to voice a complaint. On other occasions their overlong pauses or slow visible reactions cause nonreactives to think they are slow-witted or have nothing to say.

It is always important to bear in mind that the actual content of the response delivered by a reactive represents only a small part of the significance surrounding the event. Context-centered utterances inevitably attach less importance to *what* is said than to *how* something is said, *who* said it, and what is *behind* what is said. What is *not* said may be the main thrust of the reply.

Self-disparagement is another tactic of reactives; it eliminates the possibility of offending others. Such humility may draw the other person into praising one's conduct or decisions. Linear-actives and multi-actives must be aware of presuming that self-disparagement is connected with a weak position.

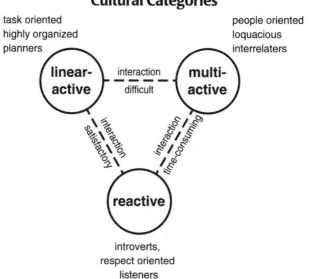

Cultural Categories

Intercategory Comparisons

Common linear-active behavior will facilitate smooth relations between, for instance, Swedes and Flemish Belgians. Likewise, a common multi-active mentality will help Italians, Argentinians, and Brazilians interact successfully. In the Vietnam War, the most popular foreign troops with the South Vietnamese were reactive Koreans. The groups shared naturally underlying similarities because they both belonged to the same cultural category.

When members of *different* cultural categories begin to interact, the differences far outnumber the commonalities. The diagrams on pages 77–78 illustrate intercategory relationships. When we look carefully at these diagrams, we can see that commonalities exist among all three types, but *similarities are fewest between linear-actives and multi-actives*. Reactives fit better with the other two because they *react*. Consequently, the trade-hungry Japanese settle comfortably in conservative, orderly Britain and also have reasonably few problems adapting to excitable Latins on account of their similar orientation toward people, diplomatic communication, and power distance.

The entirely disparate worldviews of linear-actives and multi-actives pose a problem of great magnitude as we begin a new century of international trade and aspire to globalization. How can the pedantic, linear German and the voluble, exuberant Brazilian share similar views of, for instance, duty, commitments, or personnel policies? How can the French reconcile their sense of intellectual superiority with cold Swedish logic or the American bottom-line mindset? Will Anglo-Saxon hiring and firing procedures ever gain acceptability in people-oriented, multi-active Spain, Portugal, or Argentina? When will product-oriented Americans, Britons, and Germans come to the realization that products make their own way only in linear-active societies but that *relationships* pave the way for product penetration in multi-active

Linear-Active and Multi-Active Comparison

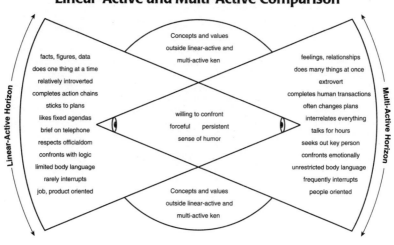

Linear-Active and Reactive Comparison

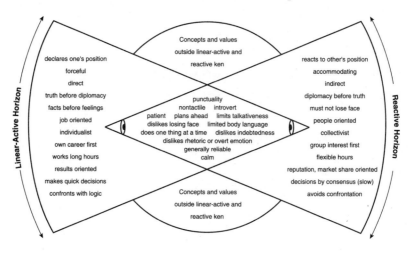

Multi-Active and Reactive Comparison

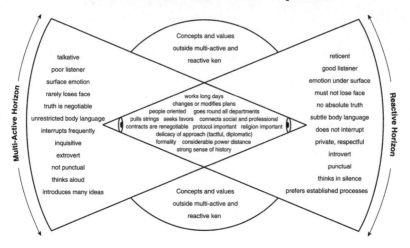

cultures? One can well say, "Let's concentrate on selling to the six hundred million linear-active customers in the world." But what about multi-active and reactive customers? The fact is, there are a lot of them: three and a half billion multi-active and just under two billion reactive customers at last count. The chart below shows predicted numbers in each category for the year 2005.

The figures on pages 80–82 summarize the salient characteristics of the three cultural categories. Figures A, B, and C elaborate on the values and communication styles in the linear world, multiworld, and reactive world respectively. Figure D, page 83, indi-

Cultural Category Population Statistics

Linear-active: 600 million
Multi-active: 3,500 billion
Reactive: 1,800 billion
Hybrid (multi-active and reactive):
    Indonesia: 220 million
    Philippines: 80 million
TOTAL: 6,200 million

cates that while some countries are convincingly linear-active (Germany), multi-active (Argentina, Brazil), or reactive (Vietnam), others are more hybrid, combining traits from two or even three categories.

A discernible thread of *extraneous* influences has begun to weave itself into the area of international business. For instance, the successful Japanese, with their logical manufacturing processes and considerable financial acumen, are becoming more amenable to Western linear thinking. Hong Kong was created to make money, a very linear and countable commodity, while Lee Kuan Yew's brilliant economic management of Singapore—the result of combining his innate Confucianism with his double first degree from Cambridge—pushed that tiny island city-state to the very borders of linear-activity, in spite of its 72 percent Chinese majority population.

Other East Asian reactive nations tend to temper their inherent reactivity by occasionally wandering along the reactive/multi-active plane. The Chinese are less interested in Western linear thinking and logic ("There is *no* absolute truth") than in mammoth gut feeling and periodic explosive assertion of their inalienable rights and dominance based on a culture that is five thousand years old. They have no interest whatsoever in Western logic as applied to Tibet, Taiwan, or human rights. Koreans, while extremely correct in their surface courtesy, actually suppress seething multi-active emotion, even tendencies to violence, more than any other Asians. They frequently demonstrate explosive rage or unreliability vis-à-vis foreign partners or among themselves. Further along this plane, Indonesians and Filipinos, after many centuries of colonization, have developed into cultural hybrids, sometimes opposing, sometimes endorsing the policies and cultural styles of their former colonizers.

Figure A   **The Linear World**

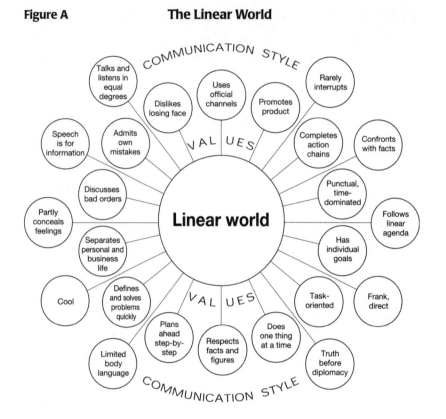

Near the end of the multi-active plane, we encounter popula-tions whose characteristics, though differing significantly in terms of historical background, religion, and basic mindset, resemble each other considerably in the shape of outstanding traits, needs, and aspirations. For example, Latin Americans, Arabs, and Afri-cans are multi-active in the extreme. They are excitable, emo-tional, very human, mostly nonaffluent, and often suffer from previous economic exploitation or cultural larceny. Turkey and Iran, with more Eastern culture intact, are somewhat better off economically, although all of this group needs either aid, debt forgiveness, better trade conditions, more medical help, or more education—or, in the case of African countries, all of the above.

Figure B   **The Multi-Active World**

What all of these groups could benefit from, at little or no cost to affluent nations, would be compassion, understanding, cooperation, and linkages where possible as well as recognition of achievement and progress.

To switch our commentary to Northern European cultures, and proceeding along the linear-active/reactive axis, let's consider three committedly linear countries that exhibit reactive tendencies (when compared with the Germanics): Britain, Sweden, and Finland. British individuals often seek agreement among colleagues before taking decisive action. Swedes are even further along the reactive line, seeking unanimity if possible. Finns, however, are the most reactive of Europeans in that their firm deci-

Figure C   **The Reactive World**

sion-making stance is strongly offset by their soft, diffident, Asian communication style (plenty of silence) and their uncanny ability to listen at great length without interrupting.

The linear-active/multi-active axis is fairly straightforward. The United States, Norway, and the Netherlands plan their lives along agenda-like lines. Australia has multi-active flashes due to substantial immigration from Italy, Greece, and former Yugoslavia. Danes, though linear, are often referred to as the "Nordic Latins." France is the most linear of the Latins, Italy and Spain the least. Russia, with its inherited Slavic soul, classifies as a loquacious multi-active, but slots in a little higher on the linear-active side on account of its many millions living in severely cold envi-

Figure D **Cultural Categorization**

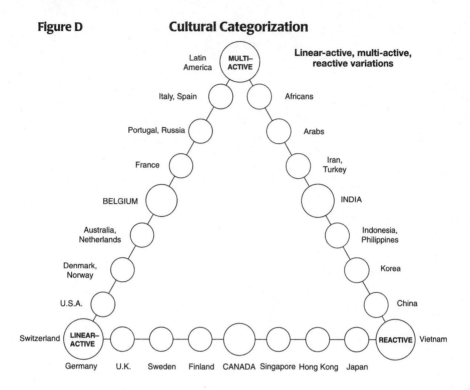

ronments. Belgium, India, and Canada occupy median positions on their respective axes. These positions can be seen as positive and productive. Belgium runs a highly prosperous and democratic economy by finding a successful compromise between linear-active (Flemish) and multi-active (Walloon) administrations. Canada, because of massive immigration and intelligent government cultural care, is the most multicultural country in the world. Indians, though natural orators and communicators, have combined these natural skills and warmth with Eastern wisdom and courtesy. On top of that they have inherited a considerable number of British institutions, which enables them to relate to the West, too.

Figure E   **Hybrid Types**

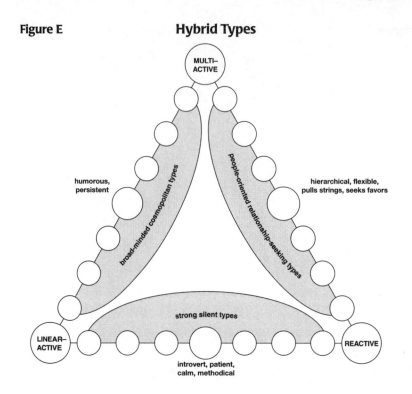

Figure E shows how certain nationalities sharing characteristics from two categories may find areas of cooperation or common conduct. Those close to the linear-reactive axis are likely to be strong, silent types who can work together calmly and tend to shun multi-active extroversion and loquacity. Those close to the multi-active/reactive axis will, in spite of visible differences, attach great importance to relationships and circumvent official channels by using personal contacts or networks. People close to the linear-active/multi-active axis, though opposites in many ways,

Figure F   **Style Variation**

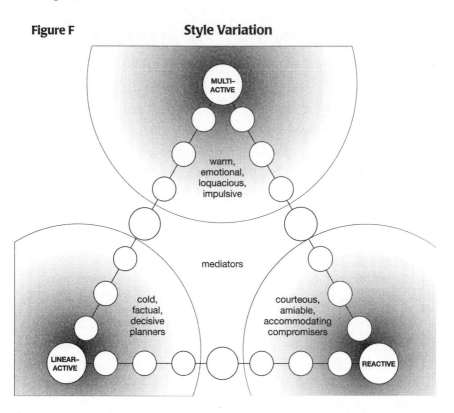

are inevitably broad-minded on account of their range of traits and are likely to be forceful and persistent in their actions.

Figure F suggests that individuals whose cultural profiles wander away from the axes and who occupy a central classification inside the triangle may possess qualities that enable them to be efficient mediators or team leaders.

Case Study: The Mexican Mindset

The Mexican psyche, even before the United States ascended to dominance, was already profoundly different from that of other European- or Asian-influenced cultures on account of the dramatic and irreversible fusion of Indian and Latin characteristics in the years following Hernán Cortés' victory in 1521. Mexicans, like other Latin Americans, derive many of their characteristics from Spain, whose language, religion, values, and lifestyle were imported by the conquistadores. The subsequent fusion of cultures was, however, quite different in Mexico from what occurred in the United States, Brazil, or Argentina, where the indigenous peoples were decimated, marginalized, or ignored culturally.

When Cortés arrived in Mexico, a magnificent civilization was already in place. It is true that the Aztec armies were defeated and the populations subjugated, but the indigenous influence remained, pervading every aspect of Mexican life: food, involvement with nature, beliefs, concepts of time and space, attitudes toward authority, and eventually the Mexican worldview itself. The readiness of the Spaniards to intermarry with Indians soon produced a rapidly expanding mestizo population and culture which gave Mexico the most Indian-oriented mindset among the major American countries.

Which are the Indian-influenced characteristics of the Mexican? If passion, rhetoric, exuberance, extroversion, and imagination are Hispanic traits, the subtler, deeper, more inscrutable side of the Mexican reveals an affinity with indigenous life. Though normally bouncy and gregarious, Mexicans frequently slip into melancholy and despairing moods, where fatalism, apathy, and a sense of powerlessness combine to produce an inferiority complex far removed from Argentinian conceit or Brazilian gay abandon. At such times Mexicans "put on a mask," concealing their feelings behind an impassive countenance denoting stoicism in adversity and a quiet understanding of human suffering. From the Indians Mexicans have also inherited the passive acceptance of the stratification of society, just as it was in the Aztec caste system: a readiness to assume a preordained role in the hierarchy, an exaggerated deference for age and its assumed wisdom, and an ability to face poverty, hardship, and death itself without undue fuss or complaint. This is a product of the Indian concept of cyclical time, presupposing that compensation is achieved when the wheel turns full circle and that no human endeavor, however strenuous, can really affect the immediate sequence of events.

Like the Indians, the Mexican believes in the solidity and comforting support of the group, where oral agreements are kept, commitments are honored, and trustworthiness is paramount. These time-honored values dominate Mexican business and social life today. Indigenous peoples, who mixed the natural and supernatural in their everyday life, lost face if they could not find sufficient sacrifices for their demanding gods. The modern Mexican is similarly preoccupied with face and credibility, far more than most Latin Americans, who are often more pragmatic. *"La dignidad del hombre"* ("The dignity of the man"), certainly a Spanish concept, is a more sensitive issue in Mexico than anywhere in Europe, with the possible exception of Sicily.

Mexican face-saving and the obsession with respect and status resemble the Asian (Japanese) variety in its finickiness and intensity. This Asian characteristic was carried over the

Bering Strait by the native populations and has lost no significance in the cultures they affected, all the way from Alaska to Tierra del Fuego. The Asian-Indian influence is also seen in the slow Mexican tempo in building relationships, the Mexicans' unwillingness to commit themselves to involvement with others if trust has not been established, suspicion of the "gringo" (how often the Indians were betrayed!), and the tendency to look for a go-between if agreement cannot be reached in discussion. Above all the Mexican mestizos are united with their Indian forebears by a sense of historical perspective and a conviction that anything that happens in the present is an inevitable result of past action and destiny. Logical thinking therefore differs sharply from the linear Western model.

If we compare Mexican cognition of the hierarchical group with the Asian view, it involves a need for *completeness,* which is not altogether dissimilar from the Chinese. The Mexican leader may have acquired his position initially by birthright or nepotism, but he will not be successful unless he takes great pains to develop a huge network of friends, business partners, and officials who will help him to consolidate his power base. As in the Aztec cacique system, these relationships are built on complex personal ties that allow favors to be sought, usually granted, and ultimately reciprocated.

In business a senior manager will command unquestioned obedience and respect from subordinates, but as in Confucian systems, he is obliged to reward them with loyalty, courtesy, and protection. The *patrón* wields his power openly and with machismo, but he will show immediate compassion for a worker's misfortunes and come readily to the aid of the worker's family in the case of undue hardship or bereavement. The patrón is himself a family man, a good Catholic and moralist as well as a shrewd tactician and negotiator. When the chips are down, he has the connections and levers of power to attain the goals of the group he leads. This is what the Mexicans mean by completeness: the cycle of reciprocity whereby the patrón exchanges protection for loyalty and respect. Subordinates will therefore not reason in any individual manner. Abstract principles count little (or not at all) with Mexicans if they contradict or clash with the views of one of their leaders.

Mexicans' cognition of time is part multi-active and part reactive. This differs sharply from linear time. Much has been written about the Hispanic mañana syndrome, which, though perhaps originating in Moorish Andalucía, is associated more closely with Mexico than with any other nation. The slow, deliberate lifestyle of the Indians hardly mitigated this tendency. Punctuality at events is not high on the list of Mexican priorities. In most hierarchical societies, the powerful make others wait, and this is considered acceptable practice. Easy access to a superior casts doubt on his status.

In Mexico life is not organized around the clock—a mere machine—but around a succession of encounters and relationships that are qualified and quantified not in linear fashion but in terms of depth of personal involvement, excitement, opportunity, or caprice. Human transactions must be satisfactorily completed, not interrupted by the ringing of a bell or a knock on the door. This is one aspect of time—the relationship takes precedence over the schedule. Another aspect, which concerns late deliveries or tardy payments, often accompanied by a paucity of communication, is an unending source of irritation to linear-active, to-the-point Americans, Germans, and others, who accuse Mexicans and Spaniards of laziness. But Mexicans and Spaniards are not lazy—they cannot afford to be! Delays may be caused by the necessity to juggle options or assets due to a lack of resources, or simply because one is not ready to make one's move yet. Cheated so often in the past, the Mexican has good reason to move slowly! Mexicans recognize that fate has many things in store for us that we cannot foresee, that the sequence of events in God's calendar may not correspond to man-made schedules and deadlines. Sometimes one has to make changes in one arena to accommodate changes elsewhere. One has to choose one's priorities. When invited to two parties on the same evening, the Scandinavian or the American will politely reject the less attractive option or the second invitation received. The Mexican, doubly honored, will please both hosts by attending the two parties, but he can hardly be punctual at both!

Chapter 5

Cultural Spectacles

Cultural conditioning, taken care of extremely well by our parents, peers, and teachers, tells us that we are "normal." Surrounded as we grow up by the norms of our own society, we acquire a view of the world that will be hard to change after puberty. As we venture abroad, we see that Russians, Japanese, and Spaniards do not live as we do. Some things that we hold dear, they do not seem to care about. On the other hand, they can appear obsessed by matters we consider of little importance. In this sense we think they are "abnormal."

What happens is that we see the world, and others in it, through a kind of filter that we might describe as *cultural spectacles*. Our own particular bias distorts our opinion of others, so that we may not see them as they really are. Certainly we do not see them as they see themselves. Energetic, speed-conscious Americans tend to see most other nationalities as lacking in urgency, commitment, and drive. Finns find Spaniards and Italians irremediably talkative and scatterbrained. These Latins, looking at Finns through their own spectacles, see them as cold, withdrawn, and slow-witted.

We are rarely aware of how others see us. It would certainly help if we could. An American wishing to relate to a Mexican would be greatly helped by being able to visualize a Mexican's perception of him or her (Yanqui) and thereby eliminate in advance some of the characteristics Mexicans find undesirable about their northern neighbors.

Few nations share a cultural heritage in terms of historical contact and traditions as close as that between England and France. The English and the French should understand each other well by now (after all, England has been an Anglo-Norman country since 1066!). They should be the greatest of friends. In fact they find it hard to tolerate each other and are quick to indulge in biting criticism. This is because, though close neighbors, they belong to different cultural categories and see each other through uncalibrated pairs of spectacles of different tints.

The following assessments—English and French, Germans and Italians, and Americans and Japanese—have been compiled by people of the corresponding nationalities. Judgments vary to such an extent that we might think we are not looking at the same people!

The English and the French

The English through English Eyes

Values and Core Beliefs. The English are a calm, reasonable people who believe in fair play, good manners, old traditions, the monarchy, cricket, soccer, rugby, tennis, and the Church of England.

Fond of dogs, cats, horses, sheepdog trials, queuing, and garden parties, we are casual and laid-back, can laugh at ourselves, and are occasionally eccentric. We support underdogs and have kind hearts that are concealed by a reluctance to appear emotional. We are reliable in a crisis, maintaining a "stiff upper lip." We admire reserve and conservatism and are occasionally vague. We often think laterally and are frequently inventive.

Communication. When communicating with others, the golden rule is "Do not rock the boat." Boasting is taboo; understatement and modesty show good form. Being too frank or brutally honest is not always appropriate. Humor, stalling, even a sprinkling of white lies emphasize diplomacy at the expense of truth. Coded speech is a good way to convey feelings without revealing criticism, anger, disappointment, or even approval too directly. We are good listeners and like to offer useful feedback and debate.

Social and Business Behavior. The English invented Good Manners, which peaked during the reign of Queen Victoria. We avoid voicing strong opinions and prefer to influence events through behind-the-scenes connections.

Initial formality at business meetings soon gives way to informality and first names. Humor and storytelling are necessary ingredients in business. As managers we are diplomatic, tactful, laid-back, casual, reasonable, helpful, willing to compromise, and inventive. We conduct business with grace, style, wit, eloquence, and self-possession. We regard meetings as occasions to seek agreement rather than to issue instructions.

Other. Punctuality is admired, but one needn't arrive on the dot. Distance of comfort is 1.2 meters. The continuing polarization of society constitutes an English "cultural black hole" (see chapter 6).

How to Empathize and Motivate. Speak with modesty, reserve, and discretion. Be as humorous as possible but avoid open sentiment. Don't pry. Be casual. Avoid intensity of feeling and expression.

The English through French Eyes

Values and Core Beliefs. The English are a rather closed, undemonstrative lot who believe they have a monopoly on impartiality and good manners. They are somewhat old-fashioned and cling to old traditions like the monarchy, cricket, croquet, country dancing, and "five o'clock tea." They are slow to modernize and in the last twenty years have fallen behind the French in technology. They are reluctant members of the European Union and may one day be thrown out. Their famous quality of reserve often leads them to be obtuse in international exchanges. They are obstinate and often very cool with Latins in general, the French in particular. They have shared a lot of history with France, but they don't seem to have learned much from it. They lack panache.

Communication. Unlike the French, who are direct and precise communicators, the English are woolly, unclear, and often devious. They think slowly and reply to our questions with phrases such as "I'll have to think about it," "It's a moot point," or "I'm not quite with you on that one." They rarely say what they mean (and often say the *opposite* of what they mean). They are condescending toward French people and tell us funny stories to distract us. They avoid precision or commitment.

Social and Business Behavior. The English are much less formal than we French, often wanting to use first names much earlier than we do. They become familiar too soon and lack respect for our position. They think they dress well, but we know better. They pride themselves on their table manners but hold a fork the wrong way up and think we are uncivilized when we (sensibly) wipe gravy off a plate with a piece of bread.

They want to follow agendas strictly and dislike discussing

important points that we want to revisit. They say things like "That was *settled* earlier." They like to appear laid-back during business meetings but often fail to give adequate attention to important matters. They pretend business is a kind of game that can be won by excelling at humor. They are always trying to pin us down ("Could we please write down what we have agreed upon?") when we obviously wish to discuss vital issues further.

Other. The British stand well away from interlocutors and seem uncomfortable when Latins get close to them. They shake hands less than we do. They like frequent "tea breaks."

How to Empathize and Motivate. We have to flatter their position and refer to the British Empire as if it still existed. We have to learn English and use it to do business with them. They can always be motivated by money. They do not always believe what we say but look at what we do. We pretend they are great humorists, though they are not as witty as we are. We make a fuss over their animals—and for this they are grateful.

The French through French Eyes

Values and Core Beliefs. A close study of European history during the second millennium reveals that France was the continent's most influential power, setting the norms for democracy, justice, government and legal systems, military strategy, philosophy, science, agriculture, viniculture, and haute cuisine.

Clear-sighted, perceptive thinkers, we French have an unrivaled historical perspective. Our sense of intellectual superiority, combined with our moral and didactic authority, gives us a clear mission—that of preserving the age-long values and philosophies that Europe cherishes. *"La mission de la France, c'est civiliser l'Europe,"* proclaimed André Malraux (former Minister of Culture).

The French excel in Cartesian logic, have quick minds, and would rather be right than popular. Individualistic and opportunistic, we nevertheless show great compassion for the weak and underprivileged, and we pride ourselves on our inherent humanity.

Communication. The French communicate clearly and precisely; the clinical nature of the French language facilitates this. Our style of speaking is personal, often emotional, but essentially rational. We tend to be extroverts. Discussion is an intellectual exercise during which problems and issues are analyzed from all perspectives. Firmness is combined with politeness.

Social and Business Behavior. The French are among the most formal of Europeans, and proper respect must be accorded to age and rank. We entertain lavishly with the best food and wine in the world at our disposal. Politics is our favorite discussion topic, and conversation is regarded as an art. Lunches and dinners can be extremely lengthy, accompanied by animated discussion.

Our businesspeople arrive at meetings well dressed, well prepared, and with clear goals. They are great orators and see no reason to compromise or fudge issues if their logic has not been defeated. They are strong on vision and imagination; during brainstorming sessions, they usually contribute more ideas than anyone else. They have long-term objectives and they try to establish personal relationships. Negotiation is not a quick procedure. Although wit and humor form a part of the discussion, flippancy is frowned upon. French managers consider not only the business at hand (e.g., investment and profit) but remain aware of their company's standing in the framework of French society and of their own personal status in the organic whole.

Other. We are often seen as anti-Anglo-Saxon in general and anti-American in particular. But we would not be human if we did not resent the rise of the British after the fall of Napoleon, the decline of the French language as a world tongue, the ubiquitous use of English in international affairs, and most of all, the pernicious Americanization of large parts of the world, including once-French-dominated Europe and even French culture itself.

How to Empathize and Motivate. We French like frequent reference to France, her history, and her many achievements. We like understanding and even closeness, once initial formality and distrust have been dispelled by reliable behavior. Money is less important than pride and social position are. We admire people who speak French well.

The French through English Eyes

Values and Core Beliefs. The French live in a world of their own, the center of which is France, and they attach little importance to the opinions of other nations, which they see as intellectually inferior. They see themselves as the natural leaders of Europe and claim to have pioneered or invented virtually everything, including tennis, which, as everyone knows, started in England. They admit that we once had an empire covering fifteen million square miles, but they see us now as a rather small, foggy island lying off the French coast. We see the French as an obstinate, opinionated people, always the last to sign agreements at such international gatherings as the GATT meetings. They make poor team members and are quick to attack others. Irrevocably chauvinistic, they know little about other cultures and believe it is their mission to civilize the rest of us. They are obsessed by theories and often ignore facts that might contradict them. Shining French ideas often blind them to the truth. They are irremediably cynical and distrust Anglo-Saxons most of all.

Communication. The French talk too much and irritate us with their excessive body language such as constant shrugging of the shoulders and frequent pouting. They are so long-winded that it is often difficult to get a word in. They, on the other hand, show no hesitation in interrupting us, and they often talk over us while we are saying our piece. They claim that they can talk and listen to what we say at the same time. We believe them. Our problem with the French is that although they are overly loquacious, they adhere strictly to logic, so it is difficult for us to win an argument. The best policy is to agree with them early on, as this stops them from talking. They are poor listeners, being convinced that a Brit can tell them nothing they don't know already. When they pin us to the wall, we tell them funny stories, which confuses them and upsets their concentration. Parables are best, as they dare not admit they have not grasped the point.

Social and Business Behavior. The French are well known for their rich cuisine and lavish entertaining. Lunches are, in our opinion, too long, and after three or four glasses of wine, it is difficult to get anything done in the afternoon. Dinners are even longer; they serve many dishes separately, whereas we often put everything on the table at one time. They have some funny manners, too, like tearing their bread up and wiping their plates with it. They eat so much at night they are unable to face a decent breakfast. They describe English bacon as "burning pig meat." We have to admit, however, that they are excellent hosts.

A business meeting with the French can be a trying affair. They follow the agenda at first but soon depart from it and want to revisit points we think have already been settled. They diverge constantly in all directions and will introduce subjects that are not on the agenda at all! They can even make a new platform out of these topics so that the whole nature and thrust of the negotiation can change completely. Their discussion is so roundabout and prolonged that we get drowned in words and often wind up completely lost. English negotiators frequently have to say, at about half past four in the afternoon, "Could we please write down the points we have agreed upon?"

Meetings scheduled for three to four hours often last until

evening, or indeed continue the following day. The French refuse to do business piecemeal and will not agree to any particular items until the whole thing has been settled. They look for "all-embracing solutions," which can be very difficult to reach.

Other. The French, along with the Spanish, are the worst linguists in Europe. We are not good either, but at least English is the international language.

How to Empathize and Motivate. One has to flatter the French and show exaggerated respect for their opinions. They don't mind fierce debate, but they want to win the argument. A good tactic is to let them win it but repackage afterward. They like your showing an interest in their family—this is another way you can "defuse" them. Use your schoolboy French as much as possible—it amuses them. Praise French cheeses.

The Germans and the Italians

Germans through German Eyes

Values and Core Beliefs. The Germans are the most honest, straightforward, and reliable people on earth. We believe in scientific rather than contextual truth and conduct our private and professional lives on this basis. We have great respect for facts and figures, the law, property, and rank. Our standards of cleanliness, orderliness, and punctuality are beyond reproach; our work ethic and efficiency are surpassed by none. We Germans stand by our commitments and keep our word. Concepts such as fidelity, loyalty, and honor are very much alive in modern Germany.

Communication. The German communication style is serious, frank, and open. Rarely are we devious; we prefer to disagree openly rather than simulate compliance. We are not slow to criticize because we believe that *constructive* criticism is helpful and beneficial. Discussion begins formally, without much small talk, which we think is a waste of time. Facts are important, and often we prefer to write things down to avoid multiple interpretations of what was said. Instructions should be given clearly—repeated when necessary. We avoid exaggerated or boastful statements and are unimpressed by flashy television advertising or clever slogans. With strangers, we don't smile a lot and are not overly friendly, but we're sincere. We Germans are among the world's best listeners; we rarely interrupt.

Social and Business Behavior. Germans generally dress well and are neat and clean in appearance. We prefer new clothes to old clothes and spend a good proportion of our budget on clothing. We are quite formal on first meeting; we shake hands more frequently than Anglo-Saxons do. A distance of a full 1.2 meters from other people makes us feel at ease, and we respect privacy more than most people do. It is advisable to knock on a person's door before entering, and please don't ask us too many personal questions. We do not use first names in the initial stages of a relationship, preferring to show respect and use proper titles.

Meetings begin formally, titles are used, visiting cards are exchanged, and seating may be hierarchical. We believe successful business is built on reliable procedures and processes, and we work hard to develop these and adhere to them. Managers usually combine a good education with solid experience and are expected to give subordinates (and partners) the benefit of their expertise. We come to meetings well prepared and often go into great detail. We try always to be logical, and our strong points are quality, on-time delivery dates, and competitive prices; we look for these qualities in others.

Other. We believe in true, deep friendships. A German friendship is a good investment. Contrary to popular belief, we admire intellectuals more than we do military or business leaders.

How to Empathize and Motivate. One should respect the German primary values of honesty, efficiency, punctuality, and *Ordnung*. We look for common ground with people, and when we find it, we love sharing. Put as much as possible in writing and don't leave things unfinished. Above all keep your word and deliver what you have promised.

Germans through Italian Eyes

Values and Core Beliefs. The Germans are always telling us how honest and reliable they are; we suspect they are comparing themselves with us. They strive to lead good, orderly lives and respect the law so much they won't even cross an empty road at midnight if the light is red. They also pay their taxes regularly, keep only one set of books and are quite ungenerous in giving little presents to officials. They all seem to want to get into Heaven rather badly, but we aren't sure we want to get into a German Heaven!

Communication. German communication style is so frank and open that we know the whole story in five minutes and wonder how we can begin to negotiate or even make interesting conversation. If we start to show a little artistic creativity with their cold facts and figures, they attack our logic and criticize us mercilessly. If we pretend to be upset, they say they are only trying to help us. Humor doesn't help either—they don't think our jokes are funny, and *they* won't tell any while doing business. We must admit they are truthful, sensible people, but they come across as a bit heavy at times.

Social and Business Behavior. Germans spend a lot of money on new clothes, but we would not go so far as to say they are well dressed. They go in for a boring charcoal grey rather a lot—it's like a uniform for executives. When we show up in tastefully designed sports jackets, they ask us if we have just arrived back from holiday. On introducing themselves, they shake hands snappily in military fashion. Mentally, they've got to be clicking their heels. They don't smile much initially (in Germany smiling is only for friends); we try hard to be their friends, but if we try too hard, they get suspicious.

They are very formal at business meetings and use titles a lot. Most of them are "Doktors." You can always tell who the delegation leader is because the others always glance at him before they say anything they think is important. Our bosses are autocratic, too, but in our case we pretend not to be. Germans expect us to arrive on time at their meetings and come fifteen minutes early to ours, before we are ready. Agendas, schedules, timetables, and contracts are all holy documents in their eyes. We like to ad-lib a lot at meetings, and they try to write down everything we say, but after a while, they give up.

Other. Germans seem to indulge in a lot of soul-searching and worry about whether they are leading good lives or not. We think they are, but they are not sure about us.

How to Empathize and Motivate. Although the Germans criticize us, we are not offended because we know that nobody is perfect. We usually agree to everything they say; we can always modify things in due course. We share the dream of a United Europe with them, and we don't challenge their leadership, as the French do.

Italians through Italian Eyes

Values and Core Beliefs. We Italians are charming, intelligent people to whom Europe owes a great cultural debt. Our Roman forebears built Europe's greatest empire, yet in spite of our outstanding achievements in the fields of art, architecture, military history, and modern industry, we remain among the least chauvinistic of peoples, exhibiting a national modesty rivaled in Europe only by the Finns. We aren't touchy (like the French or Spaniards), and we accept criticism with both grace and good humor.

Essentially gregarious and people-oriented, we combine ready friendliness with unfailing courtesy. Quick of mind, we are witty and fun; we also seek style and form and beauty. Less impressed than most by governments or the Church, our first loyalty is to family, then group or clan. Join the group and we will be your most reliable ally through thick and thin.

Communication. Eloquently loquacious, Italians are the world's best communicators, combining charisma and exuberance with ultrakeen perceptiveness and flexibility. We are winningly persuasive without being aggressive in argument. Although always wanting to speak, we are attentive listeners, and while you talk, we evaluate your personality and formulate our reply. Our goal is to try to construct a relationship based on what you say and how you say it. We rarely criticize.

Social and Business Behavior. We Italians are invariably courteous and considerate and are well mannered by any standards. We show great compassion to people in difficulties and will go to great lengths to help people who have gained our trust. We are less private than many nationalities and will share details of our personal lives, exchange photographs, borrow and lend our belongings freely, are relaxed about time, and show great flexibility concerning appointments and commitments.

This flexibility allows us to do business in a special way not always properly understood by others. To our way of thinking, bad or useless rules and regulations can be circumvented without actually being broken. There are many grey areas where shortcuts are, in our eyes, a matter of common sense. Closer to reality than most, we are not bound by ideals. We will gather you into our "conspiracy" and share the benefits with you, if you accept. We are excellent negotiators—patient and accommodating. We are always willing to rediscuss tricky agenda points; we dislike silences. Two or three conversations can be conducted simultaneously—one does things faster that way. Italy is, by the way, the sixth-ranking industrial nation in the world (in GDP).

Other. We are among the most tactile of peoples. We also use our eyes a lot. We like being friendly. Why not?

How to Empathize and Motivate. Be understanding and, above all, flexible, especially about time. Rome was not built in a day.

Italians through German Eyes

Values and Core Beliefs. Italians seem to be among the most disorganized of Europeans, with a multitude of political parties and changing governments every few months. Prime ministers and other leaders are in and out of power as if they were in a revolving door. Even failed and tainted politicians are reelected regularly and are often simultaneously in court on corruption charges. More than one ex–prime minister has been linked convincingly with the Mafia (often seen as the best-organized political force in the country). Northern Italians are so fed up with the chaotic and clan-ridden south, they have formed a party whose aim it is to split the country in two. Italians seem to have little respect for Parliament, government, law, or the Church, remaining loyal only to their own families and the clique to which every Italian male belongs. Their standards of probity and commitment fall far short of our own, and though they rank as the world's sixth industrial nation, we have no idea how they managed it.

Communication. We Germans are capable of conversing and analyzing things at great length, but we are taciturn compared with the Italians. We argue in a fairly straight line, but they go around in circles—ever-widening ones. The problem is that at the end we are not at all sure what they have said or in which direction they are heading. We usually make the agenda for meetings, but they avoid it conscientiously. When they make an agenda, it reads like a short story.

Social and Business Behavior. Italians set great store by their charm and charisma and think they can pull the wool over German eyes with their tactics. They are pleasant enough characters and confide in us greatly, telling us all about their families, their professional and social lives, where they were educated, where they go for their holidays, and so on. They don't realize that we do not want to know all these personal details—their hopes, aspirations, disappointments, and so on. *It is none of our business.* They want to get too close to us too quickly—and not only spiritually, but physically, too; they have little hesitation about touching us, even hugging and sometimes *kissing* us after only a short acquaintance! Who do they think we are—pets? However, we must admit their general manners are better than ours, and they never seem to be insulted. Although we are often very dry and ironic with them, they don't seem to notice.

Italians don't appear to understand that business in Germany is done strictly according to the law and that we follow rules and procedures rather than getting things done "through the back door" and using key acquaintances. We know that sometimes influence counts in our country, too, but we don't talk openly about it. During meetings Italians often talk two or three at a time and make a mockery of any agenda we attempt to start with. In general they agree to most of our proposals but only follow up on those that interest them. They are somewhat unreliable suppliers and late payers. When they negotiate a price, they start high and come down a lot, their final prices often being reasonable.

Other. With their relaxed nature and natural exuberance and optimism, they are in many respects the opposite of Germans, but they are pleasant companions (for a while).

How to Empathize and Motivate. We listen to their joys and woes and pretend we are interested. We go easy on the irony and play the "flexible price" game with them. We make allowances for late deliveries and payments. We hug them occasionally and try to enjoy their humanity.

The Americans and the Japanese

Americans through American Eyes

Values and Core Beliefs. We Americans—the most courageous and dynamic people of the twentieth century—have a lot going for us. Lucky to have been born in God's Country, with its protected geographical position and almost unlimited resources, we have certainly made the best of our good fortune. By conquering a vast continent and taming a wilderness, we have created the world's biggest economy, lead all others in advanced technology, and are the undisputed champions of democracy and free trade. Imbued with the frontier spirit, we Americans work hard, play hard, move fast, and are pragmatic, optimistic, and future-oriented. We seek equality and individual liberty in a land where honest toil makes anything possible and where anyone can become president. The visible achievements and prosperity that make the United States the envy of other lands confirm the reality of the American Dream.

Communication. Americans communicate in a frank, direct manner: we "spell it out," "tell it like it is," and "lay our cards on the table." In other words, we keep things simple and get to the point. We dislike devious discussion, though we may lace our message with humor. The communicative style is friendly from the outset, accompanied by smiles and the use of first names. Disagreements are expressed openly, without beating around the bush. We listen well, especially for technical details.

Social and Business Behavior. Because of the nature of the country's social history, Americans have many easy strategies for meeting strangers. We make friends quickly, seek early trust, and are relaxed about manners and dress. We pride ourselves on being the world's best small talkers. In the United States, different levels of society mingle easily; European-style snobbery is rare.

Americans are the world's best businesspeople—the U.S. economy was dominant for most of the twentieth century and shows few signs of flagging. Among the reasons for this success are the willingness of Americans to think big and to take risks. We are good at sniffing out business opportunities, we move quickly to propose deals, and we put our money where our mouth is. Hardworking and persistent, we place emphasis on competence, and specialists may have their say, free of the hierarchical constraints common in other cultures. Contracts and commitments are binding, and American businesspeople normally stick to what has been agreed. Compared with many nationalities, we Americans work at a breakneck pace and take few holidays when there is a task to complete.

Other. We Americans feel strongly about our mission as world policeman and guarantor of basic freedoms. Our military can be called to arms quickly to defend democracy or trade routes, and at the turn of the twenty-first century, we remain the only true superpower.

How to Empathize and Motivate. We like straightforward dealers who play the game and share the risks. Earnestness is important to us and is better accompanied by a sense of humor.

Americans through Japanese Eyes

Values and Core Beliefs. Americans are big, not only in their physical size but also in the way they think. Their houses are big, their cars are big, their ranches have thousands of acres. Biggest is generally considered best. They have led the world economically, politically, and militarily since 1945, and we Japanese have no quarrel with that. We are happy to be number two. Americans are well-meaning people who charge ahead with their policies, often dragging us along in their wake. It is good to have them as an ally, but we would be even happier if they tried to understand us better and learned the importance of face.

Communication. Americans always spell out their intentions in quite loud English from the outset. When we don't understand the first time, they spell it out again in even louder English. They can't understand why we are so quiet, and when we lapse into silence, it seems to make them nervous. They then speak again, even though it's our turn. They think we are devious because we are less direct than they are. They often call us "inscrutable," but really, they ought to "scrute" more.

Social and Business Behavior. They are immediately very friendly and open with complete strangers, pumping hands heartily (even violently) and saying they trust us. They are skilled at making small talk at cocktail parties, equaling the British and Canadians in this respect. We prefer restful silence, so we just drink and smile, but they are bigger drinkers than we are. We take them out to elegant restaurants, but they often gobble up their food quickly without showing due appreciation of our porcelain, table and food arrangements, and flowers. We notice they have trouble sitting on the floor. It must be their long legs.

When negotiating, Americans come straight to the point and ask us, "Do we have a deal?" when in fact we may be several months away from making a decision. They are quite happy airing differences of opinion in public, which is not at all our custom. They even differ in opinion among themselves and argue in front of us. They never spend a long enough time in Japan to set up a deal properly, always saying they have a plane to catch. When we know their departure time, we are able to use this knowledge to pressure them with last-minute changes. They seem to have no patience (compared with Asians) and do not understand how long it takes us to achieve a proper consensus. They honor their commitments but are unable to see the advantage of renegotiating a contract under certain circumstances. If we break a contract, they take us to court, even though we are good customers. They have more lawyers than we have soldiers!

Other. In spite of frequent misunderstandings and mutual sniping about protectionism, we see that U.S.-Japan trade is the biggest bilateral commerce the world has ever seen.

How to Empathize and Motivate. We motivate Americans by helping them to make money and by imitating certain of their qualities like punctuality, work ethic, and short holidays. We agree to nearly all their proposals but only follow up on those that are mutually profitable or beneficial to us. We pretend Japan is a democracy, just like the United States.

Japanese through Japanese Eyes

Values and Core Beliefs. The Japanese people are culturally very different from all others—in fact, we are unique. This uniqueness derives from our history of isolation and from the special qualities of the Japanese language. No one who is not a native of Japan can aspire to speak Japanese as we do and thus can never gain access to the superior thinking and culture of which the language is the vehicle. Japan's general remoteness over two millennia and especially her 250-year period of complete isolation up to 1853 led her to develop a distinct society that has no equal in terms of group cooperation, national spirit, and high-context understanding. All of us are instinctively proud of our nationality and culture, which has attained unrivaled standards of honesty, loyalty, self-effacement, stoicism, bravery, self-sacrifice, unselfishness, and unfailing courtesy.

Communication. Japanese communication style has as its main premise the promotion of harmony among all interlocutors. Confrontation is avoided at all costs, and great care is taken to see to it that nobody loses face. *What* is said is actually of minor importance. *How* it is said, *who* says it, and *when* it is said are the vital ingredients. Japanese speak slowly, quietly, and politely, frequently offering the partner a turn to speak. Invariably we agree with the other side's point of view in order not to offend or disappoint. It is true that a Japanese never says no. Alternative courses of action can be suggested in other, more subtle ways, and in due course after adequate reflection. We also often resort to silence, which can be soothing when shared and enjoyed.

Social and Business Behavior. The Japanese are excellent hosts who often entertain guests lavishly in expensive restaurants. We also believe in frequent gift giving, the gifts being selected not so much on the basis of intrinsic value as on the basis of their appropriateness. This activity is an example of Japanese thoughtfulness and our caring nature. Compassion comes naturally to us. In spite of our innate friendliness, however, we Japanese use surnames and titles and maintain certain formalities in social intercourse in order to show respect to the other person.

Courtesy and respect are maintained in business relations. We are patient but resilient negotiators and make unhurried decisions by general consensus. We do not often act as individuals but most often as team members. The company (*kaisha*) comes first, though we can be surprisingly accommodating to foreign partners, provided that harmony and courtesy are maintained. We prefer to do business with people to whom we have been properly introduced. Company reputation on both sides is very important. Because of the interlocking nature of Japan's "web society," we benefit from an excellent networking system from which foreign partners may also benefit.

Other. We are very honorable people who always strive to keep our word.

How to Empathize and Motivate. It is advisable to seek common ground with us; we love sharing. Oral agreements endure longer than written ones do.

Japanese through American Eyes

Values and Core Beliefs. The Japanese believe they are a unique people, and we heartily agree with them. They are so opaque! We don't understand how they think, and it would seem that other Asians don't either. The Japanese closed their country down for 250 years and would probably still have the blinds drawn if we had not opened them in 1853 with generous offers to trade. Even then their shogun was against it, but we had some pretty big guns, too. Today we can see what a great boon it was for both our countries.

Communication. Basically, the Japanese do *not* communicate; that is to say, we are usually in the dark as to their intentions. We don't speak their language; they barely speak ours. The ones who can get by in English are the young, low-level employees, who have no influence. The (older) decision makers remain isolated behind a language curtain. Of course the Japanese come with interpreters, but they are the hardest of all to understand. We suspect that because they are so polite, they never say how things are. If you tell their boss something is impossible, they think you said you need more time to think about it. When the Japanese mean "I disagree," they say, "We agree," then cock their head to one side or sigh heavily.

Social and Business Behavior. The Japanese entertain us lavishly, spending more in one evening on a fine restaurant than our salaries for a month! The company comptrollers must be blind, gullible, or both. They also keep giving us presents when we have not earned them—we suspect they are softening us up to get better terms, but they say it's just because we are so kind. They are also always apologizing for mistakes they have not made or rudenesses they have not shown. They are the most polite people on earth, unless you tread on their tatami with your shoes on. Even then they only giggle with a hand in front of their mouth.

When doing business, rule number one is to remember to give them your business card and accept theirs (tenderly). Without calling cards in Japan, it's like meeting each other with no clothes on. The Japanese prefer bowing to shaking hands, though they will offer you their limp hand to press gently. If you go in for bowing at a reception, this will go down well, but you may have a backache the next morning. They don't negotiate as we do, during a meeting. They simply state their position, two or three times, if you ask for more specificity. If you start to bargain, they look upset (or blank) and suggest your young men go with their young men to the bars that evening for a few whiskies and water. Whenever you ask an individual for a quick decision at a meeting, he will look sideways at his colleagues, who all smile at you understandingly. Decisions in Japan take a long time (often months). The comforting thing is that they are always unanimous. They are pretty reliable in the end, though.

Other. When you get to know the Japanese, you realize they are really very kind—definitely a lot more considerate than New Yorkers.

How to Empathize and Motivate. The main thing is never to be rude to a Japanese, though you will often be tempted. Drink their green tea and keep trotting out the platitudes like they do ("Our Vice President so much enjoyed playing golf with Mr. Yamamoto at Hakone Country Club"). Reciprocate their gifts—they deserve them. Don't talk about the war—it was all a big mistake.

Conclusion

Comparing the assessments above, we see a repetition of a number of trends in the way people judge themselves and others.

First, self-assessment is almost invariably made through rose-tinted spectacles. In a survey I conducted among one hundred Swedes in 1994, the Swedes chose the following ten values from a list of forty-eight to describe themselves: conscientiousness, honesty, loyalty, tolerance, equality, love of peace, love of nature, cleanliness, kindness, and modesty.

The respondents chose ten positive values and no negative ones, though the list contained many negative or neutral attributes. This euphemistic view of oneself varies slightly from nation to nation. The French, Chinese, Japanese, Swedes, and Americans are normally very proud of themselves. The British used to be—now they aren't so sure. Germans, Italians, and Finns often indulge in bouts of healthy self-criticism, while genuine soul-searching is typical of Russians at a personal level and of Dutch and Norwegians at a national one. In general, however, we humans describe ourselves in glowing terms. Prior to September 11, 2001, the American Dream was a living reality for many Americans, though fortunes ebbed and flowed.

The second conclusion we can draw is that the rose-colored tint disappears when we look at other nationalities. At best we see them through plain glass (Americans looking at Canadians, Norwegians assessing the British, Italians viewing Spaniards); in the case of *neighbors* the tint is invariably a shade on the dark side. This is often the result of traditional, age-old antipathies (Serbs and Croats, Greeks and Turks, Romanians and Hungarians, Jews and Arabs, Koreans and Japanese) or—less seriously—the irritating proximity of a differing culture (Flemish and Walloons, Poles and Germans, Finns and Swedes, English and Irish, Fijian Polynesians and Indians, U.S. Americans and Mexicans). Only Canada and the United States share a long border with relatively little friction, and even the Canadians get nervous sometimes.

An interesting phenomenon is that we tend to put on relatively rose-colored spectacles for a cultural group *on the other side* of the neighbor. Consequently, Finns view Norwegians favorably, Portuguese admire the French, Poles like Hungarians more than their neighboring Slavs, Mexicans have a sneaking fondness for Canadians, French and Scots gang up on the English, and Italians reach out over France to the British; even Israel looks over Syria to get cozy with the Turks! Humans are a funny lot.

In the global village of the twenty-first century, will cultural spectacles be put aside? Increasing international contact gives us more familiarity with other peoples in business, social, and organizational situations. But, as we know, familiarity can breed contempt! However, we can expect and hope that a general, all-round improvement in educational standards as well as a dramatic increase in tourism will help to soften some of our antipathies and remove some of our biases against strangers. After all, the French and the Germans, traditional enemies, now view each other with some equanimity. That is indeed a cultural success story.

But "opticians" need not worry too much—this century will still see good trade in spectacles. The English may go to the sun-drenched Costa del Sol, put on their rose-tinted sunglasses, and see the Spaniards in a favorable light in the euphoria of a temporary escape from rainy England. Rioja, *gaspacho,* and splendid tortillas will add to the rosiness of the lenses. But when they go home, they switch specs again. Like the myopic people we all are, we wear spectacles because we have to. If only the world's opticians made similar spectacles!

Chapter 6

Cultural Black Holes

An article in a November 1997 issue of the *Times* (London), stating its case against European monetary union, was entitled "The Black Hole at the Heart of Europe." It began, "At the heart of the Euro-constellation, shortly to be renamed EMU, yawns a black hole, threatening to suck in any economy which strays into its gravity field. The black hole is called insolvency."

Whatever the merits of the argument, the nature of the imagery caught my attention, since I am interested in black holes of an entirely different substance and category that may pose an even greater threat to European homogeneity and prosperity than the black hole offered by a single currency. These are phenomena I would describe as *cultural black holes* (CBH), which exist not only in Europe but virtually everywhere in the world.

Before I cite some examples of CBHs, it is helpful to look at a general definition of black holes of the better-known cosmic variety, as described by scientists such as Stephen Hawking and Fred Hoyle, since I will take the liberty of drawing certain parallels, in the cultural sphere, to the celestial bodies discovered by science.

A composite description might read as follows:

A black hole is a theoretical celestial body with a gravitational field so strong that nothing can escape from its vicinity. The body is surrounded by a spherical boundary, called a horizon, through which light can enter but not escape; it therefore appears totally black. Material may fall into a black hole, but no information or energy can come out of it. The radius, or spherical boundary, is also referred to as an "event horizon." In this area, gravitation severely modifies time, space, and other phenomena.

A black hole is a fearsome concept—that of a cosmic vacuum cleaner, capturing, sucking in, and annihilating anything straying too near its orbit.

Cosmic Black Hole

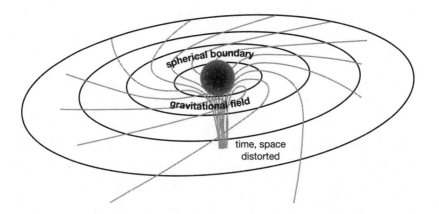

What, then, do I mean by cultural black holes? When and how were (are) they created? Who or what are the victims? How common are they? Why are they dangerous? Who, if anybody, is responsible for forming them; who is culpable?

A cultural black hole, in my loose definition, is *an undiscussable core belief of such intense gravity that it transcends or distorts any other beliefs, values, or set of principles that enter inside the spherical boundary of its gravitational field and absorbs, indeed swallows up, the precepts held by the "victim."*

To carry the imagery further, just as in the case of the cosmic black hole, light can enter the CBH, but it can never escape; that is, enlightenment as might be offered to a cultural group by another cultural group with a different set of cultural values loses all impact as it falls into the CBH and disappears into blackness, nothingness, obliteration.

Do such things ever happen? Yes, they do, all the time. Cosmic black holes, as scientists admit, are still in the hypothetical stage; none has yet been positively identified. CBHs, on the contrary, are spread across the surface of the globe. Classical CBHs often have political or religious origins. Unbridled patriotism, jingoism, religious fanaticism are cases in point. "My country, right or wrong" is a CBH, though it sounds good in times of war. This particular CBH, sucking in the normal rational and humanistic beliefs of a British soldier, enables him to shoot a German or Argentinian soldier with whom he shares a host of Western and universal values, morals, and a cultural heritage. The trenches of World War I were both physical and cultural black holes, accounting for a massive distortion of views and (unfortunately) the deaths of millions of otherwise peaceful British, German, and French young men.

"There is only one God, Allah, and Muhammad is his prophet" is a CBH, inasmuch as the assertion, when absolute, brooks no argument, dissent, or alternative. A Muslim, though perfectly amenable to reason and open to debate, influence, or persuasion in other areas, may be completely intransigent and intractable if your argument impinges on the credibility of Islam. Such is the gravity and intensity of the Muslim's belief that it transforms, sidelines, or relegates to insignificance any connected or peripheral circumstances or conditions that you may be discussing with him. Consequently, a rational analysis of the attacks of September 11, 2001, even by moderate Muslims, was a near-impossibility. It is not just Islam that is at fault. Fanatical Hinduism, Quakerism, Zionism, or any other absolute religious creed might serve equally to destroy any reasonable or enlightening discourse.

The problems caused by political or religious questions are, in fact, not the subject here, except where they intersect with cultural traits. The CBHs with which I wish to take issue have little to do with patriotism or religion, though they are closely connected with the "national programming" of various cultural groups. Most of us "own" a cultural black hole or two, and we frequently drag in those who approach us. They may be sucked in as we devalue their dis-

Cultural Black Hole

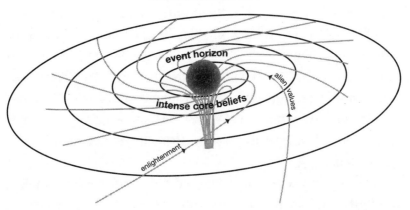

course and subordinate it to our (black) indisputable credo. Usually we are unaware that we are doing this.

Take, for instance, the American Dream, which underpins the mentality of the mainstream American culture (not the subcultures). Americans imbued with this spirit or credo firmly believe that the dream exists and is obtainable only on American soil; no other dream can coexist with it. You may arrive with your visions of the Swedish welfare state, the British quality of life, or the earthly utopia of Costa Rica, but nothing you can say or do will change or even influence most Americans in their belief in the work ethic, efficiency, democracy, the almighty dollar, time as money, and the various simplistic and often materialistic trappings of American society. Here we have an example of a yawning CBH of staggering dimensions. Its surface gravity is so strong that it enables a U.S. president to mobilize half a million troops in a few hours and dispatch them to Kuwait, Haiti, Panama, Vietnam, Grenada, Korea, or Afghanistan in the unalterable belief that only Americans can preserve democracy and free-trade routes. It took Margaret Thatcher fewer than four days to send half the British navy to the other end of the world in 1982 because "the lion's tail had been twisted."

The fact that CBHs allow politicians manipulative powers is regrettable, but what is more significant from the cultural point of view is the extent to which people are blinded when they are within the "event horizon" referred to earlier. Britons are, in the main, calm and phlegmatic people, yet the rampant jingoism in 1982 sprang from nowhere, and anyone present in the screaming crowd seeing off the troopships on their way to the Falkland Islands could not fail to be astonished at its intensity.

Massive CBHs have been created by the rewriting of history. In the late 1950s I traveled from London to Helsinki on a Russian ship; we were about one hundred passengers, mostly British. The crew and stewardesses were very friendly, meals were passable; in most respects it was a very pleasant trip. In the evenings after dinner half a dozen of the ship's officers joined passengers in the bar to socialize. From the very first evening, politics became the subject of discussion. We were subjected to vigorous political indoctrination, for the Russian officers were committed Communists. This in itself was hardly surprising, given the situation at that time. Debate with the British (many of them students) was occasionally heated, but not more so than a university debate might be. What amazed me was not so much the Russian officers' blind belief in Communism as their particular version of history. They were clearly educated men, yet all of them believed that World War II had begun in 1942. They had never heard of the Battle of Britain or the RAF. They believed the Soviet Union had won the war single-handedly against Nazi Germany. Yes, the Americans had contributed some small amounts of war matériel, for the purpose of blinding the Russians to the actuality of an American-British-German-Japanese conspiracy to surround and contain Russia after the war. Churchill was, according to the Russian officers, a British Nazi, Truman was the father of the atom bomb. Yes, we ate decently in England (they saw this every two weeks on their visits to the U.K.), but most of America was starving.

Nothing any of us could say made the slightest impression on these men. Any argument we contributed, however well documented, was simply discarded. Some of the British students, who were Communists and were on their way to Moscow, were also not believed. When the topic of discussion occasionally turned to sports, ballet, painting, or architecture, however, the Russian officers were knowledgeable, interesting, and amenable to other opinions.

In certain countries CBHs of irresistible gravitational intensity are born out of centuries of hatred for or divisions between neighbors. Examples are reciprocal attitudes between Greeks and Turks, Flemish Belgians and Walloons, Koreans and Japanese, Jews and Arabs. It is virtually impossible for an outsider to these inimical stances to make any kind of neutral or impartial statement in the presence of the contestants. They are dangerous CBHs in every respect.

Other CBHs are more benign, though no less powerful in their effect on their environment. In Japan the concept of "face" is a CBH. Few nationalities easily accept losing face, though some handle it much better than others. In Japan, China, and Korea, however, the issue of face assumes such importance that all aspects of one's behavior must be subordinated to it. Successful negotiations, contracts, and other agreements are achieved in these countries by parties constantly "giving face" to the other side. Preserving and giving face is the key to success and progress. On the other hand, a loss of face destroys any other activity in the vicinity.

Cultural Black Holes, by Country

China

A CBH specific to the Chinese is their concept of *Chung Kuo*, the "Middle Kingdom." China is the center of the world and has the oldest civilization (true); therefore, goes Chinese thinking, other countries are peripheral, young, inexperienced, often immoral, and lacking in real values—certainly not properly civilized. This belief is held not only by Chinese intellectuals but is also observable among the peasants. If you speak Chinese well enough to converse with a peasant in his rice paddy, she will politely interrupt his work for a few minutes, ascertain vaguely where you come from, exchange a few pleasantries, and then quickly resume her toil. She is not particularly interested in you (a foreigner). She is already at the center of things. This is where it is all happening.

France

The French CBH is their certainty of French intellectual superiority. I often ask French individuals if they subscribe to this belief, and they are honest enough to admit that they do. They don't consider themselves immodest. The length and magnificence of their historical achievements simply leave them convinced that they have a mission to teach and civilize others. Their political, military, and economic strengths may no longer predominate as they once did, but the French perceive no diminishment or fading of their moral and didactic authority. It is very difficult for a Finn, Swede, or Dane to convince a French individual that he or she can learn something from Scandinavians. Try telling the Frenchman that in the twenty-first century France will only be a bit-part player in world events and you will soon perceive the yawning depths of the French CBH.

Britain

In Britain, the polarization of society is a CBH, certainly as far as the upper and working classes are concerned. The British traditional capacity for reasoned debate breaks down when confronted by the "us and them" phenomenon—the unfortunate legacy of an early Industrial Revolution.

Sweden

The Swedish obsession with consensus is a more benign, though often irritating, CBH. Endless meetings, where everyone's opinion has to be heard (though not always agreed with), lead to habitual deferring of decisions, ultracautiousness, and woolly guidelines from Swedish managers. Innate fear of confrontation and overreliance on the team for initiatives slow down action and decisiveness in Swedish society.

Finland

If in countries such as France and the United States being over-confident and overtly overopinionated is CBH-related, in Finland the opposite is the case. The Finnish CBH is one of extreme taciturnity; opinions are strongly held but often unvoiced. The Finn has an obsessive talent for self-effacement. The manager of a Finnish engineering company told me recently that he sent fifteen of his engineers to service machines in a South American country for three weeks. After the engineers returned, the South American managers refused to pay the bill, saying that they had never seen the engineers and did not believe they had really been there! Modesty and self-deprecation are not unattractive values, so a CBH is not necessarily always entirely negative, though it complicates communication in no small measure!

Italy

Another somewhat positive CBH, though troublesome for Nordics, is the Italian compulsion for voluble conversation and persuasion. Italians—the most communicative of all humans—are convinced that they can persuade anybody to do anything, provided they can get them in a face-to-face situation and capture their attention long enough. They often fail to understand that this tactic may not always work with some nationalities, for example, Nordics, Koreans, and the Chinese. The Italian passion for lengthy self-expression also prevents their interlocutor from providing an adequate reply. Italians can speak and listen at the same time, but Nordics and the Japanese cannot.

Russia

The Russian CBH is suspicion. Centuries of bad governance and propaganda have conditioned Russians to regard anything said by authorities (or foreigners) to be untrue and exploitative. Stalin's "freedom" preserves its meaning only in the clandestine dictionary of laughter (a secret joke). Within the Russian CBH horizon, frames of reference are distorted to such an extent that using normal (Western) vocabulary to convey meaning or information becomes an exercise in futility.

Australia

The Australian CBH, its ironic view of authority, is perhaps only a "grey hole," since the Australians' basic cheerfulness and openness place them among the most readily sociable of humans. Nevertheless, what they call the "Tall Poppy Syndrome" is an enduring national trait and harks back to the arduous days of the convict transports and early settlements, when to rise above your mates or to associate with hierarchy would damn you in the eyes of your peers. Modern Australians will discard their normal congeniality at the drop of a hat if you show any sign of adopting a superior attitude or pulling rank, and any reasonable suggestions you try to offer after that will be devalued.

Mexico

The Mexican CBH bears some similarity to those of Russia and Australia with respect to antipathy toward power, especially if the power is North American. The gringo syndrome is centuries-old, and we are left in no doubt as to its origins. U.S. diplomats have learned that a prerequisite to any kind of reasonable or fruitful negotiation with Mexicans is the recognition of their national honor by showing the utmost, perhaps exaggerated, respect for the Mexicans' rank and credibility. This *pundonor* (point of honor) sensitivity is shared by all Latin American peoples and is evident also in Spain, where the traditional preoccupation with "la dignidad del hombre" colors otherwise normal, rational discussion. In all dealings with Hispanics, this setting or backdrop of personal, regional, or national honor will persistently intervene. In the case of the cosmic black hole, it would be called "frame dragging." Einstein's observation that black holes "drag" space and time around them, distorting the surrounding fabric, is applicable, in cultural-black-hole terms, to proverbial Hispanic individualism, use of time (mañana behavior), and dual perception of reality or truth (that of the immediate detail and that of the poetic whole).

Germany

The Germans have been model European citizens since the 1950s. They have a functioning parliamentary democracy, an excellent record in human rights, a strong environmental protection policy, and political stability. They have worked hard, not only for their own economy but also to establish a European spirit aimed at eliminating intracontinental conflict. They have eschewed involvement in military affairs to the extent possible. The German CBH is perhaps one of persistent cultural self-trust, a phenomenon also observable among Finns and the Japanese. This means that a German, Finn, or Japanese, meeting a compatriot at the other end of the world, automatically trusts him or her without necessarily verifying trustworthiness. This rather attractive trait, noticeably absent among Italians, French, Russians, and many others, nevertheless has the effect of blinkering the "trusting" individual not only to a compatriot's deficiencies but perhaps also to the merits of others. It is a fact that most Germans, Finns, and Japanese see themselves as more honestly efficient than anybody else. This is, however, a CBH with perhaps more positive than negative connotations.

It has its dangers, however. There are different interpretations of "efficiency," just as there are of "honesty." Italian efficiency may involve long hours of apparent time wasting, gossiping in a café after work. But the gossip may be gathering information useful for business or academic research or for developing a deeper relationship with a valuable client.

State-Induced Black Holes

The most frightening and sinister CBHs in recent history have been state-induced. Apartheid and fascism (especially Nazism) were the most prominent and historically significant. Nazism was relatively short-lived but horrific in its intensity. The fact that 50 million decent and educated Germans were unable to climb their way out of it under their own steam demonstrates the power of CBHs. Apartheid was slightly less vicious but unfortunately more durable. Again it was morally opposed by the majority of white South Africans, many of whom left their home, country, and livelihood in final protest. The universal popularity of Nelson Mandela after the demise of apartheid emphasizes what a futile decades-long exercise it had been. Yet it took intense and prolonged international pressure to bring about its downfall.

Extreme poverty and hunger preempt measured thinking or rational behavior in many parts of Africa and India. In the former Communist states of Eastern Europe, where toil gained little reward and idleness attracted no rebuke, there developed a gigantic CBH of apathy. This is proving hard to shake off all the way from the Baltic states to the Balkans, though inherently energetic peoples such as Estonians, Hungarians, Czechs, and Slovenians could claim some credit for accelerating the process. This apathy and antipathy to work should diminish over the next generation, but the slow take-up of entrepreneurialism by even the East Germans (and their nostalgia for Communist times) shows the depths of the CBH.

*   *   *   *   *   *

What can we do about cultural black holes? There are few grounds for optimism. Hawking has suggested that cosmic black holes may have formed in the early universe. Small ones (about the size of a large mountain) might evaporate, but gigantic ones do not. Many CBHs, as we have seen, date back to the earliest histories of humanity and may in fact have existed in prehistoric times. We consider ourselves rational and knowledgeable, yet obduracy and intransigence persist, clouding our vision, distorting the framework of our logic, and blurring the blueprint of our pattern for survival.

Like cosmic collisions, cultural collisions wreak great damage. Much has been written about when cultures collide. Will cultures ever connect?

To end on a positive note, the Franco-German reconciliation, the gradual development of at least a thin veneer of global culture, the convergence of knowledge taking place through information technology, all give us grounds for cautious optimism. We may seek further hope in the growing interdependence of nations, the common pursuit of comfort and pleasure, the ascendancy of feminine values, the healing congruence of youth, and a continuing human yearning for education and security. In the meantime, beware of black holes....

Chapter 7

Cognitive Processes

In past centuries it was assumed by Western scholars and psychologists that thought processes were universal, that people everywhere had the same strategies for processing information and drawing inferences from it. The assumptions were very much in line with the linear-active habits described in chapter 4—an adherence to linear logical reasoning, a tendency to indulge in the categorization and pigeonholing of ideas, and a practice of interpreting events in linear terms of cause and effect.

These were comforting and reassuring assumptions for the Westerner and were bolstered by the writings and thinking of a battery of Western philosophers from Aristotle and Plato right through the Renaissance and up to the early years of the twentieth century. It was only in the second half of the twentieth century, with the stunning emergence of Asian, and particularly Japanese, economic success as well as increasing attention being paid to the tenets of Confucius and Lao tzu, that credence has been lent to the belief that people in the East (and not only in the East) hold worldviews that are not necessarily those of the West.

We know now that differences in human behavior and perception are not due in any measurable degree to genetic differences. Behavioral diversity is largely culture-bound, not hereditary. Two Bolivian children transferred to Sweden at the ages of one and two (and receiving a Swedish education with Swedish foster parents) behaved exactly like Swedish teenagers when they reached their teens.

A diversity of worldviews does exist, however, especially when comparing East and West and even when juxtaposing certain Western cultures (e.g., Germany and Mexico). Much of this has been dealt with in my comments on the categorization of cultures (linear-active, multi-active, and reactive) set out in chapter 4.

The questions remain: What causes people to be linear-active, multi-active, or reactive? What diverse ways of thinking underlie the creation and formation of societal norms, rules, and comportment?

My extensive contact with Asians in academic, social, and business life has led me to believe that a *basic difference in cognitive processes* between East and West is a source of cultural diversity between the two. Reactive Asians simply do not see the universe in the pronounced linear form that Americans and Northern Europeans do. They analyze visible (and invisible) phenomena in an entirely different manner, mainly because they are using different analytical and cognitive tools. The multi-actives too, with their backdrop of emotion and penchant toward dual truth, have their own particular cognitive processes, though they are closer in concept to the linear ones than to the Asian systemic thinking patterns.

To be more specific, the basic concepts of truth, logic, and reasoning in the East and the West are arrived at by completely different routes. Linear-active Westerners believe in scientific truth—one that can be established through Cartesian, Hegelian, or other logical systems. They focus on target objects (especially those that can advance their goals).

When Asians focus on objects or things, they do so holistically, that is to say, they refuse (or are unable) to separate them from their context or environment; they see objects as parts of a whole that cannot be manipulated or controlled piece by piece. In their eyes the world is too complicated to be contained in linear pigeonholes or ruled deterministically. For the Chinese there is no absolute truth—only situational and/or temporary alignments of facts that can change at the drop of a hat or indeed be contradictory yet still valid. Something can be right and wrong or black and white at the same time, as long as the outcome is virtuous and harmony is preserved. Neither are the Japanese lovers of absolute truth, which they regard as a dangerous concept, able to destroy harmony and progress. Even multi-actives such as Spaniards and Italians do not arrive at truth in a linear or logical fashion. In Italy truth is seen as negotiable (in order to produce the best possible outcome in a given situation). Spaniards and Hispanics revel in the application of dual or double truth—one dealing with immediate necessities and the other taking into consideration the more lasting philosophical whole.

These diverse concepts of truth and reality cause the three cultural types to organize their lives in quite different ways. Everything is affected: social behavior, business methods, decision making, problem solving, communication styles, the use of time and space, considerations of hierarchy and respect, aesthetics and creativity, standards of ethics, ways of negotiating, societal obligations, sense of duty, and so on. The diversity of conduct springs from one's interpretation of how the world really is. But what cognitive or interpretive tools does one use to sense reality? Why or how do they differ from culture to culture?

Language and Thought

To begin with, there was spoken language—indeed a complete linguistic map or blueprint—to define reality for us. But there are strikingly different maps. A person embarking in life with Germans and their disciplined thought processes will have a different worldview from the linguistically freewheeling American or Australian, but the schism between them is a narrow ravine if one considers the yawning canyon between European languages and Japanese. We cannot avoid language—we are born into it. Our early mental experiences are dominated by our mother tongue, and if by chance we have a choice to speak a different language a few years later, it is already too late; the patterns of thought are already formed. Language determines thought more than the other way around. By the age of six or seven, our thought processes are calibrated for good by either clinically logical French, exuberant but vague Spanish, respect-oriented but even vaguer Japanese, or rigidly morphological (fourteen case endings) Finnish.

Writing Systems

Language is our first and most basic cultural tool for interpreting the nature of the universe. How else can we think about it? How else can our elders inform us? How else do we pass on the information to others? There is in fact a subsequent and closely related device—our own writing system. If the difference between Western and Eastern spoken languages is formidable, the contrasting nature of the scripts used is even more striking (and indeed significant).

So the American/European child of tomorrow commences the

construction of his or her worldview by two essential means—
the native language and the national writing system. The Chi-
nese/Japanese child embarks on the same venture, but what a
contrast! Indo-European children have at their disposal an analytical, logical, consequential language system—rich in nouns
and structured to handle cause and effect without difficulty—as
well as a Romanic script of 22 to 28 letters. Chinese and Japanese children are expected to wield languages rich in give-and-
take respect mechanisms, sophistication in ambiguity forms,
nonsequential reasoning features—and written with 5,000 to
10,000 ideographs (or pictographs) embodying a *richesse* of nuances, subtleties, aesthetics, and compound cultural concepts that
will take them twenty years to learn thoroughly. Given this, how
can we expect cognitive processes to be the same?

Historical reasons underlie the choice of alphabet or script by
cultural groups; they are largely accidental or arbitrary and have
little to do with mentality. Once adopted, however, certain scripts
have a tremendous impact on the thought processes of their us-
ers. This is particularly evident in East Asia, where more than
one and a half billion people use or are familiar with the Chinese
kanji ideographic writing system. This legacy, extant already in
A.D. 500, spread to Japan, Korea, Vietnam, and other parts of Asia
and had a profound influence on the way people constructed and
interpreted symbols of reality. Pictographs are in fact uniquely
suited to express Chinese—an "isolating" language consisting of
stand-alone concepts—but are hopelessly inadequate and inap-
propriate for Japanese and Korean, "agglutinative" languages re-
quiring scripts that can deal with an elaborate system of morphological qualifiers and polite endings. Koreans eventually developed a phonetic script, though kanji still looms large in their consciousness. The poor Japanese—still stuck with kanji after one
and a half millennia of struggling with it—had to create two fur-

ther scripts (hiragana and katakana), each with 48 syllables, to be able to get their spoken language on paper.

hiragana

あ	い	う	え	お	は	ひ	ふ	へ	ほ
a	i	u	e	o	ha	hi	fu	he	ho

katakana

ア	イ	ウ	エ	オ	ハ	ヒ	フ	ヘ	ホ
a	i	u	e	o	ha	hi	fu	he	ho

Unfortunate choice or not, the fact remains that the use of ideographs directs thought and perceptive abilities along channels familiar to East Asians but quite unknown to the West. Americans, with the limitation of just twenty-six (Roman) English letters at their disposal, have nothing to concentrate on except *content*. This suits their need for analysis, reasoning, and logic. The Chinese or Japanese, with thousands of symbols to call on, can express the same thoughts in many different ways, in terms of both nuances and aesthetics. The American is very concerned about *what* is said. The Japanese cares much more about *how* it is said.

There is a firm correlation between harmonious speech and aesthetic script. Calligraphy is a prized art in both Japan and China. Japanese businesspeople have explained to me that even as they read for content, they are influenced aesthetically (favorably or unfavorably) according to the combination of kanji characters. Such aesthetic appraisal of script and the meaning conveyed by it have an enormous effect (when practiced over a thousand years) on the cognitive process. In international teams factual information leading to speedy logical decisions makes little impact on Japanese team members. They are often unimpressed by, and indeed suspicious of, too much logic. On the other hand, they are better than Westerners at detecting currents of harmony and good-will (or lack of it) in the atmosphere of a meeting. Even a business meeting for a Japanese is (or should be) an aesthetic experience. The same applies to most East Asians.

In the case of the Japanese, there is an interesting implication in their having combined an ideographic (kanji) writing system with a phonetic one (hiragana). Scientists tell us that different activities are processed in different parts of the brain. The left-hand side processes logical concepts (mathematics, logic itself) while the right-hand side deals with creative concepts such as music, painting, and so forth. When one is reading English, one uses largely the left-hand side of the brain to analyze the phonetic characters. The Japanese use the left-hand side to read hiragana (and katakana), but have to switch to some extent to the right-hand side to be fully involved (aesthetically) in the ideographic kanji. This implies that they must use both sides of the brain simultaneously. It is a well-known fact that although it would be economically advantageous for the Japanese to give up the cumbersome kanji writing system, they consistently refuse to do so on account of the aesthetic loss implied. They would lose their literature.

Skills

Richard Nisbett in his excellent book *The Circle and the Line* raises this question: Why is it that East Asians excel in certain skills such as arithmetic, algebra, and spatial relations but perform poorly in verbal tests? In my opinion the Chinese and Japanese are good at mathematics because they are used to reading symbols, some of which are very complicated (the kanji symbol for *rose* consists of twenty-six different strokes; see diagram on page 136). The Japanese, particularly, like business concepts explained to them by diagrams, which they internalize much faster than words. On another plane, the Japanese predisposition to visual communication, by virtue of their calligraphic writing system, may explain the popu-

薔薇

This elaborate pictograph (kanji) means "rose" in Japanese.

larity of comics in Japan, a billion-dollar industry without parallel in any country using Romanic script. Some weekly comics sell four million copies!

The Japanese are poor verbal performers mainly because they *do not trust words*; in contrast, they have remarkable visual recall. Habitually reading 5,000 or more kanji characters sharpens one's visual memory much more effectively than an alphabet of 26 letters ever will. Put 20 objects on a table, let a Japanese look at them for one minute, then remove them from sight. The Japanese will be able to remember and list 16 to 20 of them. Most Westerners will remember fewer. Chinese, too, have excellent visual recall. "One picture is worth a thousand words" is one of the best-known Chinese proverbs. Nisbett asks why Asian students in Silicon Valley shine in the classroom in comparison with Americans, yet fall behind in creative science. The reason is that originality is not prized in Asia as it is in the West. The best Japanese, Korean, and Chinese paintings are those which most faithfully reproduce those lovely horses, tigers, fish, birds, bamboo, and landscapes from the sixteenth and seventeenth centuries. If imitation is the sincerest form of flattery, in the East it is part of the drive toward perfection. The collective nature of Chinese and Japanese thinking leads them to consider that something that has been written, painted, or invented really belongs to the public domain on account of the combined effort that went into its production. That is one reason why Westerners run into problems concerning intellectual property rights in Asia.

If linear-active and reactive people demonstrate skills in the fields of mathematics, engineering, physics, and science, multi-actives shine in "soft" subjects. High on vision and imagination, they live in a world of ideas, often articulating them expressively. Their all-round sensitivity enables them to put together helpful syntheses, and they frequently provide the social glue in a diverse group or team. They naturally excel in artistic pursuits in almost every field, as witnessed by the richness of French and Spanish literature, Italian music and opera, Russian ballet, and Mexican murals. Arguably the world's most beautiful monumental architecture was created by the Moors, Italians, and French. The last two have long dominated the world of fashion.

Collective and Individual Thought Processes

Why do most Asians think collectively, while Westerners prize and practice individual thinking? We have already mentioned that Westerners focus on objects they believe they can control, whereas Asians take into consideration a host of other related factors that add to the complexity of the situation. This leads to more compli-

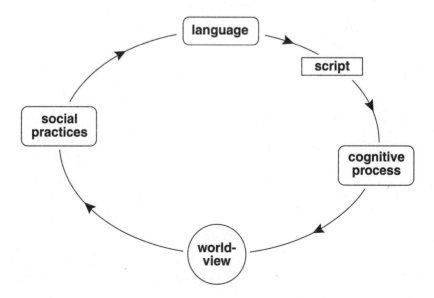

cated social practices in Asia, particularly in Japan and China, where societal role obligations are onerous. Without a doubt large populations and crowded conditions are conducive to collective thinking and consensus (consensus-prone Sweden is an exception). Collective and contextual thinking also derives from the nature of language and ultimately reinforces the original bias of the language. The diagram on page 137 illustrates this process.

The mother tongue is usually mandatory, the script arbitrary; but as I've mentioned, once chosen, the script welds with the spoken language to impart cognitive processes to the person. The filter created by the thought processes results in a worldview, which in turn lays down certain social practices and rules that typify the cultural behavior of the group. The social practices will subsequently affect the language inasmuch as it will be modified to conform to the society. For example, one would expect Swedish to be democratic in tone, Japanese to have many respect forms, and American English to contain neologisms—and one would be right. In this way the "circle" is self-reinforcing.

Let us look more closely at what happens in the West:

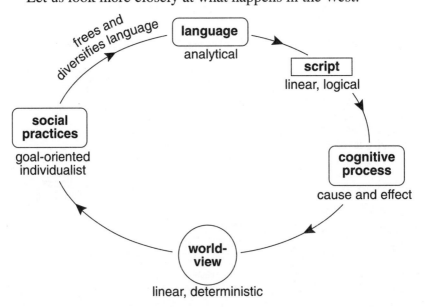

and in the East:

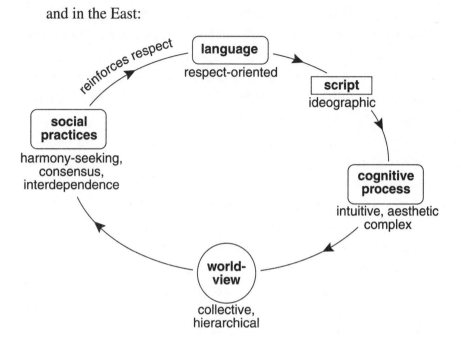

To elaborate on the diagram above, let us consider how the mutual reinforcement of language and social practices actually takes place. The Japanese language is characterized by a multiplicity of respect forms and can be spoken with at least five levels of politeness. There is even one level used only when addressing the emperor, who also uses special vocabulary. There is also what is referred to as feminine Japanese, spoken by ladies to adopt a subordinate role vis-à-vis men. Other East Asian languages also incorporate numerous respect forms (for instance, Thai has forty-six different ways of saying *you*).

The inherent politeness and respectfulness of Japanese imposes a respect-oriented manner on its speakers. In their social practices the Japanese are arguably the most courteous people in the world, which is demonstrated in their speech in a variety of ways. These are (1) choosing the appropriate status level, (2) selecting the correct vocabulary, (3) picking the appropriate deferential tone of voice, (4) displaying respectful body language, (5) timing (knowing when to speak and when to keep quiet), and (6) knowing what to leave unsaid.

All this may sound rather complicated, but to a Japanese it comes naturally because many of the tools are built into the language. The virtual absence of rude words or swearing in Japanese social intercourse contributes to the maintenance of the polite bias in the language. Grammar also unfolds in tandem with social behavior. For instance, it is considered unseemly, or incorrect, in Japan to report conversations one has had in private with others. Consequently, there is no reported-speech mechanism in Japanese similar to that in most Western languages. The question remains: Which led to which, the absence of the mechanism or the public distaste for the practice? The fact that Japanese women have traditionally reinforced their subservience to men by using extrapolite vocabulary and meek verb forms is well known. How, then, can a Japanese female manager ever succeed in giving a direct order to a male? Indeed, it is equally questionable whether a (male) subordinate can ever be assertive vis-à-vis his boss. A female subordinate is thus doubly thwarted. My daughter, who worked for a Japanese company in London, found that she had to switch to English to ask for a pay raise. The correlation of the correct language form and social or political behavior can be exaggerated to an astonishing degree. In the mid-1860s, for example, a conservative Japanese government, wishing to placate shogun Tokugawa, ordered its officials to use feminine grammatical forms in their correspondence as a symbol of submissiveness!

The Japanese language has many well-used terms dealing with honor, reputation, soul, and spirit. These concepts are strikingly visible in social behavior, particularly in the military. Following Commodore Matthew Perry's successful landing on Japanese soil in 1853, samurai retainers refused to exchange their swords for rifles, even though this left them sorely disadvantaged. In World War I, Japanese soldiers and officers clung to the weapons and tactics of the past on emotional and moral rather than practical grounds. Again, this was a question of worldview. To men brought up to honor physical courage and self-sacrifice, hand-to-hand combat, and leading from the front, devices such as tanks, machine guns, and periscopes seemed distinctly unheroic. Yet Japanese soldiers can outshine Europeans in displaying a sense of aesthetics. During the Boxer Rebellion in Beijing, even soldiers involved in looting were commended for their good taste. "The Japanese," wrote correspondent Henry Savage Landor, "were the only soldiers in the field who showed any natural and thorough appreciation of art and of things artistic. They—like everybody else, of course—looted, but they did it in a quiet, silent, and graceful way, with no throwing about of things, no smashing, no confusion, no undue vandalism. They helped themselves to what they fancied, but it was done so nicely that it did not seem like looting at all.

"I went into a house," Landor continued, "which had been entered by a number of Japanese privates. They had found a cabinet of old china, and each soldier was revolving in his supple fingers a cup or a vase or dish and carefully examining the design. 'Lovely, isn't it!' exclaimed one soldier, looking into the work with the eye of a connoisseur. 'Yes, indeed. First rate!' announced his neighbor, drawing in his breath in sign of admiration, while he tried to decipher the mark on the bottom of each cup.... One could not help being struck, especially when small, delicate articles were handled by the dainty, artistic touch of the Japanese soldiers."

This "aesthetic" behavior derives from a strong feeling among the Japanese that they are themselves a part of nature. Even indoors Japanese surround themselves with natural elements—unpainted floors and walls, wooden posts, and grass mats, which they feel with bare foot and hand; similarly, they enjoy visual contact with grains of wood and grass. Flimsy sliding doors pose the tiniest distinction between the garden and the interior and usually stand open so that one is indoors and outdoors at the same time. Japanese haiku poetry uses words from nature, and it is not unusual for a Japanese to begin a letter with sentences describing beautiful changes in the color of leaves or seasons or referring to cherry blossoms.

One can deduce from studying Japanese literature that the concept of nature has a unique history, differing from the West. In his study *The Tale of Genji*, Ivan Morris notes that in premodern Japanese literature, nature was often represented not just as a passive backdrop but as a "vital force, exerting a constant influence on characters." In fact the central role of nature in Japanese culture can be traced back to both Shinto and Buddhist influences. In Japanese Buddhism, nature came to represent the source of meaning and value. In English, nature is often depicted as threatening (rough, stormy seas, lost in the woods, etc.), whereas in Japan humans and nature are not in opposition but are part of each other (in harmony). Augustin Bergue notes that the Japanese self is "relatively permeable with its environment, both social and physical." Nature acts as a conduit between conscious and unconscious thoughts. This is a premodern Japanese tradition suggesting a continuum between past, present, and future.

Group or collective thinking and behavior are, as indicated earlier, highly contextual. In Asia lateral clearances are imperative. The Westerner looks at a situation and thinks in a linear fashion, considering alternatives and gradually eliminating them until a logical course of action becomes evident. The Asian is less interested in eliminating alternatives than in combining them in a multifaceted harmonious solution. Opposing arguments need not collide—better that they converge and eventually merge; different parts will become one whole. This way of thinking also applies to human relationships. An individual is incomplete and must be supplemented by others to have any significance.

Challenging the indivisible "I" is not new in Japanese tradition. Many anthropological studies have defined the Japanese self as relational and contextual, demonstrating that the self cannot be separated from its environment. The relative nature of the self is also reflected in the Japanese language, which has a range of words for the first-person pronoun that *change* according to the status difference between the "I" and the person being addressed as well as to the context of the exchange. This poses profound challenges to Western assumptions about the primacy of the individual. The Japanese (and other East Asians) do not see the "I" as the center from which the rest of the world is observed. Rather, they see the individual as *part* of the world. In fact the Japanese will *omit* the first-person pronoun completely if the meaning remains clear. This makes foreigners speaking Japanese (who tend to *put in* the pronoun) seem overly assertive.

These Asian cognitive processes also affect legal procedures and customs in Confucian-dominated societies. The Chinese hate written laws and make theirs vague, allowing for flexible interpretations. The Chinese base their values on human feelings rather than on legal or even religious principles and are less concerned with what is right and wrong than with what is "virtuous." This derives from Chinese fondness for enlightened and benign Imperial edicts and is hard for Westerners to accept.

The sense of belonging to a group rivals the concept of face as the dominant feature of East Asian mentality. The Chinese and Japanese just cannot accept or condone the Western sense of the individual self, which is anathema to one who sees everything in a collective context. Many Japanese salarymen still spend ten to twelve hours a day at work. The company is their *uchi*—their home and hearth. The Chinese spend more time with their family, but it is an extended family. In both cases the individual is subsumed and rarely operates singly. Japanese company colleagues go on long Saturday afternoon picnics, even though they have rubbed shoulders with each other fifty or sixty hours during the week. Tokyo's citizens pack *pachinko* parlors nightly in the tens of thousands, not in search of financial gain but on account of the sense of belonging that the mindless entertainment gives them. They are with others, they are cozy. After his Japanese soccer team won the Asian Cup in 2000, the team's French manager told his players to take Sunday night off and go out on the town as a reward for their success. They spent the evening in the team bus nibbling sushi. In China a military commander once confined a group of undisciplined soldiers to the barracks for the weekend as a punishment for their misdemeanors. Unfortunately for the commander, they *liked the coziness* of their confinement, so he had to look for a new punishment. This may seem incredible to some Westerners, but to those who have experience in East Asia, it will come as no surprise.

Logic, Logic, Logic

People who use different structures of reasoning seem illogical to each other. It has been said that Western logic tends to be *monocular*, which is another way of saying it supports one side of a proposition and pursues its conclusion in a linear fashion. Cartesian logic is linear logic. Chinese logic can be called *binocular*, meaning opposites are not necessarily seen as contradictions. Reactive in nature, the Chinese will make an effort to accommodate another's point of view without simultaneously discarding their own. Japanese logic may be seen as *polyocular*—a reactive, circular form of thinking where a multiplicity of points of view is accommodated. The fact that the Japanese are careful to protect everyone's face supports this description. The Japanese are more reactive than the Chinese in the sense that they avoid conflict or confrontation more painstakingly. Westerners often complain that the Japanese often change their minds or cancel appointments and arrangements without apparent reason. But there *is* a reason, invariably contextual and not apparent to the linear-active, more single-minded Westerner.

The Chinese, with their binocular reasoning, are much more comfortable with ambiguity than most other cultural groups. Reactive people love ambiguity because different interpretations of a situation facilitate avoidance of conflict and leave more options open for future cooperation. Linear-active people, on the contrary, find ambiguous statements irritating and often seek clarification or an unambiguous answer to a question. This in turn irritates reactives, who thought they were skillfully avoiding "rocking the boat." They fail to see why the Westerner does not wish to benefit from this clever ruse. The Chinese do not see their ambiguous stance as paradoxical. They can scream hysterically to foreign guests about the Taiwan problem while at the same time be the most considerate of hosts. They believe they are the gentlest of humans, but they execute more of their fellows than anyone else.

The Western cognitive process is facilitated by dialogue and debate. These are largely absent in China and Japan, where geo-demographic factors influence East Asians to exalt human-centered hierarchies over propositional truth in their thought systems. The hieroglyphic character and grammatical presuppositions of the Chinese and Japanese languages produce a mindset more oriented toward imagery and sympathetic understanding than toward definition and distinction. Americans try to solve problems by giving direct answers to questions. Asians avoid direct answers and wait for solutions to emerge in due course.

In summary, linear-active, multi-active, and reactive people wield logic from different starting points. Linear logic is based on facts—if possible, indisputable ones. It asserts that some things are constants. Reactive logic suggests that very few things are constant—perhaps nothing except change itself. Reactive logic is essentially contextual and cannot be separated from the situation in which it is embedded. In this light, ambiguity itself becomes more logical. Multi-active logic is more akin to reactive than to linear inasmuch as it takes into consideration a host of factors that the reactive person would also identify. It does, however, differ from Asian reactive logic in terms of being more influenced by subjective feelings and emotions. It is logical for linear-active people to follow their head. Reactives align decisions with a situation. Multi-actives follow the heart. Italians, Mexicans, and Arabs do not see actions that spring from the heart as being divorced from logical behavior. Impulsive, often emotional acts (perhaps considered by linear-actives as precipitous) seem right to them, as their heart tells them so. Multi-active reasoning strives to be all-embracing; its very depth and complexity baffle linear-actives. The events of September 11, 2001, and the subsequent reactions on many fronts (events I deal with extensively in the Epilogue) demonstrate only too poignantly the catastrophic effects of the clash of different brands of logic.

As we have seen in chapter 4, more than three and a half billion people are characterized by multi-active behavioral styles that, though differing in various respects, share the common traits of nonlinearity, acute human relations orientation, strong family ties and respect for elders, impulsive modes of conduct, and compulsive desires to live and work in groups. Non-European multi-actives (e.g., Africans and Arabs) have distinctive localized mindsets. Those of Western or European ancestry (Slavs, Greeks, and Latins, including Central and South Americans) share many values and core beliefs (including religions) with the linear North, but their cognitive processes do not in fact align with Northern European or American, inasmuch as a more emotional worldview prevails. To illustrate this difference in ways of thinking, we took a closer look at one multi-active group that has been separated physically from its European cousins and which, moreover, has received a significant "blood transfusion" from a reactive culture. That interesting example was Mexico (see "Case Study: The Mexican Mindset" at the end of chapter 4).

Now we will consider another aspect of cognitive processes—time.

Concept of Time

If you go to New Mexico, you can find a variety of concepts of time that depart wildly from the linear-active or the multi-active. With the Navaho and Hopi peoples, we are back among reactive or Asian concepts of time that found their way to the American Southwest via the Bering Strait thousands of years ago. Benjamin Lee Whorf, the famous American scholar who studied Hopi, Aztec, and other Indian languages, reported that among these cultures there is no general notion or concept of time as a smooth-flowing continuum. The Hopi language allows for no reference to time or to the past, present, or future.

In his long and careful study of the Hopi, Whorf found no words, grammatical forms, constructions, or expressions referring to what we in the West conceptualize as time. There are no tenses, as we understand them. The Hopi strives to influence events by concentrating, hoping, and so forth, but there is no notion of kinematic access to a future; rather, the future is experienced as a dynamic process or interplay of feelings and existing phenomena, all rooted in the present. Returning to the question of what is not knowable, the Hopi goes further than the Malagasy. In Madagascar the future is considered unknowable; the Hopi considers even *present* events unknowable if they take place at a distance. Distant events cannot be contemporaneous with near (observable) events; therefore they take place in what we would call the "past." The diagram below and the one on page 150 illustrate this.

Hopi View of Time

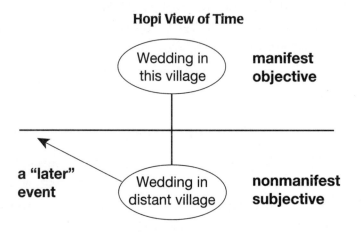

The wedding in the distant village,
which can only be known about later, is a later event.

For the Hopi there is no past and no future—only the observable and the unobservable. They conceive of these two categories not, as linear-oriented cultures would, along a horizontal axis but on a *vertical* axis. The manifest, the observable—their "present"—is on the surface of the earth, in close proximity. Looking up, they see the sky and the stars, but what is known and said about them is suppositious or inferential. In a similar manner the myths and legends they believe in originate from a corresponding distance *below* the surface of the earth (see the diagram on page 150).

The Hopi view our past and future as subjective—not pragmatic or real—just as we see the Hopi perception of time as strange indeed, and certainly not real.

The different ways of thinking about time are discussed in detail in my book *When Cultures Collide* (2000, 52–64). Here are a few more samples. The cyclical concept of time dominates in India, Thailand, and most of East Asia. Chinese, Japanese, and Malagasy peoples have specifically unique attitudes toward time due to diverse cognitive processes. The Chinese are preoccupied with not wasting time as well as with not stealing it from anybody, but they want to make sure that *adequate* time is devoted to any transaction or relationship. The Japanese are less concerned about amounts of time than about the order in which events take place; the *unfolding* of time is of major importance. The Malagasy see the past in front of them (known and visible), but the future is located behind their heads (invisible and unknowable).

No one thinks of time in exactly the same way, though the Swiss would like us to.

Changes in Cognitive Habits?

It is evident that Westerners and Asians have maintained quite diverse thought systems over thousands of years. What reasons do we have to believe that the twenty-first century will witness substantial convergence or alignment of these systems? Will some aspects of the current globalization of the economy encourage Easterners to think in a more linear fashion or Westerners to perceive things more holistically?

It is exciting to speculate. Will Asia continue to be a mystery, even to those who live nearby? Will globalization nourish the great "global tribes" of the Chinese, Indian, and Japanese diaspora? Will Asians continue to see equality as a child of Western civilization (not in nature)? Will literal-minded Asians ever comprehend Western humor? Will units such as international

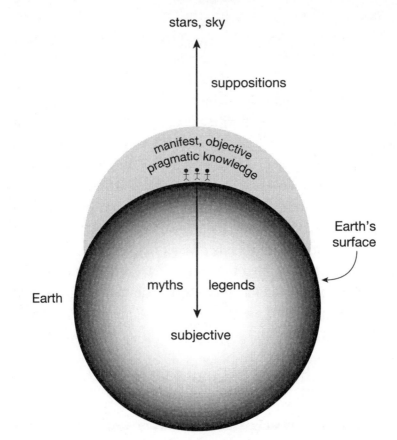

The vertical axis of experience:
manifest, observable, subjective, supposed

teams ever develop cognitive biculturalism to the extent that they can tackle problems from both ends? Can the internalization of more than one cultural style give one the ability to communicate and act flexibly from each cultural context? Will Asians begin to use the five senses for problem solving instead of looking back for the best past precedents? Is it even feasible to envisage *any* changes in cognitive processes in such a short period as one century?

Linear-active cultures are hardly seeking change. Their successful economies and pride in their democratic institutions bolster their belief in Western logic. This does not mean that they are right or as successful as they think they are. Their civilizations are younger than Eastern ones, and their colonial dominance was, in retrospect, bewilderingly brief. Asian cultures, for their part, are unlikely to abandon their basic thinking styles. The Chinese and Japanese languages will be used increasingly in this century and their ideographic depiction will continue to mold Asian mindsets. The concept of cyclical time, Eastern aesthetics, direct communication style, collective effort, sense of shame, use of silence, protection of face, and avoidance of confrontation will persevere throughout the twenty-first century, as it has for centuries in the past.

Some swings, however, might occur. The rapidly growing East Asian, Indian, and South American populations tilt the balance against a linear world, where numbers are stabilizing. On the other hand, Japan's slowing population growth and the tendency of the younger generation toward individualism (corresponding to modernization, Westernization, and welfare) may have some effect on traditional thinking patterns not dissimilar to that observable in India. The advent of the Internet has certainly empowered individuals—they can now bypass traditional authorities, even governments, in certain transactions—though the "global village" created by the Internet has in a sense increased the contextualization of actions, and it encourages a holistic approach.

Some factors that may encourage reactive and multi-active societies to embrace a modicum of Western linear-active thinking are (1) the success of globalized multinationals in outgrowing (almost "outsmarting") many governments, (2) the observed alacrity of Western colleagues in international teams, (3) the subsequent speed to market (so essential in the high-tech age), and (4) the swing toward a capitalistic structure in China.

This last development—seemingly irreversible—will not only involve more linear processes of wealth creation (following shining examples in Hong Kong and Singapore) but will also impose modern (Western) legal regulations governing international trade, investment, and corporate and property laws, thereby reducing the exaggerated submissiveness to authoritarian hierarchy (whether Confucian or communist), which for so long suppressed individualism and creativity. Gaining increased freedom while "making money" will also lessen fear (of job loss or prosecution) and foster more individualism, comparable to that seen in Overseas Chinese communities.

Having said the above (in relation to the swing to Western linear processes), I forecast that in the twenty-first century cultural trends will increasingly head in the other direction, that is to say, Asian and other reactive and multi-active values will be in ascendance and will be ultimately imposed to some degree on the currently triumphant but morally dubitable Western linear-active cultures. One reason is that linear-actives, already outnumbered by six to one, will soon constitute less than 10 percent of the world's population. Another factor is the ascendancy of feminine values at cross-century, largely due to widespread public disaffection with politicians, governments, and "ruthless" impersonal conglomerates. This disaffection, or disgust, is as pervasive in Western societies as in others and has nothing or very little to do with political affiliation. Feminine values correspond to a striking degree to Asian (and multi-active Latin and African) family values. It has been estimated that in twenty-five years' time females, non-Westerners, and nonwhites will constitute 80 percent of managers worldwide. Their cognitive patterns will have an enormous effect on the way business is conducted and, simultaneously, on the nature of international social intercourse.

   As the power of states and politicians recedes, globalized concepts (free movement of capital, mobile labor markets, cross-
border projects, mergers and acquisitions, virtual teams, and standardized production, accounting, and reporting systems) will take
over, but they will be increasingly collective and popularly supported. Early twenty-first-century statesmen have already recognized this trend, and countries such as England, Germany, Sweden, Finland, the Netherlands, and France have struggled to find
the "Middle Way." Both leftist and rightist parties have moved
toward the center; even U.S. Democrats and Republicans find it
hard to differentiate many of their policies. The rise of feminine
values, which has been a catalyst for the disaffection with political extremism, has also engendered increasing interest in religion and related philosophical doctrines or pursuits. Buddhism,
tai chi, yoga, Zen teachings, and Islam are attracting more adherents than ever before.

   Collective thinking and cognition is not going to die away. Collectivism is the most ancient of human social behaviors. In the
Stone Age tribes had lifelong companionship with *small groups*
consisting of kin and, presumably, friends. This type of relationship is mirrored in modern Chinese, Japanese, Korean, Thai, and
Indian societies. We may not be sufficiently familiar with the
chronology and ramifications of our past to be able to project our
future paths, but *culture knows the way*. We humans have powerful innate social tendencies, compelling us to seek the membership of a group. The small Western nuclear family leaves many
people with a lack of the sense of belonging, a lack of rootedness.
The human mind is designed with a fair amount of empathy, generosity, and a sense of companionship. As indicated by W. Damon
(1999), these feelings are present from a very early age. New-
borns cry when they hear others cry and show signs of pleasure

at happy sounds such as cooing and laughter. By the second year of life, children commonly console peers or parents in times of distress.

But, perhaps unfortunately, many of us (especially in the West) live under conditions which are different from those to which our genes are adapted. Industrialization, overcrowding, and separation from spouses or loved ones through work cause us stress, because these factors are suboptimal for our innate cooperative inclinations. In this age we are short of time, and what little we have is devoted to making money. It may be that when we invented industrial production, we were expelled from Paradise, and the gap between our genetic constitution and the way of living widened.

Asian cultures, consciously or not, have gone a long way toward organizing society in a way that caters more to our innate social tendencies. The problem has been to ensure that social arrangements were in harmony with those aspects of personality that were genetically determined during the long period of human evolution when we were members of small, relatively homogeneous kin groups typified by altruistic behavior. China, Vietnam, Thailand, Korea, and other East Asian countries have continued this lifestyle. This is the history of collectivism and the mindset that controls thinking processes.

*   *   *   *   *   *

The evolution of culture (and also biological change) never stops. Ultimately our genes, environment, and habits will balance, but we cannot expect evolution to come to our rescue any time soon. The process is too slow—and it may be heading in the wrong direction. The twenty-first century, with the population and economic balance tilting toward East Asia, will inevitably rise to the challenge of bringing society and human nature into harmony. But has evolution equipped us with the mental and cognitive tools needed to handle the challenge? Obviously we cannot afford to neglect or ignore any of the cognitive options on offer.

Chapter 8

The Pacific Rim:
The Fourth Cultural Ecology

After 1970 a popular prediction among economists and futurologists was that if the nineteenth century belonged to the British
and the twentieth, to the Americans, the twenty-first would belong to the Japanese. This is now less evident than it was. While
Japan's economy is still twice that of Germany, the current rate
of growth of China and other East Asian countries, as well as the
continued technological and productive resilience of California
(itself eighth in the world in GDP), suggests that an important
center of gravity in the twenty-first century will lie somewhere in
the middle of the Pacific Ocean. The Pacific Rim, as we now like
to call it, is lined not only by China, Japan, Korea, the ASEAN

countries, and Siberian Russia on the one side but also by such high-ranking economic powerhouses on the other as the United States and Canada, not to mention Australia, Mexico, Chile, New Zealand, and half a dozen other countries with potential for growth and trade.

If a Pacific culture or civilization were to achieve economic, scientific, or even political preeminence in the next century, it would, in a sense, demonstrate a certain consistency with the direction or flow of those human civilizations of which we have some record—in short, they have succeeded each other in a *westerly direction or progression.*

Transcending national boundaries and ethnic groupings and taking a sweeping bird's-eye view of the great historical civilizations up to the end of the twentieth century, we can identify three great, sequential *cultural ecologies:* the ancient riverine (Yellow, Indus, Tigris, Euphrates, Nile), the Mediterranean, and the Atlantic. All these, like the probable fourth (the Pacific), are water-based and derive their character, drive, and potential from a critical set of circumstances at a given point in the historical space-time continuum.

Humans' territorial instinct inclines them to covet land, usually for the purpose of aggrandizement. It should, however, come as no surprise that large bodies of water are the major catalysts in our drive toward progress and acquisition. Water not only makes up most of our bodies, it also dominates all forms of existence on the planet. Of all the worlds we know of, only the earth is wet. Seven-tenths of the globe is covered by oceans and seas. If the earth were smoothed out, we would all lie under two-and-a-half kilometers of water.

The earth's layer of water is four billion years old. By means of its endless cycling, the water of the seas and oceans *rules* climate and life on this planet. Vast areas of surface water evaporate and

form clouds, which send us rain and snow. This nourishes and irri-
gates the land and forms rivers along which we live. The oceans
receive two-thirds of the solar heat that reaches the earth; this "heat
sink" drives wind and weather systems. Ocean currents transport
entire heat systems great distances: the Gulf Stream in the Atlantic, for example, carries one hundred times as much water as all the
planet's rivers, and it determines the climate of Europe.

Oceans will determine our fate in ways other than climatological. Vast tracts of ocean depths remain unexplored, and it is estimated that 90 percent of life-supporting space on the planet is
ocean-held. Our food supply will depend more and more on our
oceans, as land-based agriculture gradually approaches its limit.
The world catch of fish already amounts to 18 kilograms per person per year. There is an untold number of species that we have
not yet tried to eat.

The Pacific Ocean, which covers almost one-third of the globe
and which contains the areas richest in phytoplankton (reservoirs
of life and the base of the marine food chain), looms large as the
strongest candidate for the world's fourth cultural ecology. Before delving into the possibilities of this fourth great center of
civilization, however, let us first take a look at the foundations,
characteristics, and ultimate destiny of the preceding three.

Riverine Cultural Ecology

Our knowledge of the cultures of the early Chinese Yellow River
and Indian Indus valley civilizations is scanty in terms of their
links with Mediterranean and Atlantic cultures; we do know, however, enough about the later riverine ecologies of the Tigris,
Euphrates, and the Nile civilizations to ascertain to what extent
the features of these centers heralded the development of those
that followed. The Sumerians in 3000 B.C. had invented writing
and the wheel. The Babylonian cultures, like the ancient Egyp-

tian, were concerned with architecture and construction on a grand scale—the epoch of the Pyramids and the Seven Wonders of the Ancient World. Powerful kingdoms were created on the basis of slave labor. Gods and ancient religions and magnificent ceremonial occasions occupied the front of the stage and pervaded the minds of men and women. Agriculture had put an end to wide-ranging nomadic activity, with its opportunities for freedoms and territorial advancement. Instead there was a strictly layered, static society, which heralded systems of societal structure that would prevail for four thousand years.

Mediterranean Cultural Ecology

The succeeding Mediterranean cultural ecology, with its roots in Crete, ancient Greece, and Rome, had different fish to fry. Grandiloquent architecture, from new schools of design, remained important and highly visible (particularly Greek), but political systems rapidly acquired sophistication, especially in the Greek city-states and later during the creation of the Roman Empire. Major catalytic features of this ecology were, in addition to politics, the modern religions of Christianity and Judaism, the beginnings of Western art and mathematics, the refinement of food and wine, and the exploitation of the Mediterranean Sea for ever busier trade routes. Phoenicians, Greeks, Carthaginians, Arabs, and those at the far reaches of the Roman Empire elevated trade to the preeminent form of human activity, although it was often disturbed by wars (over empires, religion, and trade itself). It was an era of limited (inland) discovery, of the beginnings of science, of certain ethnic supremacies, and of consolidation of assets in the known world (of which the Mediterranean Sea was the undisputed center).

The Arabs had a shining role in the later centuries of this cultural ecology. As the first millennium ended, Muslim Cordoba was the most cultured city in Western Europe and actually the largest city in the world outside China. The Arab/Berber army that crossed the Strait of Gibraltar in 711 soon reached France, but if the Arabs' stay there was brief, it was durable in Spain.

Al-Andalus, as Muslim Iberia was known, inspired the Western world from the ninth to the thirteenth centuries in the fields of science, astronomy, agriculture, textiles, mathematics, medicine, and personal hygiene. The unparalleled magnificence of Arab architecture in Granada survives to this day. Both Granada and Cordoba swarmed with physicians, poets, and scholars of various disciplines. Religious tolerance held sway until 1499, ended not by the Muslims but by Spain's Ferdinand and Isabella. Cordoba fell to the Christians in 1250, but Granada survived, and indeed flourished, until 1492—coincidentally the year that ushered in the next cultural ecology, courageously initiated by a gentleman from Genoa known as Cristóbal Colón (Christopher Columbus).

Atlantic Cultural Ecology

The third cultural ecology had an immeasurably vaster stage on which to play out its schemes and fantasies. The foundations of the Atlantic culture, particularly those lands bordering the part of the ocean that lay between Europe and North and Central America, were the activities of humankind striving to structure society—communal endeavors that were to develop not only more sophisticated forms of government but also to take giant strides in science, shipbuilding, astronomy, cartography, and ultimately global exploration. The Atlantic body of water was a challenge in itself. Columbus, Magellan, and others took up that challenge; the cultural ecology soon embraced both sides of the ocean. Vasco da Gama, sailing round Africa and on to India, also created a communications system between Europe and the Far East, the first information highway! This was the era of the Renaissance—the hour of Italy's glory; of enlightened monarchs such as Louis

XIV, Catherine the Great, and Frederick the Great of Prussia; and of intellectuals such as Descartes, Milton, Locke, Jefferson, Franklin, and Darwin. Acquisitions of this period were largely material—land and colonies, wealth, substance, and global exploration and conquest. Marx, late in the era, saw history as historicism—fixed laws of evolution, a process humanity cannot change. But water obeys no man-made boundaries. Wars in this period were often about colonies, trade routes, harbors, and eventually oil. England's moment of dominance came toward the end of the Industrial Revolution, soon followed by the burgeoning power of the young United States.

Pacific Rim Cultural Ecology

The Pacific Rim cultural ecology will be based not on industrial or political development but on telecommunications, electronics, aerospace engineering, and biotechnology. The silicon chip has rendered most industrial processes obsolete, and its unstoppable advance—along with that of genetic engineering, medicine, and nutrient sciences—will dictate the way we live and work and how we are governed. Large conglomerates, many of them electronics-based, command assets and powers far exceeding those of half the governments in the world. The Information Technology (IT) Revolution and the unbelievable speed at which it operates enable certain groups to bypass national decision makers at a multitude of levels.

We are at what Andy Grove (the former head of Intel) calls a "strategic inflection point" in human history. The course of human destiny has been radically and suddenly changed on numerous occasions. This may be because of an invention (agriculture or Gutenberg's printing press), an idea (individual liberty in the eighteenth century), a technology (electricity), or a process (the twentieth-century assembly line).

The latest information technology gives us *electronic proximity*. The powerful neighbors looking at each other across the Pacific—China, Japan, and the United States (notably California) will, like the other bordering nations, draw closer because of this technology. The Pacific Ocean itself, though it is so big that all the land on earth could be dropped into it, will "shrink" in terms of cooperation in information sharing. Not only will information traverse national boundaries but the electronic proximity will increase democratization of the zone, as totalitarian nations (perhaps China or Russia) may want to participate in the major new economic force of the twenty-first century. To do so, they will have to play by the rules of engagement made by the predominantly democratic nations that are starting to establish the Information Marketplace.

The Pacific nations, though differing wildly in culture, will enthusiastically indulge in the most ancient form of exchange, that of information—now on a global scale. These developments will occur worldwide—not only in the Pacific—yet one is tempted to see the Pacific Rim as *the launching pad for human endeavors and targets in the twenty-first century:* cosmic exploration, ultimate information flow, ultratechnology in medicine and genetics, to mention a few. Of the six biggest countries in the world, five—China, the United States, Japan, Indonesia, and Russia—share this gigantic ocean. Not only do they represent one-third of humanity, but also a united Korea, Vietnam, and the Philippines will be the thirteenth, fourteenth, and fifteenth most populated countries on earth, while Mexico, Canada, and Australia will play substantial roles in the development of the Rim. Land neighbors usually end up fighting, but nations facing each other over large stretches of water cannot attack each other as effectively; there is instead an obvious invitation to trade, and the trade routes of the ocean are multitudinous.

The Pacific has been described as a future Japanese lake, but this description overestimated Japan's powers and grossly underestimated the influence of China and the brilliance of researchers and scientists in California and elsewhere. China will ultimately dominate more than half of the Pacific, but not solely based on the overwhelming population of the mainland Chinese. America, Japan, and Korea will be important players, but the major organizers of Pacific affluence and dominance will be the *Overseas Chinese,* who already have most of their pieces in place. They now control 75 percent of listed companies in Thailand, 72 percent in Indonesia, 50 percent in the Philippines, about 60 percent in Malaysia, and 81 percent in Singapore.

The Overseas Chinese—not the Americans and the Japanese—are providing the capital for the development of industry within China (80 percent of the investment in the mainland has come from Overseas Chinese sources, mainly Taiwan, Hong Kong, and Singapore). The major result of the handover of Hong Kong to the Chinese will not be the "neutering" of Hong Kong but the admittance of the People's Republic of China (PRC) to the worldwide Overseas Chinese network operating in Taiwan, Singapore, Malaysia and all ASEAN countries, London, San Francisco, Vancouver, and to a lesser extent in most centers of world commerce as well as inside mainland China's Special Economic Zones (SEZs).

The Overseas Chinese, who are arguably the world's best businesspeople (certainly the most wired up), will have a heyday in the Pacific, which will be their major sphere of influence in the twenty-first century. The economies of Southeast Asia are in effect "leased" to the Overseas Chinese, who run their businesses and act as agents for a large number of European and U.S. companies who are trying to penetrate the area.

The progress and achievements of the fourth cultural ecology will be decisive in determining the future course of humanity in

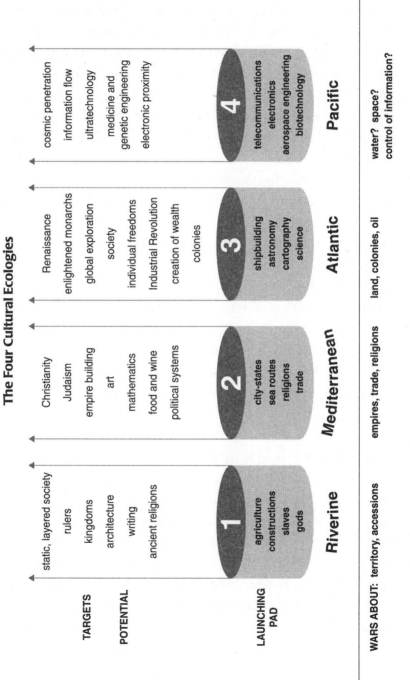

The Four Cultural Ecologies

terms of saving or ruining the biosphere. The global ramifications of our actions take place at lightning speed, judged against
natural change. The technological and demographic decisions
made by the burgeoning populations of the Pacific will affect the
lives of all peoples. With the world's numbers increasing by a
billion a decade, stresses mount on water supplies and on the
land, through erosion and deforestation. It is comforting to note
that most of the world's top reafforesters—China, Russia, the
United States, Canada, and Japan—are around the Pacific. The
area is also noted for the vigor of its agricultural research and
scientific husbandry in revolutionizing meat production. The Pacific Ocean itself may well be our last reserve and resort. Its in-
comparable vastness must be a source of great comfort to us in
the twenty-first century.

Although the economic and possibly political preeminence of
the Pacific area may well lead us to define this as the next great
civilization, it is unlikely, however, that it will constitute a pal-
pable cultural entity. The cultural diversity possessed by the nations on the Pacific Rim is too great for us to foresee any extensive coalescence. Reactive Asians, multi-active Mexicans and
Chileans, and linear-active Canadians, Americans, and Australians will pursue their separate cultural agendas. What may well
emerge, however, is a Pacific Ocean mentality which, reveling in
the new world of ultratechnology, will supersede the aging Atlantic spirit. None of the three previous cultural ecologies was
based on a simple culture. If anything, they were more diverse
than the Pacific. What they had in common was a spirit of the
age. In each case that spirit became the driving force for human
progress and development. The Pacific "age," in a time of unbelievable scientific advancement, is likely to be the most spec-
tacular of all.

Chapter 9

The China Phenomenon

In chapter 1 I made the case that world history has been recounted principally by Europeans (or people of European descent) and is primarily concerned with the history of Europe and, to a lesser extent, with that of the Near East. In this context Europe (more recently including the United States) has been depicted as the center of the world stage, not only as the political center of gravity but also as the engine room of scientific, commercial, military, and cultural activity. From the era of ancient Greece and the Roman Empire, the rest of the world was, in Western eyes, peripheral.

Of course, this was not the case. I also mentioned in the first chapter that China, for most of recorded history, was the most populous, influential, inventive, and technically advanced country in the world.

Europe, in no uncertain terms, was a latecomer. We know that Rome boasted about 350,000 inhabitants in A.D. 200. China, at the same time, had a population of *at least 60 million*. The most important city in the world (in European or Middle Eastern eyes) at the beginning of the first millennium (birth of Christ) was Alexandria. At the beginning of the second millennium it was Cordoba—intrinsically a Moorish capital—with wonderful architecture, science, scholarship, and cultural brilliance. Europe was emerging on center stage (thanks largely to the Arabs), but Xian, the illustrious capital of China at that time, had more than one million inhabitants in A.D. 800. By 1750 China's population had grown to 200 million and progressed to 530 million by 1950, one billion by 1981, and (as we all know) 1.3 billion by the end of the second millennium. Weight of numbers is only one thing, however; ancient China had other attributes, not the least of which were scientific and cultural eminence. For the sake of historical context, it is worth listing some of China's illustrious achievements, commencing at the very dawn of recorded history.

China's Achievements

8000 B.C.: Agriculture and Sailing Vessels. The earliest known cultivation of land was in the basins of the Yellow and Yangtze Rivers, thus facilitating the emergence of the world's oldest civilization. These great river floodplains were conducive to a settled agricultural economy. This, combined with the acquisition of techniques of animal husbandry, led to the systematic growing of cereal crops, which resulted in a remarkably rapid increase in population—both a cause and consequence of a more settled lifestyle. Around this same time, the Chinese learned the principles of the dugout boat to make junks, which were not dissimilar from those we see today.

7900 B.C.: Pottery. The oldest known piece of pottery found in China dates back to this date. These early pots were made by pressing clay piece by piece into molds and then leaving them to bake slowly in the sun.

3200 B.C.: Silk. The Chinese were the first people to make silk. Their detailed knowledge of silkworm biology, selective breeding, and a diet of the best mulberry leaves for the worms eventually led, many centuries later, to a thriving trade with the Middle East and Europe via the famous Silk Road traveled by Marco Polo.

2500 B.C.: Weaving, Ink. The Chinese invented a foot-powered treadle in the third century B.C., which enabled them to make intricate damask twills. Another invention at about the same time was ink, made from lampblack—a fine black soot ground up with glue.

2400 B.C.: Canals. The Chinese devised several schemes for the construction of canals beginning about this time. In 700 B.C. they started to build the ambitious thousand-mile Grand Canal from Hangchow to Beijing. It was completed nearly 2,500 years later (in A.D. 1780) and still exists as the oldest artificial waterway in the world.

1000 B.C.: Armor. By the beginning of the last millennium B.C., Chinese warriors began wearing armor made from four to seven layers of rhinoceros hide.

320 B.C.: Umbrella.

A.D. 100 to 200: Paper, Wheelbarrow, Abacus. One of the world's greatest and most significant inventions was paper, in A.D. 105. The wheelbarrow was invented in China in 118 to transport heavy loads for the Chinese army. In A.D. 190 the abacus, the ancestor of the calculator, was developed. (N.B. In 1980 China developed an electronic abacus, which proved no faster than the original one.)

500: Block Printing. This form of printing—centuries before its invention in Europe—was particularly suited to the Chinese pictographic writing system.

868: Books. The Chinese *Diamond Sutra* is generally regarded as the world's first printed book and is among the oldest surviving ones from the ninth century.

850: Porcelain. Porcelain made its first appearance in China at this time. Although Europeans imitated Chinese porcelain for hundreds of years, they did not produce a satisfactory match until after 1700.

1000: Gunpowder. Gunpowder was invented during the Tang Dynasty by Taoist alchemists who stumbled across its potential while studying its medical qualities!

1092: Mechanical Clock. Invented by a Chinese monk, the world's first mechanical clock was driven by a waterwheel.

1493: Toothbrush. Just a bit too late for Columbus' men.

China's Decline from Preeminence

Which cultural factors led to these many outstanding achievements during the centuries when Europe struggled to raise its living standards and began to aspire to higher goals? The teaching of Confucius with its emphasis on the work ethic, conscientiousness, discipline, patience, and learning surely all played a part after 500 B.C. Earlier, the huge Chinese lead in the cultivation of land 10,000 years ago resulted in a quantum leap in population. Many heads are wiser than a few, and sheer numbers undoubtedly contributed to invention on a larger scale than elsewhere. These factors, allied to the innate Chinese penchant toward entrepreneurialism and intense competition engendered by numbers, led to a cohesive form of collective behavior that served the country well.

When European urbanization began its steady growth from 1450 onward, China's population was approximately the same as Europe's. Well into the fifteenth century, China was still ahead of Europe in science and technology and was proud of its centralized decision making, extensive state bureaucracy, developed internal communications, and unified financial system. Early technical advances, together with the country's population—estimated at 380 million in 1820, compared with 170 million in Europe—made China the world's biggest economy—until it was *overtaken by the United States in the 1890s.* But if truth be told, China had already begun to slide from its pinnacle by this time. So why did Europe take off and not China? Why did China slip into an extraordinary decline, in absolute terms at least, from 1820 until 1952?

The answers to these questions probably lie in the perennially inward-looking nature of Chinese governments and most of its people. Opportunities for expansion and leadership were many. The Chinese had in fact matched early European voyages of discovery and had made informative and lucrative voyages in the Indian Ocean and off the east coast of Africa. Cheng Ho commanded fleets of over three hundred ships. Yet they soon lost interest in further exploration. Historically, China had also failed to develop military technology in the way that enabled Europeans to turn exploration into domination and conquest. Why should this be so?

One explanation for China's disinterest in development and power is that the Chinese authorities throughout the ages saw their own country as the only one that mattered. As mentioned earlier, the Chinese call their country "Chung Kuo" ("the Middle Kingdom"), which implies that other nations are peripheral.

The Chinese, historically, have shown little interest in, and even less liking for, nationals of other countries, whom they habitually refer to as "foreign devils." Like pre-1860 Japan, China for centuries did its best to shut out foreign influence, ideas, and pressure. Unlike in Japan, however, its rulers were bureaucrats whose highly centralized rule systematically prevented the rise of a merchant or entrepreneurial class. Whereas Japan reacted favorably to increasing Western technological and economic superiority in the mid-nineteenth century, China kept foreigners at bay, and those who favored opening to the outside world were overruled.

Another major reason for China's unwillingness to expand was its fear of losing control of its own vast territory, which had been a very real threat throughout its history. Consolidation of internal security has always been—and still is—a priority in the eyes of Chinese rulers. The Opium War and the various depredations and exploitation of colonial activity did nothing to lessen China's distrust of and distaste for Europeans and Americans.

The Chinese dislike of foreigners and its belief in the Middle Kingdom as literally the center of the earth was not simply a notion that has been perpetrated by its leaders. Even the peasants toiling in the fields have believed this. When I toured China toward the end of the twentieth century, I started up a number of conversations with land workers. They are a special breed of human being, conditioned by many centuries of unremitting toil. These men and women who farm the land are entirely focused on rice cultivation and live in hermetic ignorance of the outside world. Most Chinese peasants spend their entire lives within one or two miles of their home, their hands and feet underwater for a large portion of the day. They have rarely, if ever, heard a language other than Chinese, never seen a Western face, never ridden in a private car. As I started to talk to them, they still bent over their tasks. The more curious among them would raise their heads to look at us for a minute or two, mumble a couple of sentences in a friendly enough but hardly enthusiastic tone, then bend again and ignore us. This is what one means by inward-looking. We had come from the other end of the world, but they weren't interested in us. There was little we had to tell them. Their field was in

China—the Middle Kingdom—and they were at the center of things. This was where it was all happening. We had come from afar, we acted and looked strange, and we were temporarily sharing the five-thousand-year-old Chinese experience.

The peasant does not, basically, feel inferior to us, in spite of our nice clothes and our Western ways. We revolve round China, not the other way around. After all, they invented paper in the second century, when Northern Europeans were still wiping their bottoms clean with sycamore leaves. Who are the isolated, provincial ones? Of course the Chinese acknowledge and envy our current technology, but technical know-how can, of course, be transferred. What about culture? We met some Chinese Canadians in Shanghai. "The culture is all here," they told us. "All Westerners have is money."

If Chinese complacency vis-à-vis their own self-sufficiency (including food supply) has been a major cause of their ignoring others, their geographical location has been another. China was and still is to some degree essentially an isolated country, cut off from other peoples by a vast ocean to the east, jungles to the south, towering mountain ranges to the west, and freezing steppes to the north. Even in this age of air travel, it is a long way from Europe and the former centers of early civilization in Babylon, Egypt, and Rome. Why go so far to meet barbarians who had so little to teach the Chinese, anyway? Besides, the great extent of their own territory and the frequent eruptions of an unruly populace lent risk to Chinese rulers who ventured far from home. The Mongols were daring raiders and were a threat for many centuries.

Finally, there was the barrier of language. While historically many Europeans and Middle Easterners have enjoyed a certain multilingualism, the Chinese have always had difficulty communicating with foreigners. Though some East Asian cultures have adopted the Chinese writing system (Korea and Japan), their languages are structurally different from Chinese. For Westerners, Chinese is one of the most difficult of all languages to learn. Knowledge of foreign languages in China was confined to scholars. This language curtain (which can in some ways be compared with a similar one in modern Japan) inevitably discouraged the Chinese from traveling afar and for centuries diminished their voice in international affairs. Again, there is a parallel with the Japanese, who, though successful international traders, have not punched their weight in world politics.

Overpopulation is often cited as another cause of current Chinese backwardness. So what if there are well over one billion people in China and they are overcrowded? So are the Dutch and the Japanese, two of the most developed countries on earth. The population density of China is 127 people per square kilometer. In Japan it is 331, in the Netherlands, 380, and even in the United Kingdom it is 239! Large parts of China are uninhabitable, you say, but so is most of Japan.

The Political Handicap

Although China remained economically strong until the middle of the nineteenth century, the political situation worsened rapidly in the ensuing years. The Opium War with the British weakened her, and they took out a hundred-year lease on Hong Kong in 1897. Prime districts in Shanghai were taken over by British, American, French, and Russian "colonists," among others. The fall of the last dynasty and the rise of warlords led to a deteriorating situation culminating in the Manchurian Incident and the establishment of the Japanese puppet state, Manchukuo. China slipped into anarchy in the 1920s and was plagued by further Japanese incursions in the 1930s, which developed into all-out war. The Japanese, intent on creating a "Greater Asian Co-pros-

perity Sphere," occupied most of eastern China and drove the
Chinese government to relocate its wartime capital as far west as
Zhengzhou (Cheng-chou). Chiang Kai-shek rallied with Allied
help, but his ultimate victory was short-lived, ending in Mao
Zedong's triumph in 1949.

Another recent explanation of China's uneven development is
the legacy of an unfortunate political period from 1949 to the
advent of Deng Xiaoping.

Cognizant of the unrivaled durability, resilience, and opulence
of Chinese civilization as well as the accumulated wisdom and
composure of its people, I was nevertheless intensely curious to
see for myself what actually happened on the ground. In 1985
China was in a particularly acute stage of transition (there have
been many in her past). When Mao triumphed in 1949 and the
"foreign devils" were forced to abandon all enclaves on Chinese
soil save Hong Kong, the new leader imposed on China a political, ideological, and economic structure (Maoist Communism),
which seemed to fly in the face of all that China stood for. The
emperors had gone, it was true, but the hierarchical mentality of
the Chinese, embedded since Confucius (551–479 B.C.), could
not evaporate in a sudden change of dogma. Nobody in the Middle
Kingdom had believed in equality of society for 2,000 years, and
very few do today. Social discipline (essential in a sprawling,
multiethnic country like China) was based on inequality—a comforting, familiar inequality, where the rights one possessed on
one's particular rung on the social ladder were unquestionably
guaranteed. And what was all this about the primacy of the state?
The Chinese had always been collectivist in behavior—they had
to be to survive—but one's first loyalty was to the *family,* where
the unequal relationships between father and son, husband and
wife, and older and younger siblings already provided a sound
structure for a secure future and a venerable old age, when one

was cared for by one's children. Would bureaucrats in Beijing take care of the old folk in Xinjiang or even Guangzhou?

What prosperity had ever existed in China came from the hard work of the farmers and their ability to sell their produce on the best terms available or, in more modern times, their products from small family businesses, especially in that vast beehive of activity south of the Yangtze River. What about the strength of the great extended Chinese families who lived and worked not only in China but also prospered in London, San Francisco, Vancouver, Hawaii, Singapore, and throughout the peninsulas and archipelagos of Southeast Asia? Were the Wongs, the Zhangs, the Zhaos, the Chens to fade into insignificance, collectively pledging their obeisance to this unnatural structure—the Party—deriving not from any line of revered ancestors but in existence for only a blip in China's history and conjured up, of all places, in barbarian Russia?

If the Party maintained its ideological grip on the Chinese in unrelenting fashion from 1949 to 1986, it speaks more for the utter ruthlessness of Mao and some who followed him than for any compatibility between a command economy and the innate Chinese entrepreneurial spirit. Mao knew how many millions of lives had been sacrificed in Russia and the Ukraine to keep Stalin in power; if there was one place in the world where life was "cheaper" than in Russia, it was China. Nearly a billion people suffered the yoke of complete totalitarianism for one decade after another. A brilliant prime minister, Zhou Enlai, gained favor with Mao and found meaningful dialogue with the West. Unfortunately, he died in his prime and, with the Great Leap Forward, premature and ill-planned industrialization plunged China into an abyss of failure, despair, discontent, and near starvation. When wise men began to speculate, Mao smashed the intelligentsia with the inappropriately named Cultural Revolution; starting in 1966, teachers, professors, doctors, lawyers, and all manner of nonmanual workers were exiled to the countryside for five, ten, or twelve years' hard labor, thereby teaching the people the true meaning of revolution.

Chinese civilization had rarely sunk so low. After Mao's death, the Gang of Four, led by his wife, equaled him in cruelty and myopic vision. Only the rising star of the diminutive octogenerian Deng Xiaoping saved the country from further self-destruction. In 1976 he rescued the intelligentsia, liberalized the economy, and, while keeping the Communist Party in sole command, gave the green light to capitalism wherever a Chinese could find it. The people found plenty and soon started making money for themselves instead of surrendering everything to the collective. Deng declared, "It is glorious to get rich" and even allowed foreigners to come into China to advise people on how to do it.

Phenomenal China

Statistics relating to China are bewildering, mind-boggling, and often misleading. The population figures themselves are staggering when one grasps the fact that 1,300,000,000 people are equal in number to the combined populations of Europe, Russia, the United States, Canada, Mexico, and all of Central and South America! At the beginning of the twenty-first century, the GDP of this huge populace was approximately $1,000 billion—modest compared with the United States' $8,000 billion and Japan's $5,000 billion, and only on a par with the GDP of France or the United Kingdom. Similarly, the Chinese GDP per capita, at $800, pales into insignificance against Japan's $41,000 per person.

But reality is not that simple. The power purchasing parity (PPP) calculation of China's GDP suggests a comparable figure would be $4,000 billion, which brings China immediately into the big league. When Deng took power in 1978, two years after Mao's death, China was getting weaker and poorer relative to the rest of the world and was struggling to feed its growing population. Deng's solution was simple: capitalism. He introduced market prices for farmers, established property rights for the first time since 1949, opened up China to trade and foreign investment, and encouraged the importation of technology. The result was dramatic: China's GDP grew at an average of 9.7 percent for two decades and 200 million people were lifted above the subsistence line. Although accurate figures are hard to come by, there are an estimated two million millionaires or more in China; 90 million Chinese earn more than $30,000 per annum; and Chinese individuals have more than $400 billion outside the banking system, "under the bed." There are 10 million cars on the road; if China follows the United States and Japan in proportionate car use, there may not be enough oil in the world to keep them all running. There were 220 million credit card holders at the end of 2000.

Other statistics are no less amazing. Professor Yeh of Beijing University told me in 1995 that the government planned to move 200 million people from the countryside to the cities as part of the drive toward intensified industrialization. Recently I read that 420 million people are to be moved. There must be a big housing program under way. In fact we are told that 10 million people sleep on the streets in the big cities. It is hard to digest such figures, whether accurate or not, and equally difficult to forecast China's development in the coming decades by juggling numbers of this magnitude. Some economists tell us that inevitably, China's economy will overtake that of the United States by 2010. Or will it be 2020? The current health of the American economy suggests that it will be later rather than sooner.

When making predictions about China, it is perhaps safer to distance oneself to some extent from the bewildering statistics inevitably linked to such a huge nation and populace. Predictions based on such numbers have been wildly inaccurate in the past.

Who could have foreseen the incredible commercial success of Japan or even that of war-torn South Korea? Optimistic forecasts in the 1960s relating to the huge potential of giant countries such as Argentina and Brazil were never realized. On the other hand, tiny states such as Singapore and Taiwan surpassed all expectations. Less difficult to predict is how a country with a long, unbroken culture will behave. As François Guizot said some years ago,

> *When nations have existed for a long and glorious time, they cannot break with their past, whatever they do; they are influenced by it at the very moment when they work to destroy it; in the midst of the most glaring transformation they remain fundamentally in character and destiny such as their history has formed them.*

The 1917 Revolution established seventy-odd years of Communism in Russia but failed to eradicate enduring Russian traits, many of which stubbornly resurfaced after perestroika. After World War II, Polish, Hungarian, and Czech Communists reshaped their nations' destinies, only to see entrenched national traits overturn their plans in the 1980s and 1990s. Outsiders have even less success in effecting cultural change. Finnish culture survived more than seven hundred years of Swedish and Russian rule. African states reverted to ancient tribal alignments after independence from European powers that had redrawn their borders. Maori culture, after considerable assimilation with white New Zealanders, is currently reasserting its character inside a democratic framework. The older the culture, the more resilient the basic traits (which, after all, have stood the test of time).

China has a longer and more glorious past than any of us. Which of its cultural traits will persist in the twenty-first century? If we have to deal with the Chinese, or wish to, in the coming decades, what can we rely on?

Enduring Chinese Cultural Traits

When a nation believes in its own intellectual superiority, it does not abandon its ways lightly. This is particularly true when it perceives its superiority as having derived from moral and spiritual values, as China does. These are in abundant supply in Chinese self-assessment; they include wisdom, patience, gentleness, purity, impartiality, pride, sense of duty, filial piety, kindness, courtesy, respect for hierarchy, sincerity, family closeness, loyalty, tenacity, stoicism, moderation, respect for learning, diligence, self-sacrifice, thrift, and humility.

Looking at these self-ascribed qualities, the Westerner might conclude that such nice people will be easy to deal with. When faced with a dilemma, obviously they are going to do the right thing. Unfortunately, there are some complications. For instance, what, in Chinese eyes, is the right thing? They see us though their cultural spectacles, as we see them through ours. If we Westerners place truth before diplomacy and the Chinese reverse that priority, how should we assess their veracity? How can we come to terms with their inherent Confucian belief in human inequality, the basis of their respect for hierarchy? If, as collectivists, they perceive intellectual property rights as the product of the achievements of generations, how do we react if we see our technology appropriated without payment? How can we become reconciled to the view that human rights in the Western sense can only be fully granted after the stability of society has been guaranteed?

These dilemmas are engendered not so much by differences in basic, universal values (kindness, sincerity, loyalty, etc.) as by different *notions* of these concepts emerging from centuries (even millennia) of philosophical, spiritual, political, and locally pragmatic conditioning. The Chinese *will* comport themselves in the way they view as morally upstanding. We can predict with some confidence that the Chinese people and authorities in this century will pursue their core beliefs such as diligence, moderation, stoicism, respect for the elderly, conscientiousness, patriotism, and pride. The West's relations with China will improve only to the degree that we make an attempt to gain insight into their cultural patterns and behaviors and learn to interact with them more effectively. Which characteristics are going to predominate throughout the century, and how should we deal with them? I list what I believe to be the most important traits in random order below.

Confucian Tenets

The Confucian ethical system has prevailed in China since 500 B.C. and will continue to set the tone for Chinese behavior in the twenty-first century. To review, Confucianism teaches that people are not equal, that they play different roles in society. People are also regulated by specific relationships that dictate their obligations toward other people. When the Chinese are engaged with Westerners, they will act in accordance with these ancient tenets. We must remember they do not have "free hands."

Guanxi

Guanxi is a special relationship within the Confucian framework, governing the exchange of favors and usually involving position or rank. Westerners operating with the Chinese in the twenty-first century will not be able to remain wholly outside the guanxi system. It is an important part of building positive personal relationships and entails reciprocal gift giving, which is seen as a social investment. Through guanxi eventually two people are linked in a relationship of mutual dependence. Gift giving and exchange of favors are *not* seen by the Chinese as a form of bribery. Guanxi is intuitive, not calculating, and it is not limited to the business scene. The weaker party may expect to receive more and contribute less to the exchange—this is another form of Confucian unequal relationships and laudable in Chinese eyes. Westerners should be generous when circumstances afford and when the relationship is important. The guanxi process should begin *before* actual business or social transactions take place; it is more elegant that way. Incidentally, once begun, the process never stops—so be cautious!

Face

The concept of "face" in Asia is unlike face anywhere else. Face (personal reputation) completely dominates everyday behavior in China, Japan, Korea, Vietnam, and, to a lesser degree, in other Asian countries. The Westerner dealing with the Chinese must learn to coexist with and respect face as a living reality. To the Chinese, one's personal dignity, reputation, and honor are precious attributes, to an even greater degree than is the case with sensitive Spaniards, Mexicans, and Sicilians. Latin honor is often intertwined with macho aspirations, bravery, and the like; Asian face involves moral repute, basic integrity, trustworthiness, and even such disparate qualities as kindness, competence, and conscience. May the Westerner beware of imputing any base motives or deficiency of character that might impinge on or in any way threaten the Chinese perceived wholeness. Should we do so, our own integrity will be shattered as well, and any further relationships will be difficult, if not unattainable.

Virtue

The Chinese consider virtue more important than truth, for they believe there is no absolute, scientific truth. Truth depends on circumstance and is at its most meaningful in a virtuous context. A good example of this is seen in the Chinese saying, "A lie is not a lie if it prevents shame." This is no more illogical than the Western saying, "A thing of beauty is a joy forever." Is beauty any more durable than truth? Saving face and preventing the embarrassment of another is obviously virtuous, so there you have it. It will take the Chinese more than a mere century to change this view. Virtue has, over the centuries, been of paramount significance for the Chinese. It is one of the goals of life. They also believe they are more virtuous than others. Truth and honesty are ambiguous concepts, open to many interpretations. Virtue shines brightly; it is unmistakable.

Harmony and Patience

The Chinese idea of harmony is similar to the Japanese concept of *wa*—a system of conciliatory relationships and actions that smooths the running of business and the functioning of society. First meetings in China are devoted to the creation of early stages of harmony and attempts to establish trust and status. There may be several meetings of this kind, interspersed with no little amount of socializing. The Chinese prefer not to start discussing business seriously until at least a modicum of harmony with the other side has been achieved. Americans, in particular, are often impatient to "get the show on the road" and begin meetings and even negotiations at an early stage. This does not and *will not* work in China. The Chinese will continue to establish social and work relationships according to *their* timetable, which will inevitably involve many preliminaries and "toing-and-froing" that will test American and European patience. The Internet and the electronic proximity it provides may speed things up a trifle, but the essential getting-to-know-you procedure will continue. It is a well-tried and essential component of Chinese cultural procedure.

Which brings us to the question of patience, for which the Chinese are well-known. They are in fact two or three times as patient as the British, who are not known for their impetuosity. Americans would certainly not even be in the top ten. The Chinese, now well aware of Westerners' impatience, often use delaying tactics to gain advantage, frequently causing Westerners to make errors of judgment born of imprudent haste. The maxim "More haste, less speed" is true nowhere more than in China. The Chinese qualities of patience, perseverance, and stamina are factors to be seriously reckoned with in the future. They can—and most likely will—outlast all of us.

Humility

Humility, as prescribed by Confucius, is one of the cornerstones of Chinese behavior; any form of ostentation or boasting is an absolute taboo. The greater one's ability to demonstrate personal humility, the higher the esteem one will enjoy. Westerners, though they will never be able to plumb the depths of Chinese self-abnegation, would do well to try to achieve at least some degree of modesty if they wish to win respect. An eighty-year-old Chinese master carpenter visited his son in the United States. The son introduced him to a prospective temporary employer (an American), who reportedly had the following conversation with the carpenter:

Employer:	Have you done carpentry work before?
Carpenter:	I don't dare say that I have. I have just been in a very modest way involved in the carpenter trade.
Employer:	What are you skilled in, then?
Carpenter:	I won't say "skilled." I have only a little experience in making tables.
Employer:	Can you make something now and show us how good you are?
Carpenter:	How dare I be so indiscreet as to demonstrate my crude skills in front of a master of the trade like you.

Hierarchy

Hierarchical differences—another Confucian feature—are greater between Chinese of different ranks than between Americans, Britons, and Northern Europeans. The Chinese social or business pyramid is rarely flat by Western standards, and seniors are normally approachable only on their own terms, though kindness is expected to radiate downward. One can foresee a reduction in hierarchical extremes in the twenty-first century, as the Internet and more facility with foreign languages will enable many Chinese to bypass their superiors, but the general hierarchical principle will endure. Westerners should respect it. Frank, open exchange between colleagues of different ages and ranks is not going to be typical of Chinese office routines for decades to come.

One must always bear in mind that one of the basic premises of Confucian philosophy is that inequality creates stability in human affairs. Chinese, Japanese, and other Asians feel uncomfortable when having to deal with people of exactly equal rank. Equality engenders rivalry, competition, perhaps confrontation, conflict, or dispute. Subordinates on both sides suffer confusion without clear directives from above. Superiority or inferiority settles the issue. Superiors may command freely, while demonstrating kindness and compassion as well as wisdom. Inferiors are happy to obey wise instructions, and they benefit from benevolent advice, while demonstrating loyalty and trust. They are also absolved from responsibility and blame. It is a mutually satisfactory and essentially comforting situation. New generations of Chinese may seek to moderate the steep slope of the pyramid, but they are hardly likely to envision horizontal communication.

Indirectness

"Brutal" frankness on the part of Westerners is indeed brutal (or barbaric) to the Chinese. Enough has been said in other parts of this book to remind the reader that indirect, oblique—often opaque—speech is a keystone of Asian communication. Criticism, appraisal, even laudatory comments are all couched in hesitant, woolly forms of expression that allow the listener to read between the lines and enjoy the protective ambiguity that such parlance offers. It is the same with questioning. The more indirect the question is, the clearer the answer is likely to be. The Chinese excel in such courtesies—the Westerner should listen and learn the game.

Wizened and Wiser

Confucianism also bestows power on elderly men. This has been noticeable in postwar years in the structure of Chinese leadership. It is not easy in Asia for a younger man or woman to command seniors, and Chinese look askance on visiting American and European executives who are rich in titles but poor in years.

We can expect exaggerated deference to age to diminish in China in this century as the technological age fortifies its most enthusiastic adherents—the young—but it will be advisable for Westerners to pay exaggerated tribute to the age, wisdom, and experience of their Chinese partners for a few decades yet. Perhaps at midcentury a better balance between age and experience on one side and youth and talent on the other will have been achieved.

Collectivism

The shining individual brilliance often displayed in the West—and certainly strongly in evidence in the early years of the IT Revolution—is not greatly prized in Chinese or Japanese society, although among younger generations of Japanese a new form of tentative individualism is on the rise. Even young Chinese habitually subordinate personal goals to those of the collectives. Many see their personal and collective goals as being the same. The collective feeling—that of belonging to a group—is so strong in China that the average Chinese does not feel whole, or complete, as a single human unit. Only by being a useful component of a caring group, assembly, or organization can he or she experience complete self-fulfillment. Western egotism or persistent individualism is an entirely alien concept to a Chinese. How can such selfishness—conceit—be possible? Western businesspeople would do well to respect the Chinese collective spirit, which is in harmony with the rest of Asia and will not disappear in this century.

Conclusion

Successful engagement with China in the twenty-first century will depend on the West's ability to develop a more sophisticated approach than that adopted from 1950–2000—basically a yo-yo-like ricocheting between extremes of sympathy and antipathy. The least sophisticated—and most dangerous—policy would be that of isolationism, on either side's part. In the past favorably strategic geography (with two vast protecting oceans) has allowed the United States to flirt with the illusion that it can live in isolation from the rest of humanity and would stand to lose little by doing so. This is no longer viable. *Technology*, in the form of electronic proximity, *has replaced geography.* China, for its part, has nearly 5,000 years of relative isolationism to set aside. Such a long history of ethnocentrism and inwardness will not be easy to overcome, but the IT Revolution will take its toll on Chinese seclusionism. Europeans, historically, have few isolationist policies to answer for, though no doubt the Chinese would have preferred that they had, instead of the adventurist, imperialist campaigns that caused China so much angst.

China's path out of isolationism and sequestration lies in its increasing involvement and participation in global and regional institutions—the United Nations, the World Trade Organization, the Asia-Pacific Economic Cooperation, and so forth. If the United States and Europe encourage China's membership in these bodies, Western debate on China's role will be less likely to continually return to those troublesome dichotomies we are so familiar with—trade versus human rights, wealth versus morality, cooperation versus obstructionism. The West's prediction (and hope) is that in the coming decades, the market economy will prove not only beneficial but also incompatible with centralized power. That power is currently held by the communists, but if China continues to open up, the system may not be able to hold to the party line much longer. Liberal logic would suggest that if growth continues to gather momentum, the Party will eventually be damned, and if the economy worsens, it will be damned anyway. The only thing wrong with this argument is that oppressive regimes have a habit of staying around—Cuba, Indonesia, and Iraq are examples.

Again, a safer route to follow in forecasting China's evolution in the twenty-first century is the cultural one. Which aspect of the Chinese mentality will predominate in the next twenty years? Traditional centralization from Beijing and the traditional north? Adventurous entrepreneurialism among the people living south of the Yangtze? Another retreat from the meddlesome "foreign devils"?

If there is one dominant trait in the Chinese people, it is a unifying one—their patriotism or, better expressed, their sense of nation. Even more intriguing, this persuasion is also embraced by the Overseas Chinese. When we talk of the Chinese, we should remember that the mainland Chinese, though comprising 95 percent of all Chinese, are only one part of a big picture. The sixty million Overseas Chinese (fifty-five million live in Asia) have a combined GDP estimated at $900 billion, which makes them the *eighth largest economy in the world,* on a par with Brazil and well ahead of tenth-place Canada. Just over a decade ago, Hong

Kong's five million inhabitants had greater purchasing power than the PRC's one billion! Overseas Chinese in Taiwan, Singapore, London, Paris, Toronto, Vancouver, and in many parts of the United States share this prosperity. More importantly, they share hopes of a flourishing Pan-Sinic future for all Chinese. More than any other nationality, the Chinese act like they are all members of one big family. When a Zhang in Hong Kong needs extra capital to invest in Shenzen, he or she might well contact second cousin Zhang in Vancouver, or perhaps cousin Zhang in Kuala Lumpur.

The presence of a few million Chinese in Southeast Asia should also not be overlooked. Overseas Chinese are thought to control over 80 percent of listed companies in Singapore, over 75 percent in Thailand, 72 percent in Indonesia, 60 percent in Malaysia, and more than 50 percent in the Philippines. How have Chinese Southeast Asian residents been so successful in taking over businesses? In Taiwan, Singapore, and Hong Kong, where people are almost exclusively of Chinese origin, the answer is obvious, but what about Indonesia, Malaysia, Thailand, and the Philippines? The answer probably is that the work ethic possessed by Confucian disciples is much less evident in Muslim cultures and even less so where Buddhism is prevalent, as there are certain taboos concerning materialism and the amassing of wealth in both religions. Be that as it may, nearly all of Southeast Asian business is virtually leased out to resident Chinese, who often adopt local names and set about integrating themselves into the local economies.

The Overseas Chinese have been largely successful over the years, acquiring cosmopolitan and international skills, while simultaneously establishing an acceptable relationship with other nationals. They were slaughtered unmercifully at the time of Sukarno's demise in Indonesia, but this was a political reaction rather than any lasting desire on the part of the locals to take over business. The wide-ranging international experience of the Overseas Chinese living in Southeast Asia, the United States, Canada, and in major European cities will prove of enormous benefit to the development of the PRC in the coming decades. The family feeling is strong and enduring. The Overseas Chinese contributed more than 80 percent of all foreign investment in the PRC during the last decade of the twentieth century. Even Taiwan, despite the ongoing animosity between the two governments, is eager to get in on the act, financing factories and contributing managerial skills across the straits. The devolution of Hong Kong to China in 1997 is, naturally, of enormous value to the PRC in terms of commercial know-how, as a source of capital, and as a premier outlet for trade.

These connections are also valuable to the West. British, North Americans, and many Europeans are accustomed to a local Chinese presence that can walk and talk with Westerners who accept their trade and eat in their ubiquitous restaurants. PRC authorities, far from shunning their ring of capitalist brothers and sisters abroad, will seek their help and connective skills. This in turn will help Americans and others to communicate, empathize, and ultimately deal extensively with China. It will be a long and slow process, probably with many setbacks, but in a sense it is inexorable. Overseas Chinese are ideal go-betweens (itself a Chinese concept). They will remain capitalist, but at the same time they will remain Chinese. Mainlanders will become increasingly aware of the feasibility of this duopoly.

Chapter 10

Americanization versus Asianization

The American Era

In the immediate postwar years, a large number of Northern European companies—in Germany, Belgium, the Netherlands, Scandinavia, and the United Kingdom—felt the need to "Americanize" in order to emulate the forceful and palpably successful business techniques in production, marketing, sales, budgeting, and reporting emanating from the other side of the Atlantic. This trend toward Americanization (initially financed by the Marshall Plan) has to a great extent remained in place and has served its purpose, not only in the decades of rising production but also in periods of ubiquitous mergers, acquisitions, downsizing, and delayering.

Americanization of business was not restricted to Europe. In the Asia-Pacific zone, Australia is openly Americanized, while Japan, Korea, and the Philippines were by no means unaffected. Because the most pressing need of people in war-battered countries was to quickly raise their living standards to an acceptable level, the Americanization phenomenon was most immediately visible in the areas of industry and commerce. Almost unconsciously, however, many Europeans and some Asians, seduced by the success of the United States, permitted certain American notions and values to influence their lifestyles. Some of these were related to dress, sport, language, music, and other forms of entertainment. Other more subtle but enduring influences were in attitudes toward freedom, societal structure, the role of youth, and the reaction to government. Thus, what was ever more frequently referred to as the "Americanization" of Western Europe had, by the early 1950s, become clearly evident in such countries as Germany, the Netherlands, Sweden, Denmark, Ireland, and Britain—less so in countries such as Italy, Spain, Greece, and, particularly, France. In the Southern hemisphere, Australia followed the trend. Among Asian countries Japan, the Philippines, South Korea, and Thailand to some extent embraced elements of American lifestyle with some enthusiasm.

The Japanese Model

Since the mid-1980s, however, the four Asian Tigers (Korea, Taiwan, Hong Kong, and Singapore) as well as the burgeoning economies of Thailand and Malaysia have substituted *Japan* for the United States and Europe as their *industrial role model*. Vietnam, the Philippines, Indonesia, and, most importantly, China and India are following suit. China and Vietnam may well be the next two tigers.

What does this mean for the West? The biggest markets of the next quarter of a century—China, India, and rapidly developing Southeast Asia—will be drawn toward people whose business methods—marketing, sales, negotiating, reporting, personnel policies—they understand and admire. That is to say, they will conduct business most readily with the Japanese and each other.

Western nations have demonstrated convincingly since World War II, and particularly since the recession of the 1990s, that they are ill-equipped to empathize with Asian cultural sensitivity. Cultural barriers at the national level frequently prove insurmountable, even irremovable.

At the level of corporate culture, the story is occasionally different. A handful of Western firms—ABB, Nestlé, Levi Strauss, AT&T, McDonald's, and Motorola are among them—have proven that Westerners can adapt to, attract, and sell to Asians. Any European or U.S. company wishing to capture Asian markets during the twenty-first century will probably find it advantageous to embark on an Asianization policy, just as so many European firms Americanized their business culture and approach in the 1950s and 1960s.

Asianizing

In the 1980s and early 1990s, in the wake of Japan's economic miracle, many U.S. and some European firms embraced certain Japanese methods, especially in production and personnel policies.

For cross-cultural purposes, Asianization would seem to be a more meaningful and comprehensive concept than Japanization. An underlying common denominator of values, attitudes, and behaviors in Asia transcends Japanese methods and incorporates values and motivating forces across a vast community stretching from the Indian subcontinent in the west to Japan in the east and Indonesia in the south. China, of course, is the beating heart of this mentality.

Asianization is not overly difficult to achieve, but it has to be learned, and it demands intense focus. Without internalizing certain concepts, values, core beliefs, and communication styles, Westerners will never deal successfully with Asians. On the other hand, acquisition of a sound basis of understanding and cross-cultural competence will quickly elevate them to a position from which they can compete successfully with Asians.

Toward the end of the twentieth century, a significant shift in emphasis occurred in Western values. This is a phenomenon of great complexity that is influenced by sweeping political change, the dismantling of whole empires, the resurgence of indigenous philosophies, and dizzying technological revolution. In this heady and often euphoric atmosphere, one discerns a pervasive weakening, even discrediting, of age-old "masculine" values and a corresponding rise in the long-suppressed "feminine."

Various cross-culturalists have discussed and written about masculine and feminine cultures. These terms need some elucidation inasmuch as they do not correspond closely to gender issues or to the ratio of men to women in different societies. The United States answers the description (by Geert Hofstede) of a masculine society, though women have equal rights in that country. Irish society, too, has many masculine traits, though women easily outnumber men. Sweden, with its taciturn males descended from Viking warriors, is classified as the most feminine culture.

What do we mean by the terms *masculinity* and *femininity* in describing the nature of a culture? My own interpretation is that masculine societies focus on power, wealth, and assets as opposed to the feminine focus on nonmaterial benefits. Similar masculine-feminine corollaries would be facts versus feelings, logic versus intuition, competition versus cooperation, growth versus development, products versus relations, boldness versus subtlety, action versus thought, results versus solutions, profits versus reputation, quick decisions versus right decisions, speed versus timeliness (doing something at the right time), improvement versus care and nurture, material progress versus social progress, individual career versus collective comfort, and personal honor versus sense of proportion.

Masculinity and the Western Intellectual Tradition

Richard Tarnas in his *The Passion of the Western Mind* (1991), traces in admirable detail the historical masculine bias of the Western mind.

If we examine the progression of Western philosophical, political, and economic development and practice, we see that it has been produced and canonized almost exclusively by men. Plato, Aristotle, Paul, Augustine, Luther, Copernicus, Galileo, Bacon, Descartes, Newton, Locke, Hume, Kant, Darwin, Marx, Nietzsche and Freud, to name but a few, have made significant contributions to a masculine mindset.

Tarnas emphasizes unswerving masculine dominance as follows:

> *The masculinity of the Western mind has been pervasive and fundamental, in both men and women, affecting every aspect of Western thought, determining...the human role in the world. All the major languages... personify the human species with words that are masculine in gender: anthropos, homo, l'homme, el hombre, l'uomo, chelovek, der Mensch, man.... [It] has always been "man" this and "man" that—"the ascent of man," "the dignity of man," "man's relation to God,"...and so forth. The "man" of the Western tradition has been a questing masculine hero, a...biological*

and metaphysical rebel who has constantly sought free-
dom and progress for himself, and who has thus con-
stantly striven to differentiate himself from and control
the matrix out of which he emerged.

(It is interesting to contrast this view with that of Thai adaptation to nature, or general Asian collectivity in general).

Tarnas considers this masculine predisposition to be largely
unconscious but essential to the evolution of the Western mind,
which seeks to forge an autonomous, rational human self by sepa-
rating it from the primordial unity with nature.

Western philosophy originated in Greece and with it began the
kind of reflective, critical and analytic thinking that led to development and discovery. The tendency toward masculinity over
earlier matrifocal cultures emerged four thousand years ago with
the great patriarchal nomadic conquests in the Levant and in
Greece.

This trend has been evidenced in the West's patriarchal religions, from Judaism onward, in its rationalist arguments from
Greece and in its objectivist science from modern Europe. The
quest was for the establishment of the individual ego, the self-
determining crusading individual (read *man*)—unique, separate,
and free. (This contrasts strongly with Confucian and other Asian
concepts of communitarianism and duty-consciousness). It is
deceptively easy to attribute masculinity to Asian societies because of the apparently restricted role of women. In reality women
are powerful behind the scenes, operating effectively in cultures
that are based on feminine values such as intuition, ambiguity,
trust, and cooperation.

Suppression of the Feminine

The Western drive toward rationalism and science led to the establishment of laws and religions that left little room for the femi-

nine, the ambiguous. Laws were often principally rhetoric in the interest of (masculine) rulers. Religion has frequently been associated with deception. Protestantism in particular bases itself on masculine values—separation of right and wrong, absolutism in justice and truth, work ethic equating with success, and so on.

Both Protestants and Catholics saw rhetoric as a virtue, developed for competing in new areas of politics and commerce, highly visible today with modern lawyers, politicians and salespeople. Contrast, for example, Chinese and French behavior in meetings. The former grope for "virtue" and veracity; the latter are more interested in winning the argument than in discovering truths.

Tarnas points out that

> *the evolution of the Western mind has been founded on the repression of the feminine—on the repression of undifferentiated unitary consciousness, of the participation mystique with nature: a progressive denial of the anima mundi, of the soul of the world, of the community of being, of the all-pervading, of mystery and ambiguity, of imagination, emotion, instinct, body, nature, woman—of all that which the masculine has projectively identified as "other."*

The Cost

Ultimately, the pursuit of the materialistic, the scientific, the essentially rational, and the objective must produce a longing for what has been lost. Feminine values, though suppressed or ignored, have been a dormant presence all the time—important, all-embracing, and vital to human nature. The late twentieth century obsession with science, material gain, and exploitation of the planet's resources has led to a crisis of its own making. It is a masculine crisis—a rapidly developing feeling of solitude, of alienation from family and community. This crisis is observable in the breakup of families, in the rise of crime, in various forms of pollution, in the erosion of values, in the growing disgust of public leaders in business and politics, and even in the distrust of government itself.

The Backlash

A startling reverse trend is now emerging strongly in Western culture—a shift to more feminine values. Tarnas continues:

> ...[It is] visible...in the...growing empowerment of women,...the rapid burgeoning of women's scholarship, and gender-sensitive perspectives in virtually every intellectual discipline,...in the increasing sense of unity with the planet,...awareness of the ecological and the growing reaction against political and corporate policies supporting the domination and exploitation of the environment,...in the accelerating collapse of long-standing political and ideological barriers separating the world's peoples, in the deepening recognition of the value and necessity of partnership, pluralism,...in the growing recognition of an immanent intelligence in nature,...in the increasing appreciation of indigenous and archaic cultural perspectives such as the Native American, African, and ancient European.

He concludes that a drastic shift is taking place in the contemporary psyche, a union of opposites, between "the long-dominant but now alienated masculine [strongly associated with the West] and the long-suppressed but now ascending feminine [inherently Eastern in character]."

East and West

As I consider this phenomenon from its East-West aspects, I believe a parallel fusion of Eastern and Western values and systems is also imminent. In fact much of the confusion of the modern era results from the fact that this evolutionary drama is now reaching its climactic stage. The twenty-first century is going to be different. The almost magical IT Revolution has made the East and West intensely aware of each other. Speed of communication among members of diverse cultures is eliminating barriers previously erected by government, ideologies, and cartels. How will Eastern and Western cultures affect each other, spiritually, mentally, and economically? The Asian model of society and of doing business seems destined to dominate. Weight of population, as said earlier, and the enormity of the Chinese, Indian, and Southeast Asian markets will probably be the decisive factors.

The rise of the feminine in the West coincides with the necessity to accept Asian values. Let's see what Eastern values and feminine values emerging in the West have in common:

- Communitarianism and cooperation
- Leadership by the strong but protection of the weak
- Intuition, mysticism, and instinct seen as factors to be reckoned with
- The influence of the family
- The importance of educating children
- Thrift, frugality, prudent saving
- Networking
- Patience, endurance, persistence
- Balanced perspectives and a sense of proportion
- Ascendance of morality over materialism

Cross-culturalists such as Samuel Huntington focus on Asian strength, declaring that the West must abandon its universalist aspirations. China, Japan, the East in general, Muslims, and Africans are poor candidates for anything more than surface Westernization. The "Davos Culture" annually brings together one thousand businesspeople, bankers, government officials, intellectuals, and journalists in the prestigious Swiss resort. Those assembled control virtually all the world's international institutions and the bulk of its economic and military capabilities. The group's formula for progress is individualism, market economics, political democracy, the application of technology, and rapid globalization—a combination that would appear irresistible. Yet outside the West, less than 1 percent of the world's peoples share this culture. Huntington looks at the growing hegemony of China, reflects that culture follows power, and forecasts that Japan, Southeast Asia, and possibly India will drift away from the West and enter into conflictual relations with the United States, in particular.

Other culturalists, such as William Rees-Mogg, hold a different view. They hypothesize that Japan may grow increasingly alarmed at the prospect of Chinese dominance in Asia and may, along with India and most of Africa, exhibit continued dependence on the ability of the United States and Western Europe to counterbalance China. Rees-Mogg does not believe that Asia would coalesce in hostility to Western culture while it is still in the process of establishing its own balance of power with China. He sees the emergence of a new layer of culture, neither Western nor Eastern but rather both, where consumerism, education, travel, fitness, spirituality, fashion, trends, and the Internet combine in what he calls "a yearning for ecstatic experience"—not the West versus the East, but the new versus the old. His conclusion is that the next age in Asia will belong more to Bill Gates than to Confucius.

Given the durability of Confucianism, I rather doubt this, but the fusion of technology, art, and traditions; of Eastern and Western strengths; of masculine and feminine values seems ultimately inevitable and desirable in the twenty-first century. When Prime Minister Datuk Seri Mahathir Mohamad of Malaysia told the assembled heads of European governments in 1996, "European values are European values—Asian values are universal values," he hardly addressed an enthusiastic audience. What were the grounds for such a sweeping judgment? No doubt he had in mind that while the current Western civilization is usually considered as having emerged about A.D. 700, Chinese civilization is five thousand years old, Indian, nearly four thousand. It may well be that the West since the advent of Christianity, the Renaissance, Magna Carta, and the Industrial and IT Revolutions believes it has mended the world, but three billion people east of Suez have another version. Huntington advises us "to preserve and renew the unique qualities of our Western civilization." This is surely a worthy goal. If we can also embrace a degree of Asianization, just as we grabbed Americanization in 1945–1946, we will pave the road to better spiritual understanding, intercultural harmony, and better business.

In order to go about this, we must take a closer look at Asian political and management systems and how they are affected by Asian values, communication styles, and organizational patterns; then we must write ourselves a manual for adopting and benefiting from Asian ways and methods.

Values

Western	Asian
Democracy	Hierarchy
Equality	Inequality
Self-determination	Fatalism
Individualism	Collectivism
Human rights	Acceptance of status
Equality for women	Male dominance
Social mobility	Established social classes
Status through achievement	Status by birth, through wealth
Facts and figures	Relationships
Social justice	Power structures
New solutions	Good precedents
Vigor	Wisdom
Linear time	Cyclic time
Result orientation	Harmony orientation

Differing values are at the heart of intercultural friction and will not change quickly under any circumstances. The Westerner has no alternative but to accept them. He or she may, however, begin to gain insight into the positive features of, for example, relationship building, harmony, and the following of good precedents. Is there such a thing as real equality? Is there not an element of fatalism in Western religions?

Communication Styles

Western	Asian
Direct	Indirect
Blunt	Diplomatic
Polite	Very courteous
Talkative	Reserved
Extrovert	Introvert
Persuasive	Recommending
Medium-strong eye contact	Weak eye contact
Linear-active	Reactive
Unambiguous	Ambiguous
Decisive	Cautious
Problem solving	Acceptance of the situation
Interrupts	Does not interrupt
Half listens	Listens carefully
Quick to deal	Courtship dance
Concentrates on problems	Concentrates on agreed items

If different values are the root of conflict, it is usually the inadequate communication of them that leads to misunderstanding. In this area mutual progress is often achievable. It is much easier, through training, to acquire communication skills than it is to swallow alien core beliefs embedded in another's psyche. Increasing international contact and technology will play an important role in improving cross-cultural communication.

Organizational Patterns

Western	Asian
Individual as unit	Company, society as unit
Promotion by achievement	Promotion by age
Horizontal or matrix structures	Vertical structures
Profit orientation	Market share priority
Contracts as binding	Contracts as renegotiable
Decisions by competent individuals	Decisions by consensus
Specialization	Job rotation
Professional mobility	Fixed loyalty

Western companies embracing a degree of Asianization will hardly abandon their own organizational structures. What is required is an appreciation of the nature of Asian frameworks. Asian variations from their own patterns may appear positive or negative, but a better orientation toward them will be advantageous. Is there anything inherently horrid about renegotiating a signed contract? Decisions made by consensus are usually slow, but they are often sound.

The Asian Model

It is only natural that the West cherishes its own institutions; yet many of them—the electoral system, social justice, equality for women, individual rights, limited government, equality of opportunity, the sacred nature of property rights, social and professional mobility—are relatively recent inventions, with little currency in the West before the late nineteenth century. Slavery was abolished (with some difficulty) in the United States in 1865; women could not vote in Britain until 1928 and in Switzerland, not until 1971! Double standards in repelling aggression, promoting democratic movements, and preaching for nonproliferation are still evident in Western practice.

Criticism of Western universalism (seen by others as imperialism) from Asian and other sources has led scholars and businesspeople in the West to pay closer attention to the Asian way of doing things, and they see many attractive features. These include a genuine work ethic (encouraged by Confucius), a collective entrepreneurial spirit, an emphasis on education, high savings rates, positive government involvement in export expansion, dynamic community spirit, unanimous directional effort inside companies, loyalty to firms, a comforting focus on people, a high duty-consciousness, professional obedience among employees, basic trust as opposed to mere observance of legalities, and—in the case of Japan, Korea, Taiwan, and Singapore—vigorous reinvestment of profits in research and development and improvement of resources and infrastructure.

Asians, for their part, have adopted certain Western features as they have modernized. Examples are Sony's development of a marketing strategy that was highly successful in Europe and the United States and Samsung's graft of Western techniques onto its authoritarian corporate structure.

The Asian Mind

The common (and beneficial) features of the Asian business model, noted by the West, derive from an Asian mentality that merits close scrutiny by those who wish to trade with Asians or, indeed, enter into ever closer commercial relationships. When we talk of the "Asian mind," we call up visions of behavior typical of Far Eastern countries such as China, Japan, and Korea— confident adherents of Confucianism—but as mentioned earlier, there is an underlying common denominator of comportment in Asia, incorporating the values and traditions respected by a vast community from Japan in the east to the Indian subcontinent in the west. In this respect the Asian mind is a reality, even though it spans an awesome expanse of territory and a plethora of diverse religions and creeds. The basic Asian values and rules regarding courtesy and respect, humility, filial piety, hierarchical society, emphasis on formality and ritual, sense of collective duty and welfare, faith in education, closeness of family, and loyalty to friends are as real and imperative in Bombay and Djakarta as they are in Tokyo and Beijing.

Government Control

Asians believe, in line with Confucianism, that business is a *low form of activity* and therefore must be subject to government control. This has political overtones in China, Vietnam, and North Korea, but it is visible in more voluntary form in Japan ("Japan Inc."); in South Korea, where massive government funding enabled the *chaebol* to compete with the Japanese *keiretsu*; and in Taiwan, Thailand, Malaysia, and Singapore, where government leaders were conspicuous in promoting the national economy.

This general attitude toward the role of business and the involvement of public figures is often puzzling to Western businesspeople. In Asia business must be seen "to help the country." Profit is of course necessary, but it is secondary. There is a "correct way of doing things," and Asian rulers, believing in their innate superiority, tend to be autocratic, "as they know best." Power, however, is derived ultimately from sincerity and competence; therefore, "bad rulers" may be overthrown. Opposition parties may be disloyal. Asian students are entitled to revolt if abused. This happened regularly in South Korea, occurred once or twice (with tragic results) in China, and is becoming a reality in Indonesia.

The downside of the Confucius-inspired government interference with business is that bureaucracy has too much power and also has exaggerated respect for authority figures. The emphasis on harmony (hopefully unanimity) leads to legal action being viewed badly. (This has often cramped the style of American firms who feel hard done by in Japan and Korea.) The reality is that in most cases it is better not to sue but to improve one's relations with government officials (who occupy an honored position in the Confucian scheme of things) instead.

Asian Logic

Although I discussed logic and culture in chapter 7, here the focus is on Asian logic, which differs so markedly from Western thinking that it often simply appears illogical. Things that seem obvious, or cut-and-dried, in Europe or the United States are not at all evident to Asians. Westerners often refer to black and white, right and wrong, good and evil. These are threatening concepts to most Asians, who are completely at ease with the ambiguity of seemingly incongruous components functioning in harmonious coexistence. One can present two contradictory hypotheses to an Indian, for example, and he or she will courteously endorse both of them, beaming all the while. Truth itself is ephemeral, being regarded as a dangerous concept in Japan and subjected to "virtue" in China.

Only four cultural groups use "scientific" truth as a tool for discussion and conducting meetings. These groups are (1) Nordics, (2) North Americans, (3) Germanics (Germans, Austrians, Swiss Germans), and (4) Australians. These groups believe that facts and figures constitute a sound foundation for reaching decisions and conclusions. Other cultures have more subtle interpretations of truth, usually connected with an unwillingness to confront or a desire to protect face. Asians, Arabs, Africans, South Americans, and many Europeans will indulge in a certain amount of "window dressing" when describing a situation. In Italy and Greece, truth is negotiable, in England it is sometimes seen as offensive (unless coded), in Polynesia it may be considered too outspoken for comfort, and in Russia, outright perilous. Asians do not see an unbreakable bond between truth and logic.

When constructing arguments, Asians do not normally follow Western linear logic. Instead their thought moves toward an objective in a sort of spiral. The Westerner is confused by frequent non sequiturs. The Westerner uses argument and counterarguments, evidence, facts, and explanation, tackling problems and seeking solutions. Asians avoid taking sides, counterargument, any kind of confrontation. They seek agreement not by proving a point but by "zoning in," in ever decreasing circles, on what appears to be a mutually congenial state of affairs. Argument itself, in Asian eyes, is seen as a scattered number of points that, through discussion, gradually converge and eventually unify.

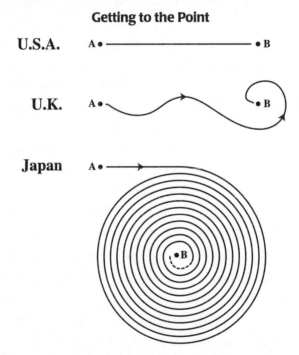

Getting to the Point

As if this is not difficult enough for the Westerner to comprehend, Asian Zen concepts about the changing nature of things complicate matters somewhat further. What is said today may be rather different tomorrow. What was done yesterday may be seen in a different light today. The Chinese, particularly, see change as a constant. It is hard for the Westerner to swallow that the only constant is change itself, but this old Asian belief has been fast gaining currency elsewhere at the beginning of the twenty-first century. "Managing change" is a popular seminar topic in the United States and Europe. Asians have long believed that one's actions must be changed on a daily basis to achieve the best results. Every business relationship is in constant transition; therefore, one must continually pay attention to all aspects of business. Japanese, Chinese and Koreans—basically reliable in their arrangements—often cancel meetings or appointments at a few hours' notice, to the great chagrin of Westerners. The reason usually given is, "Circumstances have changed."

Attitudes toward the West

Most Asian countries are very nationalistic, with a strong ethnocentric mentality. Western excesses during colonial times resulted in lingering xenophobia, particularly against former colonial masters. Indians direct their criticism mainly against the British, the Indonesians against the Dutch, and so on. Rancor is, however, not so biting as to inhibit trade relations. Indians are still courteous to British visitors, Indonesians use Dutch technicians and engineers, and Filipinos share many ideals with Americans. Countries that were never colonized are selective in their xenophobia. Americans are very popular in Thailand, and the English enjoy their reputation as "gentlemen" in Japan.

In all cases red-carpet treatment is accorded by Asians to business partners, including generous hospitality, respect, protection of face for all parties, gift giving, and so on. Asians attach tremendous importance to form, symbolism, and gesture. Of course they expect all their courtesies to be reciprocated, but they are unlikely to fail in these respects when receiving foreign visitors.

These gestures should not, however, be mistaken for genuine warmth of relationship. Asians are quite prepared to build relationships, but there remains a lot of work to be done!

Variations in Mindset

While Westerners often find Asians opaque, distant, closed, impassive, "inscrutable," and strange in other ways, one should bear in mind that Asians, for their part, are often equally bemused by Western "idiosyncrasies." Some Western peculiarities are a source of unease to most Asians, who tend to be literal-minded and can, therefore, easily misinterpret Western humor. When an American opens a seminar or a presentation with a joke or a wisecrack, Asians may think it is an integral part of the presentation. They sometimes think that Americans (and some other Anglo-Saxons) commercialize, trivialize, or "humorize" matters that for them are human events of great import.

Most Asians believe that the West suffers from a certain relative decadence, an abandonment of moral standards that are both visible and deeply held in modern Asian life—respect for parents, frugality, thrift, saving, politeness, collective spirit, and so on. They perceive a lack of solidarity and a fragile loyalty in many Western firms and among consumers (particularly in the United States, where employees frequently switch to the competition and shoppers abandon brands and stores without a second thought). Criticism of such declining morals is rarely so overt as that expressed by many Islamic cultures, but it is often an undercurrent in Asians' cautious dealings with Westerners. Asians grope for trust and respect; they respond warmly in due course when these are confirmed. Westerners are aware of and sometimes obsessed with their "quality of life" and are increasingly in search of it. This expression still has little meaning in Confucian Asia, where working hard is preferred and Westerners are seen as somewhat slothful. The Japanese pay ready tribute to the German work ethic but fail to understand how Germans can take a six-week vacation (and enjoy it!). Asians feel a certain amount of guilt about taking holidays and often curtail these in the company's interest. With increasing mutual awareness of each other's lifestyles, one can hope that traits now considered idiosyncratic will be recognized as interesting human variations not necessarily leading to conflict.

Negotiating

Fundamental variations in Western and Asian mindsets are readily observable in the different approaches to negotiating. The most important thing for a Westerner to remember when negotiating with Asians is that *the real negotiations rarely take place in the context of a formal meeting.* Americans and Europeans hold meetings to negotiate terms, make decisions, and initiate action. In most Asian countries the primary aim of a meeting of the partners is to gather information and to compare the positions of the two sides. There will be little attempt to persuade the partner to change his or her position. In Japan, particularly, one does not air differences of opinion in public. The correct procedure is to clarify positions, note the differences, show respect for the other side, and then escape for internal discussion. Once the gap between the respective positions has been properly analyzed, a new stance can be taken up that, through skilful modification, will be more acceptable to the partner. Asians assume that the other side will be taking similar steps to narrow the differences of opinion. Before the next formal meeting, informal contacts are usually made between the two parties, often at a lower level and probably in a social context. The numerous bars and clubs of Tokyo, Hong Kong, Taipei, Seoul, and Singapore witness many such encounters each evening. Younger middle managers are often involved, sounding out their counterparts and discussing possible strategies for furthering the business. They are in fact negotiating in an informal but effective manner. In such a situation concessions may be discussed without loss of face and without directly involving senior figures. Westerners should take full advantage of such discussions, whether at elaborate Chinese banquets, cocktails at the Imperial Hotel, or lunch at the Oriental in Bangkok.

When senior people on the Asian side feel that positions are closer, further "negotiation meetings" may be held. The purpose of these meetings is to confirm or ratify progress that has been made in the interim and to create further harmony between the parties at all levels. Concessions that have been made will be pleasantly referred to; sticking points may be mentioned in an indirect way without exaggerating their importance; confrontation will still be avoided. There is plenty of time for differences to be sorted out—Asians have great patience. Westerners, and particularly Americans, who have much less patience, will make a mistake if they press for quick concessions. *Asians will not be rushed.* In Hong Kong, Singapore, and Seoul the pace is often faster, but only when it suits the Asian counterparts. In the PRC, Japan, Vietnam, Thailand, and Southeast Asia the tempo is much slower than Americans and Northern Europeans are accustomed to. Asians, who are looking for long-term agreements and solutions, prefer discussions to be protracted. Basically, they are trying to decide if you are really the type of company (or person) they want as a long-term partner. The diagram on the next page indicates American impatience to discuss and get on with the deal, as opposed to the Asian preference to defer real business discussion until the parties involved have socialized sufficiently to feel confident that the partnership will be successful.

Asians' courtesy and amiability during negotiations should not, however, blind the Westerner to their aims and intent. For Asians, the objective of competitive business is total victory. This makes

The Courtship Dance

Deals	Scarcity	People you can trust
Nice people to drink tea with	Plenty	Products, deals

Analysis (left) — Integration (right)

United States	Japan
Do the business quickly.	People who enter into business quickly may depart abruptly.
Discuss the product.	Discuss other matters.
Why waltz round each other?	The waltz is full of clues to the quality of relationship expected.
Separate the person from the contract.	You cannot separate the person from the contract.
Courtship is a waste of time.	A relationship that goes sour after 3 to 4 years is a *real* waste of time!

them highly pragmatic. They do not have the same sense of business ethics as Anglo-Saxons and Northern Europeans do. They believe in "situational ethics" leading to pragmatism, usually in their favor. With partners, they are not overly concerned with division of profit but rather seek *business advantage* such as joint venture control or significant market share. When actually negotiating, they apply pressure gently but persistently and continue to do so until they are firmly stopped. It is a mistake to make concessions without asking for something in return. They easily misinterpret generosity for weakness. When they apply pressure, it is advisable to "revolt" early on—in an amicable way, of course.

When an agreement is finally concluded and a contract signed, the Westerner must understand that the document is a *statement of intent* and not fully binding in the Western sense. Asians honor their word—more than most of us—but as change is viewed as inevitable and constant, they have no compunction about seeking modification of terms if market conditions alter. This is especially difficult for Americans and Germans, who attach great importance to the written word. Latins are less perturbed, as "renegotiation" is not unknown in their world. Chinese, Japanese, and other Asians rarely have difficulty in renegotiating with each other, as force majeure is in plentiful supply in Asia, where it sits well with the continental fatalism.

Decision Making

The Asian tendency toward fatalism is evident in their decision making. Much has been written about the famous Japanese *ringi-sho* system, where ideas are bandied back and forth between workers and middle managers before ascending (after considerable time has passed) to the senior echelons, where ratification will take place. Suffice it to say that decisions in Asia take longer than they do in the West. Another basic cultural difference is the *manner* in which decisions are made. The diagram on the next page indicates how Western managers are essentially problem solvers, whereas Asian managers often accept situations as fate or God's will and make the best of them. This does not mean that they allow a negative state of affairs to continue, but instead of starting from scratch, they look back to see what their company (or another one) did in similar circumstances. Life and experience are long, and there must be many good precedents. There is little new under the sun. Managers who are willing to base their business policies on the strategic thinking of Sun Tzu in his book *The Art of War* (published in the fourth century B.C.) are quite

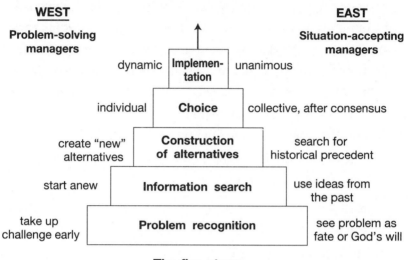

Decision Making

WEST   **EAST**

Problem-solving   **Situation-accepting**
managers   **managers**

dynamic | **Implemen-tation** | unanimous

individual | **Choice** | collective, after consensus

create "new" alternatives | **Construction of alternatives** | search for historical precedent

start anew | **Information search** | use ideas from the past

take up challenge early | **Problem recognition** | see problem as fate or God's will

– The five steps –

happy to search for historical precedents to show them the way forward.

If the Westerner considers this manner of decision making lacking in spontaneity and originality, the Asian replies, "So what?" In Confucian Asia as well as in India skillful imitation is prized more than originality. This is obvious in the repetitive sequence of Asian art, where masterpieces are faithfully imitated by succeeding generations. Just as painters do not believe they can surpass their old masters, so modern Asian managers are reluctant to think, in all humility, that they can make new, epoch-making decisions in business. Indians are exceptions inasmuch as they are risk takers, but even they see failure as God's will, or karma.

Asian Concept of Leadership

Westerners used to dealing with managers who have risen to the top via meritocratic achievement need to reorient themselves when encountering leaders or top managers in Asian countries. There are, of course, a large number of professional managers in Japan,

Korea, and India who have great competence and qualifications, but even they stand on rungs in a rigid social ladder spelled out by Confucius many centuries ago. The Chinese philosopher was especially concerned with the concept of an organized, hierarchical society led by wise men. Most Asians at the beginning of the twenty-first century are still governed by Confucian discipline, as indicated in the following maxims:

1. Society is based on unequal relationships.

2. It is organized in a strict hierarchy with a strong leader or leadership group at the top.

3. In theory leadership is made up of wise men (even scholars) who possess vision and are eminently capable of leading.

4. Orders from a superior are to be obeyed without question.

5. Strong obligations exist both top-down and bottom up in the hierarchy.

6. Subordinates owe allegiance; superiors owe guidance and protection.

7. In theory if leaders abuse their power (fail to protect), they may be overthrown.

8. It is up to intellectuals (possibly students) to expose such abuse and to act to remove abusers.

9. Except in communist regimes, leadership is gained through birthright (traditional upper-class families, wealth, etc.).

10. Such leaders are expected to rise to the aspirations and expectations of those to be led.

11. Subordinates are generally satisfied with their place in the societal and business hierarchies.

12. Suggestions for promotion are expected to come from above.

13. Promotion is granted more in reward for loyalty and seniority than for merit or brilliance.

14. The leader is seen as the father of a big family, where every-one thinks collectively.

15. The leader should place the welfare of employees before or on a par with the creation of profit.

16. Asian leaders are situation-accepting managers rather than decision makers.

17. When making decisions, leaders look for precedents in the past.

18. Most decisions are made through consensus.

19. Leaders should achieve unanimity through soft persuasion.

20. Though leaders must display paternalism, power distance remains great.

Confucianism

Confucius taught that stability in society is best achieved through a hierarchy based on unequal relationships between people. He itemized five basic relationships, each with very clear duties.

A ruler or leader (today this might mean top manager or CEO) commands absolute loyalty and obedience from his people (employees). He must, however, strive to better their lot. A husband rules over his wife in a similar manner. She must bear him sons. Children must be loyal to their parents, who will educate them.

Confucianism's Five Relationships

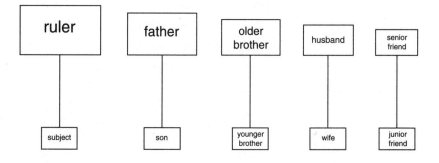

Children must look after their parents in their old age. Older brothers advise their younger brothers, who must accept their advice. The same applies to older and younger friends. Such unequal relations do not sit well with people raised in Western democratic societies. French and German managers often conduct business in an autocratic manner—and expect discipline—but such expectations serve pragmatic ends rather than theoretical ones. The Confucian husband-and-wife relationship might work in Sicily or some South American cultures, but it has changed radically in the Anglo-Saxon world and Northern Europe. Filial piety survives in Latin cultures, especially in Italy and Hispanic countries, but the seniority of older brothers and older friends carries little weight in many other parts of the West. It is, however, a present-day reality in Asia, where advice from older siblings and friends is generally followed. Japanese managers often compare the date of their university degrees to decide superiority.

Other features of Confucianism are humility, courtesy, and enduring loyalty between friends. While all these things are quite acceptable in the West, their very intensity in Asia can sometimes be overwhelming. Westerners have difficulty adjusting to Asian levels of courtesy and often feel "upstaged" by the host's attention to details of the guest's comfort as well as by lavish entertaining and gift giving.

Face

In Confucian societies and in other parts of Asia, "face" dominates everyday behavior. Some Europeans hate to lose face more than others (it is a serious matter in Spain, southern Italy, and, to some extent, Finland), but in general the Anglo-Saxon and Northern European commitment to compromise and flexibility of opinion make loss of face a fairly acceptable matter—a gentle climbdown or admission of mistakes made. One can be persuaded to negate one's previous affirmation without having one's integrity questioned. This is not the case in modern Asia, where it is unacceptable to criticize another's statement in public or to expose an error in front of others. Mistakes may be noticed and should be corrected by indirect means in due course, but in public one simply nods in agreement and holds one's tongue. This may seem hypocritical to many Westerners, especially outspoken Americans, Dutch, and Australians, but saving face is not far removed from Italian diplomatic bearing or indeed the British reluctance to "rock the boat."

Whatever the Westerners' opinion, however, they must protect Asian face at all times. Not to do so would shame the critic more than the person criticized. The damage would also be difficult (or impossible) to repair. It would probably mean the end of a business relationship not only with the victim but also with all who witnessed the incident. Even if the hapless foreigner causes someone to lose face unintentionally, the situation may be irretrievable. When one does so inadvertently, it is best to immediately withdraw the remark (with some good excuse) and to praise the victim as quickly as possible. One constantly has to bear in mind the status of all present and to accord them the respect that their rank or status commands. This involves treating people differently and occasionally being (in Western eyes) somewhat obsequious to "superiors." At the same time, one must show courtesy to "inferiors." The ability to imitate Asians in their protection of face can be the Westerner's key to success in business or social relations all the way from India and Pakistan to Japan. If one bears in mind that *every decision or action* of one's Asian partners is taken against a background of protecting face (yours and theirs), one is led to a better understanding of behavior that might appear enigmatic or lacking adherence to Western logic.

The notion of face is not going to change in the twenty-first century—at least not in Asia. Thousands of years old, it is embedded in every Asian culture. It is in itself a defensive weapon against greater force, gaining momentum in adverse circumstances. Westerners mostly understand the concept. What they must adjust to is the difference in degree.

Summary

Where We've Come From

- After 1945 many European nations (and some others) accepted a strong dose of Americanization, imitating U.S. business techniques in production, accounting, marketing, and sales. It did not kill them (or their cultures), and the material benefits outweighed the disadvantages.
- The negative effects of Americanization were experienced in the gradual erosion or dilution of (European) values, as impressionable youth embraced many aspects of American lifestyle.
- American business and management techniques lost ground in the 1970s and 1980s, as the Asian Tigers adopted the successful Japanese business model.
- In the 1990s the West frequently demonstrated that it was ill equipped to deal with Asian cultural sensitivity.

Whither the Future?

- Westerners need to establish a successful modus operandi for the new century if they are intent on globalizing their business and exports.
- Linear-active (Western) societies have everything to gain by developing empathy with reactive and multi-active ones.
- Technology has now made East and West intensely aware of each other; some synthesis of progress and cooperative

coexistence will eventually emerge. The size of Asian populations and markets suggests their eventual dominance.

- Just as there were benefits to be obtained from Americanization in 1945, there are advantages to be gained from an Asianization policy in the twenty-first century. Both Europeans and Americans would do well to consider this.
- Acceptance of a certain degree of Asianization now would facilitate better understanding of Asian mentalities and perhaps preempt future Chinese hegemony in the commercial and political spheres.
- The West should study Asian values as well as patterns of communication and organization and learn from these. There are visible benefits in Asian systems.
- The West should also study the "Asian mind" and how it perceives concepts such as leadership, status, decision making, negotiating, face, views of morality, Confucian tenets, and so forth.
- Fortunately, the rise of feminine values in the West at cross-century smooths the way for Asianization, as many of these values coincide with Asian values.

Just as the Americanization (of Europe) progressed from influencing business practice to permeating the social scene, a similar phenomenon will occur with Asianization. That is to say, Westerners will be influenced by and adopt aspects of Asian lifestyles that will have a lasting effect on social behavior, aims and aspirations, sense of morality, concept of duty, and attitudes toward politics and government.

*   *   *   *   *   *

The implications of such a shift in Western thinking and comportment are mind-boggling, if not cataclysmic. Societies such as the French, American, Swedish, and possibly the British and

German are successful in their own right and may be less inclined to modify their culture in an Asian direction than are less powerful nations. The Americans currently find little wrong with their economic model, nor do the French with their cultural one. Nevertheless a degree of feminization has already taken place in most Western countries, and the growing distaste of the younger generations for the hard-nosed exploitation of people and natural resources will make Asianization an attractive policy. After all, business is business, and there are billions of customers out there.

Chapter 11

Culture and Globalization

"I'm all for progress—it's change I don't like."

—Mark Twain

The second half of the twentieth century witnessed cataclysmic change and upheaval in the world order and the interrelations of nations. The Marshall Plan and the semi-Americanization of Western Europe accelerated economic recovery in war-battered Germany, France, and Italy. Britain, France, Belgium, and the Netherlands lost huge empires, and the Cold War set in for forty-five years (encompassing hotter wars in Korea, Vietnam, several countries in Africa, and the Middle East). In the 1970s Japan and the Asian Tigers roared, China began to flex her muscles, and the Russians and Americans ventured frequently into space. In the

223

last decade of the century, Germany was reunified, the Soviet Union disintegrated, Saddam Hussein went into and out of Kuwait, and the United States emerged as the only true superpower. All in all, it was a memorable, momentous period in human history.

Yet it is possible that the closing two decades will be remembered, indeed distinguished and branded, not by events of a political or military nature but by sweeping developments in the field of technology. This was the IT Revolution. Its implications for educating the masses, personalizing e-commerce, accelerating international trading, globalizing business, and—dare we say it—standardizing cultures are still far from clear. It is on these last two items that I wish to comment in this chapter:

1. What do we (currently) mean by the term *globalization,* and will commerce soon be globalized?

2. To what extent will the IT Revolution (and the Internet) lead to globalization?

3. Will culture itself be standardized? If so, when and to what degree?

Globalization

One definition of *globalization* might read as follows: an aggressive program for the imposition on indigenous industries and agriculture of Western norms of national economic management, economic deregulation, and market development, facilitating their takeover by multinational companies.

Significant cultural problems are bound to arise out of such a program, and we must examine these. One must also keep in mind, however, that globalization is not necessarily negative, and the concept is not as groundbreaking as one might think. In many ways the world economy around the year 1900 was as globalized as it is now, but World War I and its nervous aftermath led governments to impose trade barriers and capital controls, causing national economies to turn inward. Successive recessions in the 1920s and 1930s accentuated this trend. Even after World War II, global trade continued to be severely hampered by conflicting ideologies and national enmities. The economics of geography did not function efficiently either, as neighboring states such as Japan, China, Russia, India, and Pakistan failed to take advantage of proximity to each other. In Europe, the Iron Curtain caused similar problems.

In the 1980s many economies began to boom, and international trade blossomed. Significant recessions slowed down the process, but states such as Taiwan, Korea, and Singapore bounced back fairly rapidly, and the resilience and commitment to international trade in Japan and Hong Kong were always givens. In the main, the progress of internationalization, globalization, and the eventual global integration of world trade went forward, aided in no small measure by information technology.

Globalization, however, is only a word, not yet a tangible reality, subject to different interpretations and not a few misgivings. In the first place it is a Western recipe drawn up by the richest and most advanced nations. Its values are essentially materialistic (growth and creation of wealth). Billions of people in Asia and elsewhere—concerned with concepts such as face, national pride, collective welfare, inner harmony, and religion—place less emphasis on material benefits and see the globalization program as a self-serving ideology. Even before the turn of the twenty-first century the globalization model was being challenged. More trade, yes, but an intellectual consensus on global economic policy would eventually have to take into account Asian, Middle Eastern, African, and Latin American views and needs.

The actual assumptions of international economic deregulation and integration are of recent origin and have not yet stood the test of time. Trends may well be reversed, and already some multinationals and governments have changed their tune, advising partners to concentrate on national economic development and domestic savings—a strategy that has worked well in the past in Japan and Korea, where statist protectionism and export-led growth have been strong features. Governments now promise to "civilize" globalization (whatever that means!)

With different interpretations of globalization, it is inevitable that the process itself will be slowed. Latin Americans, for instance, will ultimately welcome a hemispheric economic partnership with the United States and Canada but will expect a concurrent "globalization of respect," in other words, explicit recognition of their social equality with Anglo-Saxons, perhaps even of their cultural superiority (which they believe exists). The French do not wish to enter into a global economic partnership with anyone except on similar terms.

For multi-active Africans, globalization sounds good in terms of facilitated emigration, more jobs, more export markets for their products, more aid and debt forgiveness, and more opportunity. Poverty is their main problem; their chief contribution to global cooperation will initially be cheap labor. For Arabs and many other Muslims, hindrance to global cooperation is political. Until current conflicts are resolved, globalization of their commerce (apart from the sale of oil) is a distant prospect.

Reactive Asians see a globalized world where meaningful partnerships with Western countries will integrate their own ambitions and expansions and will afford them greater opportunities for travel, leisure, and cultural exchange. Asians' contributions will be significant—skilled and semiskilled labor at an acceptable cost, sophisticated technological and consumer products, stable populations, commercial expertise, energy and work ethic, and, above all, huge, hungry markets to sell into.

It will not be easy to reconcile these different concepts of a globalized world. For at least a decade or two, acting local will be a necessary complement of thinking global.

Information Technology and Globalization

The greatest ally of globalization is the power and flexibility of information technology. It is the driving force that opens markets, accelerates business opportunities, and hopefully creates more jobs than it eliminates. In the past 45 years global computing power has increased a billionfold. Thomas Watson, the chairman of IBM who predicted in 1943 that there was a world market for 5 computers, was way off the mark (now over 300 million). The economic benefits offered by IT are huge, not the least of which is helping markets work more efficiently. It also speeds up innovation and experimentation. The tools get less expensive every year, and above all the Internet is truly global. Asian countries such as Taiwan, the Philippines, Thailand, Malaysia, and even China derive benefits not only from the ready information but also from being heavily involved in the manufacture of much of the computing equipment. A Nokia cell phone may be designed in London and made in China from parts produced in Canada and Sweden on the orders of a headquarters located in Finland. Economics and multinationals are impressively interconnected.

For most of human history the average growth in world economic output averaged less than 0.1 percent per annum. The spurts resulting from the invention of steam power and the Industrial Revolution (1780–1840), the advent of railways (1840–1890), and the coming of electricity and cars (1890–1950) fade into relative insignificance when compared with economic growth during the Information Age. It is a dizzying experience. We are inundated with far more information than we can ever process. This involves a hidden cost that is only partly counterbalanced by the reduction in price of hardware. Now technology changes so fast that the payback must be three to four years for infrastructure investments. Home products become obsolete in about the same time period. The convergence of technology brings competition to a level where speed and time-to-market count for everything. The customer is beginning not to care which technology is used. Whoever gets the market share becomes the standard (Microsoft). Success is the strongest reinforcer of e-commerce culture.

The euphoria surrounding technology must be seen, though, for what it is. The economic benefits are enormous, but the laws of global economy still apply. The Internet, though epoch-making, will not turn conventional economic wisdom on its head. A period of continued structural change lies ahead.

The Internet culture is still in its infancy, but some interesting trends are already emerging. This fledgling culture encourages entrepreneurialism and Western-style individualism and necessitates a rapid decision cycle. It is a risk-taking culture that must take into account changing end-user needs and the necessity to change tack quickly to accommodate them. The centralized branding system, which involved consistent brand architecture across countries and product lines (color, logo, etc.), is now old thinking. The Internet enables brand individualization and customization. Suppliers have more information about customers, so pricing and specialties can be dynamic. They try to create "communities" who feel particular loyalty, "friends and families" services, and interactive chat forums. In such ways the Internet actually demands more human interaction, not less, and presupposes extra cost with more people, effort, and creativity. Trusted consumer brands (such as Virgin) may enter unfamiliar markets (e.g., telecommunications services) and drive them with a "lifestyle" image. The key to success is for the incumbent to transform its organizational culture better and faster.

The Standardization of Culture Itself

The globalization and integration of world commerce is one thing—inherently difficult and complex, a process that will take decades, even if it continues to be a desired goal among the major nations. The standardization of culture, if one can imagine such a situation, will be immeasurably more complicated. During my seminars on cross-cultural issues, I try to make meaningful comparisons about the behavior of different societies. If one has lived and worked abroad for thirty years or more, one is led to the conviction that the inhabitants of any country possess certain core beliefs and assumptions about reality that manifest themselves in their comportment. People of different cultures may share a host of common basic concepts (truth, honor, justice, etc.) but view them from angles and perspectives that others might consider irrational or prejudiced.

Such is cultural diversity. It is not something that is going to disappear any time soon, enabling us to plan our strategies on the assumption of mutual understanding.

Scholars around the world are fond of cultural diversity. For them it is a phenomenon with its own riches: it is exciting to explore, and new insights constantly add to the body of knowledge and help us in our attempt to understand the universe. Politicians like cultural diversity, too; the well-defined and closely held beliefs of a group give them something to identify with, perhaps champion, and thereby gain popular advantage. The use of jingoism, patriotic exhortations, and even regional or tribal advancement is seen frequently in modern times, as it was in the past.

The business community, however, is considerably less enchanted by the prospect of continuing divergence of cultures. While they perceive that a multinational team might conceivably possess greater strength than a national one, they see even more clearly the advantages that convergence of multinational cultures would achieve (wearing a Western face, of course). Multinational giants like IBM, General Electric, Unilever, and Coca-Cola would benefit greatly if they could standardize procedures and systems worldwide. They weigh the economies of scale that would be realized if all their branches and subsidiaries used the same accounting systems, personnel policies, production techniques, marketing strategies, modes of remuneration, and so on. Imagine if they could run the same ad in 120 countries....

Participants in my seminars study the divergence of national characteristics attentively, but sooner or later the same questions always pop up: Won't we all behave the same way in twenty years? Aren't cultures changing quickly? Won't diversity soon disappear? My answer to all of these is invariably no. The assumptions, values, and beliefs of cultures change slowly, not quickly—in some cases they hardly change at all. It is all too easy to associate the rapid acceptance of worldwide technology and surface behavior and appearances with cultural change. Absorption of modern techniques, fast-food chains, and fashion has virtually nothing to do with deep-rooted core beliefs. For five decades we have seen Japanese executives traveling the world wearing Western suits, shirts, and ties; they carry the same luggage, briefcases, calculators, alarm clocks, watches, and cameras as we do (or we carry theirs), but this does not mean that they think like we do, or even want to. We standardize our dress and accessories for convenience, but the mental agendas remain hidden and inviolate.

The Media

Yes, you say, but the impact of mass media is unstoppable—it, if nothing else, will clone us. Personally, for many years, I have bought Japanese cameras, German cars, and Portuguese shirts. My willing acceptance of these fine products does not, however, make me feel Japanese, German, or Portuguese. I have not upped my *yamato damashii*, wallowed in *saudades,* or felt any Weltschmerz. The more the Americans pound me with baseball on TV, the more I like cricket.

One has to acknowledge the strength of the U.S. media and the role it plays in selling American products and lifestyle through newspapers, television, magazines, movies, and the Internet. People who have been oppressed, and especially the young of many nations, are particularly susceptible to these influences. But to assume the trappings of another culture does not mean at all that one accepts its values. I read an account recently of four Palestinian youths being apprehended by the Israeli authorities. They were eating McDonald's hamburgers, drinking Coca-Cola, and wearing American-style T-shirts and Wrangler jeans. They were in the process of making a bomb to blow up an American building.

The media can sell products and lifestyles, but it cannot sell one country's culture to another. It cannot sell rules, norms, customs, or religion. American attempts to convert Europeans by televised evangelism are disastrous—viewed as unconvincing and distasteful in the extreme. We may live in a utopian information society, but present-day mass media, like old-time village gossip, is fragmentary, incomplete, and usually filtered. A recent documentary on Swedish television featuring a lot of "authentic" footage projected a picture of a Mexican population consisting of a small group of immensely rich persons, a large majority of extremely poor people, and a mass of *olvidados,* thereby conjuring the middle class entirely out of existence! Other Western documentaries present East European countries as being populated entirely by new-style Mafiosi and old-style apparatchiks (often the same people).

Another difficulty for those who believe that culture can be exported through the media is that some cultures receive many more messages than they send out, while others receive virtually none at all. The great majority of films are made in the United States, India, and the Chinese diaspora. While U.S. films and programs are exported vigorously, they fail to convey many of the positive values of American society. Indian films (several hours long and combining a love story, murder, history, music, and dance in one feature) would convey a very confusing message to any Westerner who might happen to see one. Most Chinese films are viewed locally. High-quality films made in France, Italy, Japan, Britain, Poland, Australia, the Czech Republic, and elsewhere often serve as modest promotions of their respective cultures (e.g., British comedies) but have little impact outside the West. If the American media is the only one enjoying truly worldwide currency and exposure, does this mean that other cultures will gradually become Americanized? The French do not think so; neither do the Chinese, Japanese, or Indians, to name but a few.

Education

What evidence is there from education to support the theory that cultures are changing fast? Academics will tell you that while modern curricula in subjects such as mathematics, all branches of science, technology, and medicine have changed beyond recognition in the last few years, syllabi in the social sciences lag far behind. A Canadian professor told me recently that he felt history is being taught the same way it was thirty years ago; arts subjects—languages, literature, music, classics—possess a natural adherence to tradition and continuity; curricula in sociology, demographics, and civics have shown some expansion but, like theories of economics and political science, are often confusingly cyclic.

Changes in education systems in any country (apart from racing technological innovations) have proved to be slow and cumbersome. Why is this? Educators are reluctant to tamper with culture—it is, after all, the blueprint for a nation's survival.

Intransigence

As discussed in earlier chapters, if we examine the roots of culture, we identify four decisive factors:

1. language

2. religion

3. geography and climate

4. history

Even if change is desirable (and many believe it is not), there is not much we can do about any of these influences. Language changes slowly (we easily understand versions of our own written language from two or three hundred years ago). Few of us can influence our mother tongue, though James Joyce, Kemal Ataturk, and various French governments have tried. Religious tenets and dogma are difficult to change (e.g., the Pope's battle against abortion for the last few decades). Hinduism, Islam, Buddhism, and Catholicism dominate the behavior of billions of people. The earth's geography, apart from a few exploding volcanos and global warming, changes little in a human lifetime; climate still determines the conditions in which we live.

History also influences culture change and is the one area where we can decide and act. In recent times we have witnessed three dramatic culture changes as a result of historical and political events. One of these was the depressing spectacle of the change in lifestyle for the millions of people under the decades-long yoke of international communism. Though communism has now largely run its course, its cultural effects will need another generation to fade away. The second and third cultural changes were caused by the traumatic defeats of Germany and Japan in 1944–1945. The decisive switch from aggressive stances to the embracing of peace and economic objectives proved extremely beneficial to both countries and, indeed, the world.

Generational Change versus Cultural Change

Both Germans and Japanese, albeit looking at different horizons, still retain the values and beliefs of their ancestors. Even atom bombs cannot disintegrate culture. Ah, but look how different young Japanese are from their parents and grandparents, you say. It is true that when Japanese nineteen-year-olds go to university, they wear jeans and baseball caps, throw stones through windows, drink beer with abandon, and occasionally kidnap professors. But when they are twenty-four, they put on dark blue suits, white shirts, and conservative ties to go for their interviews with Mitsui and Mitsubishi. Even Finns, Swedes, and Germans will assert that their children behave in a very different manner from the way they did in their youth. They often forget that what they are witnessing is generational change, not deep culture change. Wait until those kids are forty.

I had close connections with many Japanese university students in 1966. Today they behave as their parents did then. I lived for several years in Portugal and Finland in the 1960s. Apart from their improved facility with languages and some knowledge acquired by travel, I see very little difference in the basic behavior of Portuguese and Finns after three or four decades.

Why Is Culture So Deeply Rooted?

Culture is deeply embedded. A Danish colleague of mine recently went to give a one-week intensive English language course to a group of Greenlandic fishermen. The program was jointly sponsored by the Danish Ministry of Education and the Greenland Department of Tourism. The students, twenty strong (mixed Inuit and Danish blood), were almost beginners in English but keen. For two days they practiced attentively. On the third morning one of them near the window sniffed, muttered five words in East Greenlandic, and the whole group rushed out of the room and disappeared for half an hour. They then returned to their seats and awaited further instruction. When my colleague asked what had caused them to depart so suddenly, they explained that the wind had changed. They all had had to move their boats.

The next day lessons were in full swing, when a Greenlander stuck his head through the door and shouted five more words. The entire group rushed out again, but they did not come back this time. When the teacher, curious, eventually followed them outside to find out what was happening, she saw them all on the beach (with the rest of the village) pulling in a whale. For the next few hours the whole community was feverishly occupied in cutting up the huge animal into a large number of pieces and putting them into barrels and buckets. It was twenty degrees below zero and dark (January). They all went home to wash the blood off themselves and came back to the lesson at 10 P.M. Normal behavior.

Are we really at liberty to change our culture? Why is it so innate, so embedded? In the first place it is passed on to us, orally and by modeling, by our parents when we are very young and impressionable. What two- or three-year-old child will disbelieve his or her parents' advice? What alternatives are we given? Then comes kindergarten and school where the message is reinforced by (influential) teachers. It is in school that another very important factor creeps in—peer pressure. Brave is the child who acts differently from or in opposition to classmates! Peer pressure continues all through schooling and eventually into the workplace. Religion and patriotism might be added to the mix at some stage. Our culture is also dosed to us by our literature, our arts and folk craft, our music. Soviet pragmatism, for example, was unable to distract the Russians from their love of ballet. Food, too, is part of our culture, and few of us, though exposed to foreign delicacies, are likely to desert our bacon and eggs, our *köttbullar*, our *hapan leipä*, our sashimi and sushi—those foods we crave.

If our likes and appetites persist, so do our dislikes and grudges. It is part of the cultural makeup of the Greek to hate the Turk. Membership in NATO cannot obliterate this thousand-year-old antipathy. The English do no better with the Irish. Latin America resents the traditional supremacy of the United States.

The Answer: Cultural Adaptation

Strong and Weak Cultures

Successful cultures live to be old—they have preserved the qualities that enable them to survive. Why should Chinese take advice from anybody, when they are still strong after five thousand years? The culture of India has lasted more than three thousand years. The Jewish nation, in spite of numerous persecutions and the lack of a homeland, is still around after two thousand years of harassment.

The student of ancient civilizations sees only too well that culture change can lead to collapse. In recent times the Incan, Mayan, and Tasmanian cultures were unable to withstand the changes imposed upon them by forceful Europeans. The Inuit, Native American, and Aborigine cultures, undergoing traumatic culture change at this time, are hardly likely to survive. The Maoris of New Zealand, with their rich traditions, music, and folklore might just manage it.

Management of Diversity

The objective of culture is survival and eventual prosperity. If their cultures have brought them so far, no major nations will embrace rapid change in their way of life. The European Union, NAFTA, ASEAN, and multinational corporations need to learn how to *manage* cultural diversity, not hope to eradicate it.

Micro- and Macrolevel Cultural Adaptation

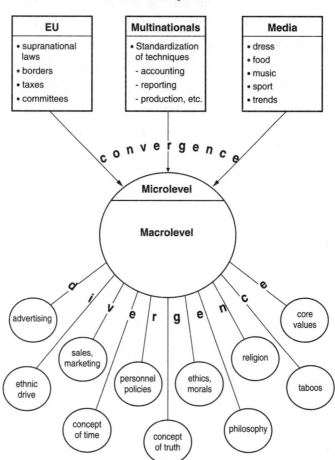

The management of cultural diversity, in terms of sensible adaptation to others and efforts to establish common ground, faces many challenges at the practical level. The above diagram illustrates some of these.

It is tempting for huge multinational and transnational companies to seek universal management solutions that would prove acceptable and feasible in their branches and subsidiaries. Corporate policy would be strengthened, training procedures would be simplified, and standardization of many processes would decrease cost. Unfortunately (or perhaps fortunately) multinational firms cannot submerge the uniqueness of different cultures. Although the corporate culture that is imposed may be strong, local staff are reluctant to give up their background or preferred ways of doing things. They may be willing to adapt, but in moments of uncertainty they will dig in their heels and revert to their own core beliefs and cultural values.

When it comes to supranational organizations such as the EU, NAFTA, ASEAN, MERCOSUR, and so forth, there is a general willingness to accept regulation and standardization of conventions when they are clearly to our benefit. Examples of such instances are the Schengen Agreement on border controls, the substitution of identity cards for passports between certain countries, waivers of visa restrictions, lowering of tariffs, the European and International courts, the extra protection against crime afforded by Interpol, the GATT rounds, and so on. The success of numerous international student exchanges and scholarships abroad as well as the universal welcome of clubs such as Rotary and Lions in every land are further examples of people's willingness to join international activities in certain fields. Yet there is a certain reticence about supranational control in other areas. Standardize European taxes? Ask Britons to carry identity cards at all times? Allow foreign police to chase criminals across your frontier in hot pursuit? Abandon the pound, dollar, Swiss franc? These are all questions that may well be settled sensibly in due course as Europe continues to integrate. Would Asian countries integrate likewise? And all the Americas?

Of more immediate import to the globalization of business is the extent to which large multinationals (and with the many mergers at the present time, they are getting ever larger) can effect economies of scale and ease of management through sensible standardization and the establishment of universally acceptable business models. As I have stated elsewhere, business models for the twenty-first century are not going to be national ones. Companies functioning across borders and cultures, if they wish to be successful, will have to sculpt or fashion business models that take into account the problems of macrolevel cultural divergence (see again the diagram on page 237). They will have to accept that there are contemporaneous processes of *convergence and divergence* in the development and restructuring of their overseas subsidiaries. Standardization of production techniques, reporting systems, general accounting, and even R&D and IT departments pose few major hurdles. When it comes, however, to sales and marketing methods, advertising, personnel policies, pay and compensation packages, leadership initiatives, staff training, legal disputes, and relations with local authorities and government, to name but a few, cultural divergences will seriously hamper standardization, and firms will have to make unfamiliar judgments on a case-by-case basis. It is not only a matter of refraining from making drastic changes in the normal business procedures of the local company that is required but, more importantly, a matter of entering into the cultural world of the partner, with all its inherited complexity of ethics, morals, core beliefs, taboos, religious tenets, age-old philosophies, and deeply embedded concepts of time, space, truth, status, prestige, face, honor, revenge—in all, a particular worldview.

This represents an enormous challenge to chief executives and managers at policy-making and decision-making levels. The fashioning of workable multicultural models is by no means impossible and has been achieved on numerous occasions. Companies such as Unilever, ABB, Nokia, Ericsson, Hewlett-Packard, Sonera, Deutsche Telekom, Nestlé, and Motorola have been both greatly concerned with and successful in international structuring and in training their managers diligently in cross-cultural issues.

Clearly, companies that are globalizing often wish to apply their worthy corporate policies and efficient business models; to them, simply "going with the flow" is neither acceptable nor advisable when entering a foreign business environment. Every model has its faults, but the local culture will have its deficiencies, too. Clearly, there must be a compromise—a harmonizing of methods and intent. Companies would do well to observe, however, that the positive qualities of head office culture may not be seen as entirely beneficial by the local society and may in fact have many negative connotations of which the head office is not aware.

Management of Cultural Values? A Different Story

People's adaptation to an alien cultures' concepts is deceptive. At the microlevel, for example, fashion, new styles can be adopted with ease, even enthusiasm. The same certainly applies to food, as the proliferation of French, Italian, Chinese, Indian, and Thai restaurants in London and New York demonstrates. The media influences our tastes and appetites continually, and at the microlevel we enjoy cultural diversity.

At the macrolevel, however, culture is far from being standardized. Americans, particularly, are doomed to disappointment if they think their core values, ethics, morals, and so on are being—or will be—adopted by other national cultures (see again the diagram on page 237).

The chart on the next page indicates how some American qualities (surely positive in American eyes) may be viewed quite differently in other lands; it illustrates why at the macrolevel cultural standardization is still a long way off.

American Qualities...As Seen by Others

American Qualities	Others' Perceptions
Democracy and equality	Don't exist; impractical anyway (Asians)
Individualism	Lack of concern for others (Asians, Swedes)
Competitiveness	Aggressiveness (French)
Speedy decisions	Too rushed (Japanese, Chinese)
Hard sell	Over the top (Germans, Finns)
Frank, direct	Rude (Japanese, French)
Optimism	Lack of realism (Scandinavians)
Charisma	Charisma is suspect (Germans, Dutch)
Change and improvement are good	Doesn't protect status quo (Saudi Arabia)
Results oriented	Lacking in people orientation (Italians, Asians)
Self-confidence	Arrogance (South Americans, Arabs)
Informal, smiling	Lacking respect, insincerity (Germans, French)
Future orientation	Lacking tradition (Chinese)
Defender of democracy and free trade	Defender of U.S. interests (Russians, Arabs)

The chart below shows how the Germans—serious, well-meaning and worthy people—can be frequently misunderstood by other cultures!

German Qualities...As Seen by Others

Others' Perceptions	German View
They complicate things too much.	Life is not simple.
They are tactless.	The truth is always the truth, why pretend?
They have no sense of humor.	We don't waste time wisecracking in business meetings.
Their speeches are long and boring.	We want to know all the facts. We are good listeners.
They are too formal.	Formality and use of surnames show respect.
They criticize and complain.	We are trying to help you improve. We are perfectionists.

The last chart in this chapter is meant to bring home to you the inherent difficulty of one's being diametrically opposed to the core beliefs of certain cultures. Try convincing these people about the following:

Arabs	Religion and business should not be mixed. Forget Islam while you're with us.
Americans	Money is not important.
Germans	Your weakness is that you get bogged down in details.
Japanese	Make decisions individually; it's faster!
Hispanics	Mañana behavior signifies laziness.
Chinese	Always be frank and tell the truth, whether anybody loses face or not.
French	You are bit-part players in world business and politics.
Russians	You need not be suspicious of foreigners—they want to help you.
Koreans	You have good neighbors.
British	Funerals are more entertaining than cricket matches.
Canadians	You are really Americans.

The preceding charts highlight the phenomenon that different cultures perceive things firmly from their habitual standpoint, their worldview, in fact. Americans see their own qualities as obvious examples of modern progress and human advancement. Who could possibly argue against democracy, frankness, and future orientation? The answer is: most people. Germans, for their part, are honest and diligent citizens who try to lead their lives in a respectable and responsible manner. Yet many nationalities frequently mock their seriousness.

Finally, the last chart illustrates that many deeply embedded habits, like Japanese or Chinese collective behavior or Russian and Korean suspiciousness, are closely connected to the "cultural black hole" mentality, where one simply does not see a better alternative.

Chapter 12

Empires—Past, Present, and Future

Scholars, scientists, economists, and various "think tanks" often engage in predicting the future. More often than not, they are wrong. Their forecasts may be based on long-range economic trends; breakthroughs in science, medicine, and technology; political shifts and alliances; military buildups; demographic developments; population explosions; even climatological change. In my opinion, these factors, even in combination, have been and will continue to be notoriously inaccurate signposts for what will happen in the long term.

A scrutiny of past history might well be a better guide, but this in itself reveals how often the experts have been wrong in forecasting events. Despite widespread expectations, the world did not end as A.D. 1000 dawned. Who could forecast, at the end of the first millennium, the rise of the Mongol and Islamic-Turkish empires, the significance of the purchase of Manhattan Island, the astonishing growth of the human race, the amazing multiplication of human wealth, or the forays to other planets in the solar system? On a more modest scale, who could predict how a tiny nation like Japan would make a huge mark on the world economy or how communism would take hold of half the globe in forty years and how it would come apart at the seams in less than a decade?

Cultural Traits as Predictors of the Future

This book has not been written as a foray into futurology. I believe, however, that if one were to attempt to forecast certain trends in the twenty-first century, *the most reliable guide would be the scrutiny of cultural patterns*, not just as we perceive them but as they have revealed themselves in history.

Cultural behavior is not accidental or whimsical. On the contrary, it is the end product of millennia of collected wisdom, filtered and passed down through hundreds of generations and translated into hardened, undiscussable core beliefs, assumptions, values, and persistent action patterns. The enduring structures of human society, which transcend and outlive political change, give us some indication of what our future will be.

By focusing on the cultural roots of national behavior both in society and in business, we can forecast and calculate with a surprising degree of accuracy how people will react in the future. They are not likely to change their way of life drastically in a short time span like a century. Deeply rooted attitudes resist sudden transformation of values (or alliances) when subjected to pressure or expediency. The Chinese today behave very much as

Confucius advised them to long ago. Post-perestroika Russians exhibit behavioral traits strikingly similar to those recorded in tsarist times. Reliable guidance for guessing what will happen in the coming century is likely to be found by examining the social history of culture—the cultural achievements of different civilizations—which is more significant than political boundaries or military exploits. We should be concerned less with the particular events of history than with broad movements—for example, massive migrations or the spread of the world's religions, the advent of historically significant tools and artifacts, the domestication of different animals, the establishment and permanence of agriculture, the eventual industrialization of large parts of the globe, and the IT Revolution.

By offering a short list of famous predictions that seem preposterous today, I hope to dispel any doubt that forecasts based on scientific breakthroughs, technology, economic trends, and so on simply aren't reliable.

The following quotations are statements or predictions made by individuals of considerable eminence in the fields of philosophy, science and medicine, business and industry, exploration, transportation, entertainment, and political and military affairs. These people included recognized experts (Foch, Watson), professors, bankers, surgeons, leaders of industry, two prime ministers, and a king. While nobody is infallible, it is not unreasonable for the man (or woman) in the street to assume that such people, by virtue of their privileged position or special knowledge, would be able to produce a fairly accurate forecast of events. For different reasons (miscalculation, shortsightedness, lack of imagination, political expediency), they could not and did not produce accurate forecasts.

Famous Forecasts

- "All men are born good." (Confucius 500 B.C.)
- "So many centuries after creation, it is unlikely that anyone could find hitherto unknown lands of any value." (King Ferdinand of Spain 1486, before Columbus' voyage)
- "Rail travel at high speed is not possible because passengers, unable to breathe, would die of asphyxsia." (Irish professor 1835)
- "Drill for oil? You mean drill into the ground and try to find oil? You're crazy!" (U.S. executive 1859)
- "The telephone has too many shortcomings to be seriously considered as a means of communication." (Western Union corporate memo 1876)
- "I'm sorry, Mr. Kipling, but you just don't understand how to use the English language." (Publisher's rejection letter 1889)
- "The horse is here to stay. The automobile is only a novelty—a fad." (a banker advising Henry Ford not to invest in the Ford Motor Company 1903)
- "Airplanes are interesting toys but of no military value." (French military strategist Marshal Foch 1911)
- "The wireless has no imaginable commercial value. Who would pay for a message sent to nobody in particular?" (Friends of RCA founder 1920)
- "Can't act. Can't sing. Balding. Can dance a little." (MGM executive 1929, about Fred Astaire's screen test)
- "I have no political ambition for myself or for my children." (Joseph Kennedy 1936)
- "Hitler has missed the bus." (Chamberlain1940)
- "I think there is a world market for about five computers." (IBM Chairman Thomas Watson 1943).
- "For the majority of people, the use of tobacco has a beneficial effect." (Los Angeles surgeon 1963)
- "No woman in my time will be Prime Minister." (Margaret Thatcher 1969)

Past Empires

Eurocentric and Americentric, we see the British, French, Spanish, Dutch, and Portuguese empires as dominant events in world history and culture. In fact, they were not very durable, especially in modern times. The British lasted 200 years in India; 170 years in America;100 years in Canada, Australia, and New

Zealand; and a mere 80 years in Africa. The French managed 100 years in Africa and Indochina and 229 years in Canada. The Dutch held on to trading posts for 250 years in Indonesia, and the Belgians ruled the Congo for 80 years. Italy with 50 years in Ethiopia and Germany with 35 years in Africa were the shortest-lived colonists. The Portuguese and Spanish, ostensibly in search of souls, did somewhat better in Africa and South America, with 450 years each. The Mongols did well to rule a stretch of land from the Pacific Ocean to the Black Sea for 500 years.

The empires that exhibited substantial durability were the Roman, which in theory lasted 1,650 years but lost its Western half early on, the Islamic Arab-Turkish (1,200 years), and the Chinese (2,100 years and in a sense still going strong). It is perhaps noteworthy that the empires founded for purposes of prestige (the Italian and the German) were the shortest-lived. Those based on resources, raw materials, and trade (British, French, Dutch, Belgian) did only a little better. The toughest empires were those based on or inspired by an *idea*—Spanish and Portuguese Catholicism or the Islamic faith. The Chinese empire—or civilization—probably owes its longevity to the fact that it has been mainly inward-looking.

Impending Chinese Dominance

Much has been written about the growing hegemony of China and its impending dominance in the twenty-first century and beyond. Samuel Huntington, as I mentioned earlier, warns against possible Chinese triumphalism in the twenty-first century in view of the country's huge population, considerable territory, and rapid technological advancement. But do we not tend to exaggerate the likelihood of Chinese expansion or aggression? We should remember that *for most of recorded history,* China has been the largest, most populous, and most advanced country in the world.

During the millennia of its existence, China has shown little in-clination to conquer others for any length of time. It was the Mongols who rode into Europe (twice), not the Chinese. More-over, China, less interested in internationalism than most of us, has never formed a lasting alliance with another country. China trusts itself and is only half-concerned with the fate of others. Strident in its claims on Taiwan—yes—and unbending and im-placable on the issue of Tibet—true—but China sees these as its own territories, close to home. China has shown little inclination to interfere with the fate of its neighbors—Russia, Korea, Japan, and India. International communism led to Chinese military in-volvement on behalf of North Korea and to an uneasy aligned relationship with the Soviet Union, but there were no cultural ties to cement these alliances. Chinese "punitive incursions" into Vietnam, politically motivated, had little to do with any lasting desire to acquire Indo-Chinese territory. Although the Chinese display no fondness for their Japanese neighbors and scream for apologies for Japan's having invaded China in the past, still China does not indicate an intention to counterpunch in Japanese terri-tory any time soon.

Confucian, patient, self-sufficient, inward-looking, the Chinese will most likely pursue a twenty-first century cultural path of traditional self-containment, domestic consolidation and control, and continued industrial and commercial development. In the last respect they will be greatly aided by the wisdom, experience, and energetic activity of the Overseas Chinese, "whose club they joined" with the reacquisition of Hong Kong and good relations with Singapore. The Chinese global communication network (through *people*) is second to none and reduces need for aggres-sion abroad.

Future Alliances: Who Wants China?

East and Southeast Asia

The Chinese inclination or disinclination to expand and dominate is one thing. The attitude of other nations is another. Will other Asian nations ally themselves with China to resist the West? The cultural record suggests otherwise.

Japan. Japanese culture has been going strong for 2,000 years and has no reason to change course. The Japanese people learned all they needed to learn from China about 1,500 years ago, when they adopted their religion (Buddhism); their writing system; styles in painting, music, architecture, pottery, and other artifacts as well as the teachings of Confucius. When Japan opened up shop (after its self-imposed isolation from 1600 to1853) during the Meiji era, it was to the West that Japan rushed in its quest for modernization. We all know the success of that choice. Apart from the hiccup of 1935 to 1945, Japan seems well-set to maintain the status quo of its distinguished position vis-à-vis the West and its status in variousWestern cultural and financial institutions. In spite of the disparity in size, Japan's economy is well ahead of China's and is likely to remain so for the next decade or so. Furthermore, Japanese culture has diverged immensely from that of China since the sixth century and its very strength enables Japan to enjoy an independent role in Asia and in the world.

India. Will India team up with China against the West? Even more unlikely than Japan. India may soon become more populous than China and has its own culture of four thousand years, which is arguably richer and more varied than the Chinese. Buddhism originated in India, not in China. The Hindu religion has more adherents than any other. Economically, India has a lot of ground to make up but is likely to progress most quickly in alliance with the West. English is India's only truly national language and is descended from an Indian language—Sanskrit—in any case! The sharing of an Indo-European language mindset with many Westerners suggests that India will face away from China rather than toward it.

Korea. The well-known Korean trait, *hahn,* precludes warm relations with anybody who is not Korean. The fact that the Korean peninsula, with its vulnerable location between China and Japan, has maintained its territorial integrity for two millennia suggests that Koreans will continue to go their own way—working hard, exporting vigorously, and trying to maintain their position in the world economies. When reunification takes place, as it *must* during this century, it will give them additional economic clout.

Other Southeast Asian Nations. Who are the other candidates for alignment with China? The Vietnamese regard China as their natural enemy and have sustained a mutual hostility for over a thousand years. They have had their own dreams of empire, lording it over the Laotians and the Cambodians. The Vietnamese say today that their favorite foreigners are *Americans,* and they are anxious to pursue reconciliation with the Americans, albeit at their own snail's pace.

Thailand and the Philippines are influenced more by the United States than by China. The large number of Thai and Filipino students at any one time in the U.S. (often aided by American grants) carries a certain assurance of continued American closeness with those countries.

Indonesia, Malaysia, Pakistan, Bangladesh, and Brunei are all largely Muslim and share few cultural tenets with China. It is hard to imagine them firmly aligned with a Confucian culture, whose work ethic and discipline they do not share. It may well be half a century before Indonesia can achieve a position commensurate with its huge population (220 million), especially as the nation has severe internal difficulties at this writing. A breakup of this scattered nation of three thousand islands is by no means impossible, given the population's dislike for the dominant Javanese prevalent on the large islands such as Sumatra and Borneo. If this happens, the separate entities will probably form a type of federation similar to that of Malaysia but with more regional autonomy.

Islamic States

The Islamic states, which often join China in criticism of Western morals and U.S. foreign policies, are poor candidates for an alliance with China. Lacking a core state (with the largest—Indonesia—out on a distant limb), the Islamic states will find it hard to coalesce as a political force. Even the Arabs have great difficulty speaking with one voice. The different creeds of Iran, Turkey, Indonesia, Pakistan, and so on in the Muslim world reduce Islamic influence to being a cultural entity like Christianity or Buddhism, spanning many frontiers but lacking political unity. Iran and Iraq, both Muslim (but of different sects), fought each other viciously in recent times. Such divisions in allegiance are not restricted to Muslims. Christian Europeans fought against each other in two world wars.

Russia

As we continue to look further afield, the prospect of a sinicized world fades markedly. Russia, in the fullness of time, must end up in the EU. Where else can it go? Most Russians are of the European physical type, they speak a European language, and almost all of their cultural heritage is markedly European—their literature, art, sculpture, painting, music, ballet, theatre, and architecture. Russia's Asian empire was huge but brief in tenure. Siberia remains for the time being, but it is too vast for Russia to allocate the resources needed to develop it. The mind-numbing distance between Moscow and Vladivostok suggests that the Russian Far East will probably become a separate political entity in due course. The region already enjoys a certain autonomy and commercial ties are currently being established between local entrepreneurs and the nearby Japanese.

After the dismantling of the Soviet Union, there was a Turkish move to set up a Turkic trading bloc with five ex-Soviet Central Asian republics. This idea would naturally evaporate with Turkish accession to the EU. Oil- and gas-rich Kazakhstan, Uzbekistan, Azerbaijan, and Turkmenistan are currently nonaligned in the confusion resulting from Soviet dismemberment and the profusion of natural resources. Kyrgyzstan borders China (this might possibly cause her to lean eastward), but the other republics are likely to be tempted by Western oil companies and remain as wild cards in the future world order.

The European Union

In the twenty-first century Europe itself remains the great enigma. The EU will have little alternative but to gradually extend its membership to all the continent's 28 countries, plus Turkey for good measure. The union is unlikely to be a cohesive political force before the end of the century. We must not forget that it took the United States approximately 150 years (1776 to 1920) to achieve political significance. Economic cohesion came first, as it probably will in Europe (with lowering of tariffs and regional rationalization of production). The obstacles to rapid European unification are of course cultural. Europe has 28 distinct cultures and 35 languages, not to mention a host of antipathies. Some of these have cooled (e.g., Germany and France), but others are still not far from the boiling point (Serbia, Croatia, Bosnia).

Nevertheless, one can assume that, given an entire century, a tougher EU can emerge, but it may well be a close thing. Who will be the last entrants—Albania? Macedonia? Kosovo? Georgia? Armenia? If Turkey joins, would Israel become a candidate?

The Pacific Rim

The Pacific Rim, as discussed earlier, is an attractive concept economically. Culturally, however, it is a nonstarter, as the nations surrounding it have different mindsets and agendas. The Rim may well, however, prove a useful mechanism for technological cooperation and cultural *exchange*. Australia's proximity to parts of Asia has encouraged successive Australian governments to woo Asian leaders with a view to achieving integration with that continent through increased bilateral trade. This worthy initiative has been received with less enthusiasm than it deserves. Again, culture is the guide. Technically, Australian raw materials, minerals, and food production are a perfect fit for Indonesian and Japanese consumers. Culturally, the Australians are blatantly Anglo-Saxon and very blunt blokes at that. Australian schoolchildren are making brave attempts to learn Japanese and other Asian languages, but the British cultural core of tea, beer, cricket, rugby, golf, tennis, the monarchy, and fish and chips makes an Asian veneer hard to come by. New Zealand, too, has a geographical remoteness problem and will be wise to foster close relations with Australia in the coming decades.

The chart on the next page summarizes the cultural traits that are most likely to persevere and lead to possible alliances in the future.

The Prevailing Cultural Characteristics and Possible Alliances

Country or Region	Persevering Cultural Traits	Future (optional) alliances	Rationale
Japan	work ethic, collectivism, harmony, face, duty, and obligation	U.S. and Korea	Powerful ties in trade and industry
India	Hinduism, sense of spiritual superiority, growing nationalism, and feeling of power	U.S.	democracies counterbalance China and Islam
Russia	cultural traits mirror those of Western Europe	EU	Western heritage and proximity
China	sense of intellectual superiority, collectivism, strong families, self-centeredness	No permanent alliances	self-sufficiency, sheer numbers
Korea	work ethic, competitiveness, energy, face, obsession with survival	U.S. and Japan	powerful ties in trade and industry
Latin America	Catholicism, Iberian characteristics	U.S. and Canada	geographic, Western heritage
North Africa	Muslim, French, and British influence	EU	proximity, shared labor market
Sub-Saharan Africa	varied tribal	internal, continental (loose and shaky) arrangements with EU	continued dependence on Europe, familiarity with Europeans, relative proximity
Australia	British, with U.S. influence	Anglo-Saxon	rejected by Asians
Central Asia	Muslim	U.S. and Russia	joint exploration (oil and gas)
S.E. Asia	Buddhist	ASEAN, with Indonesia	counterbalancing China
Indonesia	Muslim (liberal)	ASEAN, Australia (unlikely)	natural market for ASEAN products, too far from main Islamic countries for effective alliance
Islamic States (Middle East)	Muslim	mainly cultural and spiritual	countries are too dispersed geographically for effective commercial or political alliances.

Most Nation-States to Survive

I see the twenty-first century as witness to the formation and continuing existence of huge trade blocs and associations such as the EU, NAFTA, ASEAN, MERCOSUR, and so on, but *I do not envisage any real coalescing of cultures*. They are too strong, they are blueprints for survival, they have stood the test of time. Cultures coincide to a large extent with the nation-state within which they dwell, and who would predict the disappearance of any of these? Taiwan may well be incorporated into the PRC. Some of the smaller African states might at some point unite, although the precedent set by North African Arabs is not too promising. I feel confident that Japan, India, China, Russia, and the other major powers will remain intact during the remainder of the twenty-first century. I do not see Vietnam, Korea, Thailand, or anyone else, for that matter, surrendering their national status or cultural identity. There will probably be even more nation-states and cultures than there are today. Slovenia, Croatia, the Czech Republic, Slovakia, Macedonia, Namibia, and East Timor are recent newcomers! Perhaps Chechnya or Aceh will be the next. There are sixty-odd autonomous republics inside the Russian Federation alone (several of them anxious to get out). We should not make the mistake of thinking that small nations can be easily subjugated or eliminated. History has proven that countries with one million people or more can defend themselves vigorously against huge opponents. The Russo-Finnish War of 1939 to 1945 is the best example. Others are the conflicts involving Israel, Afghanistan, Kosovo, East Timor, and Vietnam. Estonia, the smallest of the three tiny Baltic states, proved to be the toughest in demanding independence. As I have suggested, the European Union is likely to survive to 2100, but it is hard to say in what form. It may well be a multicultural union where each member nation has "national state rights" like the U.S. states' rights, but stronger.

Political Systems

Just as the study of cultural traits in history foretells a predictable path for nation-states in the twenty-first century, it also indicates that political issues and ideas on the best ways to govern are by no means settled. Francis Fukuyama, in his book *The End of History and the Last Man* (1993), offered the theory that political development has run its course, that Western-style democracy has triumphed as the best political system. This is by no means apparent at the beginning of the twenty-first century.

There are few democracies in Asia, mainly because Asians don't feel comfortable with them. Asians see Western democracies as having double standards; they prefer hierarchical systems. Although India has the world's largest democracy and Japan appoints her government by electoral means, these two states are not democracies in the Western sense—not India, because of the huge gap between rich and poor; and not Japan, because of factional strength in Parliament and the collusion between politicians and big business. Filipino democracy lives on after Ferdinand Marcos but hardly functions efficiently. In Europe the Nordic democracies seem to be healthy. Britain boasts the oldest Parliament, but an awful lot of bickering can be observed there, now more apparent by virtue of TV. African democracies are fragile, the unfortunate peoples of that continent first having had their old traditions dismantled or obliterated by their colonial masters, then having been abandoned before they had sufficient familiarity with Western institutions to enable them to develop a workable alternative.

The United States

The U.S. version of democracy naturally comes under closest scrutiny (on account of the country's prominence) and in many ways is viewed with misgivings by Asians and Europeans alike.

Of common concern is the general razzmatazz of the American
political scene, its domination by the media, its Hollywood-in-
fluenced presentation, its focus on "good looks" or abundance of
hair in presidential candidates, its manipulation of statistics, its
background of criminal influence (the Mafia) and assassination,
its facile slogans, its disregard for intellectuality, and its frequent
oversimplification of vital issues. Why do Americans call their
intellectuals "eggheads" and generally refuse to consider them
for the Oval Office? Why do they *reelect* presidents of doubtful
morals (Nixon and Clinton)? How can they allow economic success to blind them to more significant issues?

These questions do not imply that the American democratic
system or leadership is totally flawed. We should all be grateful
for the role of the United States in defending freedom and human
rights. The task of world policeman is a thankless one. Nonethe-
less, it seems that the U.S. could do itself better justice, present
itself to the world in a better light, and improve the image it sends
out in innumerable films and TV broadcasts. Is America really
like *LA Law* or *Dynasty* or *Dallas*?. We who know the U.S. know
it is much better than that. But many Asians, Africans, and Europeans don't. Even South Americans, closer in geography, consider themselves culturally superior to the yanquis. The British,
along with the Germans and Scandinavians, are probably
America's best friends but have the uneasy feeling that they are
witnessing the decline of a civilization before it has reached its
peak.

At all events, the American course of action, its might as a
superpower, and the incredible resilience of its economy will be
key factors in the unfolding of all our destinies in the twenty-first
century.

Conclusion

At the end of chapter 1, I posed certain questions regarding possible cultural trends during the twenty-first century. Are human values and modes of behavior standardizing or coalescing? Are cultures aligning themselves? Will national prejudices and feuds disappear? Are we approaching the end, not of history, but of irrelevant cultural diversity?

I remain firm in my belief that most cultural groups, and the sovereign states to which they adhere, will enjoy continued and diverse longevity throughout the century. Although it may continue to foster disagreement, cultural diversity is far from irrelevant. Culture is dynamic, not static. It is a process of change over time, but it is a cautious process that clings to vestiges and memories of past experience, however faintly perceived they may

261

be. Change occurs only if the cultural group acquires a *new vision of the future* (one which is best inspired by and derived from a *new vision of the past*). Such changes are beneficial only when they spring from a culture's roots, not if they are the result of the uprooting of an indigenous culture by others—misfortunes that have befallen the Aztecs, Incas, Sioux, and, more recently, Inuit, Lapp, and Aboriginal communities.

The recorded history of even the oldest known cultural communities is merely the tip of an iceberg reaching back through the millennia. We cannot understand the aspirations or direction of a culture without taking into account its earliest known history and placing this against the backdrop of prehistorical findings. These trace the progression: hunter-gatherer-fisher, nomad, agriculturalist, migratory man, sedentary man, scholar, inventor. Only in very recent times have cultural groups in the Arctic, Papua New Guinea, Australia, and the Amazon emerged from the first category. Fortunately, China, India, Japan, the Middle East, and latterly Europe afford us a richesse of historical clues. Clearly, the more we understand the past, the more accurately we can forecast the future.

What can we do to responsibly manage cultural diversity? Twenty-first century people seem disposed to tackle this question (perhaps for commercial gain). Whatever the motive, it is a worthy aim. The catastrophic events in Russia, the Middle East, and the Balkans at the end of the last millennium have given us stern warning that national and regional squabbles (sadly allied to cultural and religious differences) are not yet a thing of the past. One important factor is *culture shock*. Whether we are talking of negotiating international business deals, managing an intercultural conference, or sending an international peace-keeping force to a war-torn country, culture shock will almost certainly make its presence felt.

Culture Shock

When crossing borders, people of all countries experience culture shock. The more experienced or well traveled the individual, the less traumatic the shock, and vice versa. One is in the main fully conscious of its impact—exhaustion, confusion, frustration, a feeling of spinning one's wheels—though its effect on the subconscious may also be considerable. It is naturally a two-way process in which shock is experienced in equal measures on both sides.

Culture shock interferes seriously with the smooth running of international meetings, diplomacy, negotiation, and management. Not infrequently, it is very disruptive. Let's take business as an example. With rapid globalization of trade and ubiquitous mergers and acquisitions, businesspeople are having to make, daily around the globe, on-the-spot cultural decisions and assume hasty cultural stances for which they are neither prepared nor trained.

The biggest gaffes and greatest frustrations are usually witnessed early on, after a brief honeymoon. Mergers and international expansions, undertaken with hardly any or no concept of the cultural minefield entered into, often have disastrous and quickly deteriorating results in terms of reduced profit, huge job losses and layoffs, and tumbling share prices. DaimlerChrysler is a recent example.

This need not be. For every aspect of culture shock, there is an antidote which might be called a *culture shock absorber*. What do we mean by this? Again using business as an example, culture shock absorbers must be prepared and held at the ready by a trained team of key executives whose job it is to meet and interact, at an appropriate cultural and authoritative level, with a counterpart team from the merging or acquired partner. These teams need not be large in number (perhaps six to twelve), but they must be sufficiently influential and part of the decision-making process vis-à-vis the marriage of the two parties.

Knowing and Entering the Cultural Habitat of the Other Culture

How can one absorb (or help another absorb) culture shock? This is facilitated by knowing and entering into the *cultural habitat* of the other. What is a cultural habitat? It is a kind of "room" or "house" put together by a cultural group, inside which one holds a plethora of beliefs, attitudes, and assumptions. Within those walls one behaves in a prescribed manner. By entering into that habitat, by following the "house rules" and sharing its assumptions during one's stay there, the "visitor" can eliminate the phenomenon of culture shock.

Why do the people in the "house" behave as they do? To begin with, they are not free agents. They are restrained by attitudes inherited from origins long forgotten. The mind is a refuge for ideas dating from many centuries ago. One pays attention not only to the guidance of one's family and peers but also to the experiences of previous, more distant generations as passed on by culture. One should not underestimate the influence of that part of the past that is still alive in people's minds today. The momentum of two thousand years is not easily stopped.

The "visiting" team should enter the host's cultural habitat with ease, without fear, and with shock absorbers at the ready. Strategies are numerous and available and only need to be known. To give one or two brief examples, there are *mindset alliances*. Often the quickest way to establish empathy with a different mindset is to find a third mindset you can both laugh at or criticize. This strategy is less naïve than it sounds and is utilized in all corners of international business. It is well known in Northern Europe that the quickest way to get a Finn on your side is to make fun of Swedish pomposity, whatever your business objectives may be. There are many other Finnish house rules, but there is nothing like getting off to a good start. Large countries with vigorous, influential cultures or economies are tempting targets (especially neighbors), so Italians and Spaniards are quick to find a shared aversion to (alleged) French "arrogance," Southeast Asians line up against the Japanese, Latin Americans together scorn U.S. insensitivities, savvy Europeans bash the insular Brits, while the poor, honest Germans catch it from any number of alignments from less successful colleagues.

Shared mindset bashing is only one strategy for creating empathy and is only appropriate when a dominant player risks being accused of cultural imperialism. A surer entrée is gained by having a sound knowledge of the house rules and—even more important—by not misreading them. Returning to the Swedes, we must be aware of expectations inside a Swedish cultural habitat. These include an ambience of absolute correctness and properness, calm principled discussion, no surprises, persistent pursuit of consensus, and steady avoidance of confrontation. Observe these tenets in the Swedish house and the Swedes will soon trust and even begin to like you. You may be bored out of your mind, but you will not run into trouble. This sober behavior is neither required nor particularly advisable inside an Italian cultural habitat. Such controlled rectitude would not only bore Italians but would make them uneasy. An entirely different approach is required. What might be seen as the fragility of certain items of Italian cultural baggage—poor timekeeping and payment schedules, low legal consciousness, clannishness, inadequate degree of commitment, backroom influence, and so on—must be dispensed with at the very outset. These characteristics are background, a kind of Mediterranean scenery. More importantly, other attractions are on offer. These include immediate warmth, praise, accommodation, physical and mental closeness, a sharing of emotions, mutual help in difficulty, willingness to share conspiracy and to use the influence of friends, and free interpretation of the rule book if need be. For your part, you should value acquaintances that are introduced to you, expose at least one personal weakness for the Italian side to protect, be unafraid to seek advice—all this in an implied context that only Italians really understand what makes the world go round.

Your cultural stance will have to change rapidly and drastically when you leave such a house and enter a German or Japanese one. Chameleon-like behavior will be required. *There is nothing immoral about this.* You will retain your core beliefs and values. You are simply in someone else's house and you are obeying the rules, which you have taken the trouble to learn. Thereby you gain not only their respect, but their liking. *To make people like you should be one of the primary objectives of your approach to international business.* It may well be that the Americans will do business with anyone who buys and sells good products, but Asians, Latins, Arabs, and Africans do business with people they like. *Four-fifths of humanity put relationship before product.* Linear-active cultures often have difficulty remembering this.

Can the West Integrate with the Rest?

If we see the possibility of the West integrating with the rest (particularly the East) rather than the other way round, some reconciliation of worldviews might come on stream. There are increasing indications from the reactive and multi-active communities (five billion people) that age-old traits will not readily disappear. These are—among others—family closeness; group cooperation; coordinated, collective action; "group pursuit" tendencies; interdependence; and general personal respect in a hierarchical framework.

The linear-active West has shown some signs of departing from many of these values. This is evident in the dysfunctional family, the early separation of children, the discontinuance of personal care of aging parents, abandonment of religion, the lack of traditional rituals, the litigious nature of society, the decline in morals (porn on the Internet), the loss of the sense of unity with nature (still existing in Japanese, Thai, Aborigine, and most nonlinear societies), the creeping impersonalization of human contact (voice mail, the Internet, faceless corporations, etc.), and the single-minded pursuit of individual aims at the expense of others.

A reversal of many of these tendencies would facilitate integration into a global village where the headmen (and -women) would be relationship oriented, reactive, or multi-active people. If the benefits of Western education could enable us to see things from a *broader perspective*, a measure of cultural integration is not impossible. What we make of other people depends on what we know of them and the world, what we believe to be possible, what our memories are, and what loyalties we have to the past, present, and future. Nothing influences our ability to deal with the challenges of life as much as the context in which we view them. The more contexts we can choose from, the more options we have. An open mind would consider not only a national, European, or American context but one benefiting from a wide variety of past precedents (taken from all cultures and all humanity).

Is it too much to expect that we can shed our American or Northern European model and meet Asians, Latins, and others with a more all-embracing approach? Can we acquire an orientation toward Asian thinking? Are we willing to accept certain ambiguities or indirectness? Can we incorporate more feminine values into our activities and think of the place of the organization (or leader) inside society? Can we learn to use forceful tactics (if we have to) like Asians and Latins do, by applying gentle, persistent pressure? Can we reconcile hierarchy with egalitarianism and democracy? Are we willing to refrain from attacking head-on such Asian anomalies as lack of human rights, snail's-pace decision making, and an overconcern with face?

In the last analysis, the linear-active Westerners may ask themselves, "Is it worth the trouble? Do we *need* to integrate?" The fifteen most linear-active countries in the world are the United States, Canada, Britain, Australia, New Zealand, Germany, Switzerland, Austria, Sweden, Norway, Denmark, Finland, the Netherlands, Luxembourg, and Flemish Belgium. Their citizens are well aware that their linear, disciplined, largely Protestant-influenced way of life differs sharply from that of multi-active and reactive populations. They are also very aware that their fifteen economies account for 50 percent of world production and that in the GDP-per-capita league, all of them except New Zealand are in the top twenty countries. (Two of the others—Singapore and Hong Kong—have strong linear-active influences.)

Judged on the scale of the Human Development Index (published by the United Nations), which estimates quality of life, linear-active countries—this time including New Zealand, Singapore, and Hong Kong—do even better, occupying seventeen of the first twenty places. Only Japan (reactive) and France and Italy (multi-active) creep in for qualification. It is not surprising that the "Linear Fifteen" see themselves as the advanced economies and from time to time, when referring to others, use such terms as emerging or developing economies or Third-World countries.

But other indices may erode Western complacency. In the last decade of the second millennium, China was by far the fastest-growing economy (over 11 percent per annum), and only *one* Western nation, Ireland, appeared in the top twenty! Ireland has a basically linear-active lifestyle diluted by marked multi-active tendencies (also supported heartily during the decade by generous EU subsidies).

The writing is on the wall, and it is largely pictographic. In two, three, or four decades at the most, China's economy will surpass that of the United States. At the beginning of this century, the world's ten biggest economies are, in order of size, the United States, Japan, Germany, France, Britain, Italy, China, Brazil, Canada, and Spain. By midcentury the ranking is more likely to be, again by size, China, the United States, Japan, India, Brazil, Mexico, Germany, France, Korea (North and South), and Canada. Linear-active champions in the top ten will have been cut down to the United States and Germany, with multicultural Canada squeezing in. Britain may not make it.

We are, of course, only talking economics. If we look at population size, the only linear-active country in the top ten is the United States (third). By midcentury the U.S. population may have been overtaken by those of Indonesia, Brazil, Pakistan, Bangladesh, Nigeria, and probably Mexico. The total linear-active population will probably be approximately 3 to 4 percent of the world's total. Even now it is no higher than 8 percent and is decreasing daily.

A Tilting Balance

We cannot consider these statistics (of economic growth and burgeoning populations) without drawing certain breathtaking conclusions. Since the fall of Arab civilization in Andalucía in 1492, Europeans and their North American descendants have dominated world affairs politically, commercially, militarily, and culturally for five centuries—half a millennium. This was largely thanks to mammoth China looking inward and letting the rest of us get on with it. Even now, it is unlikely that China will try to dominate the rest of the world in this coming century. They have a very good record of noninterference.

However, we are approaching a watershed. Whatever Chinese intentions may or may not be, *the twenty-first century will be the one in which the balance tilts*. During the century, the economic growth of Asian and Latin American countries will enable them to call the tune in international commerce and politics. Not only will most of the mightiest engines of industrial production be located in China, India, Japan, and Korea (as well, of course, as the United States), but the world's hungriest markets cannot fail to be the burgeoning populations of India, China, Indonesia, Pakistan, Bangladesh, Brazil, Mexico, and Nigeria. Their needs, requirements, tastes, and appetites will transform not only the world economy but also the way the world works and lives.

In other words, we come back to culture. Whatever is churned out by the engines of revolution, war, economics, trade, supply and demand, technology, science, environmental development, and progress in health and medicine, it is *culture that will count in the end.* It has accounted for the incredible durability of the Indian, Chinese, and Japanese civilizations; it has in its fascinating variety engendered and nursed along such incredible European achievements as the Renaissance, philosophical brilliance, the opening up of the Western hemisphere, the Industrial Revolution, and the development of electronic and space technology. It has preserved for all of us the age-old traits of family, group belonging, cooperation, kindness, generosity, aesthetic inclination, and a curiosity that fosters invention. We should take the best from this wonderful heritage, in whatever part of the world we find it.

Epilogue

After September 11

All previous chapters of this book were written prior to September 11, 2001, the events of which serve to underline the irresistible potency of culture and the enduring grip of history.

The explosive occurrences of that fateful day were hardly anomalous when viewed as sequential episodes in a continuing series of retaliations to perceived wrongs. What was inevitably exceptional (and deeply shocking to Westerners and Muslims alike) was the *unsurpassed concentration of evil intent* behind the annihilation of close to four thousand of God's creatures in the space of a couple of hours. An eye for an eye, a tooth for a tooth—this is a maxim that has weathered well in most cultures and religions for several millennia, but the sickening attacks on the twin towers and the Pentagon and the failed attack that crashed

271

in rural Pennsylvania were heart-stoppers for people of all creeds. If there is any comfort to be gleaned from September 11, it is the hope that it might call a halt to a specific variety of madness.

As we have indicated in chapter 3, Christianity, Judaism, and Islam all originated in the same part of the world, roughly in the same era, and share a plethora of principles, laws, core beliefs, and even prophets. If we compare these religions with Hinduism, Buddhism, and Shinto, we see how different the three monotheistic religions are from Eastern religions—and how similar they are to each other. Yet the rivalry between Christianity, Judaism, and Islam and the heights of bitterness to which they currently aspire threatens to tear the world apart. People in the Far East, less involved in such religious rivalries, must sometimes wonder what all the fuss is about.

The September 11 attack has been deemed by a majority of governments and authorities as an act of terrorism, not the outset of a war between Muslims and the West, or indeed between Islam and Christianity. Others, including some scholars, have, however, declared that it *is* the onset of a religious conflict. We must hope the latter are wrong. In this respect the general condemnation of the attack by a congress of fifty-six Muslim states is timely and comforting. If Islamic authorities resist the concept of a worldwide religious conflict (and eventual conflagration), it is essential that the West not fall into the trap of envisaging perpetual Muslim conspiracy and hatred. Avoidance of this trap is best served by looking closely at the history of Christian-Muslim interaction. What it contains is arguably more good than bad.

The Rise of Islam

No single event in world history during the millennium between the fall of the Roman Empire and the European voyages of discovery was more significant than the rise of Islam. By the end of the sixth century A.D. the once-mighty empires of Rome and Persia were exhausted, both riven by religious dissent. Muhammad, born in Mecca in A.D. 570, is considered by Muslims as the last and greatest of the long line of prophets. Islam, emanating from the teachings of Muhammad, became the newest and last of the three major monotheistic religions. By 625 the new religion, with its message of compassion and mercy, began to expand to the Fertile Crescent and beyond. The vitality of the Arab conquerors as they surged through Arabia and Palestine, then east to the Tigris and the Euphrates and into Asia Minor and Persia, was the driving force behind their military victories. From the beginning of their expansion, however, the *spiritual* conquests of Islam rivaled, possibly exceeded, the conquests on the battlefield. Muslim principles were firmly codified in the Qu'ran and were warmly embraced by poor and underprivileged peoples throughout the region.

Initially, Islam was not a proselytizing religion. Muhammad showed great respect for Christianity and Judaism. He regarded their prophets, from Abraham to Jesus, as his own precursors. Under the caliphs that succeeded him, Jews and Christians were allowed to worship as they wished. A persistent historical characteristic of the Muslim religion has been its open tolerance of other faiths. Jews, with their two-thousand-year-old record of persecution in the Mediterranean and in Europe, have seldom (until recent times) been mistreated by Muslims and enjoyed perhaps their brightest moment of history in their participation in Islamic Spanish society in Al-Andalus (Andalucía) from the eighth to the fifteenth centuries. The "golden age" of Spanish Jewry ended, and religious tolerance with it, when Islamic Granada fell to the Spaniards in 1492.

The Moorish Legacy in Europe

One way for the West to enhance its social and political understanding of and communication with Muslim countries is for it to
delve consciously into the riches of the Moorish European legacy.
We can easily appreciate and honor modern Italy in memory of
Europe's great cultural debt to the Renaissance. Few would dispute the contribution of British Parliaments to democratic governance or American and German achievements in science and technology. Is the West aware of the past splendors of Arab civilization existing, moreover, on European soil? In fact, many of us
are. In the year 2000 twenty million tourists visited Andalucía to
enjoy not only the beaches but also the artifacts and relics of
history and culture. They are dazzling.

Reference has been made in chapter 8 to the illustrious era of
the Moorish civilization in southern Spain. In view of the pre-
ponderantly negative perception of Islam subsequent to the strike
of September 11, this might be an opportune time to balance the
scales somewhat by giving a kindly backward glance at the
Moorish culture. It is said that Charles Martel saved the Western
world by stopping the advancing Moors at Poitiers in 732, but
from what? From a splendid Arab civilization that was shortly to
develop in North Africa and the Mediterranean, a civilization
where Jews, Christians, and Arabs would have lived together in
peace and fruitful creativity. At that time the Islamic faith showed
far greater respect for Christianity and Judaism—sister religions
also based on the Old Testament—than the Christian Crusaders
ever did toward the "heathens." The Europeans in "conquered"
Andalucía all spoke Arabic, published their books in the language,
and even wrote Arabic poetry.

In the year 1000 (just a millennium ago), Cordoba was the
greatest city in the world, far larger than London, Paris, or Rome
at the time and far more advanced in art, science, and civic splen-

dor. The Cordoba medina contained some 80,000 shops and work-shops, and the city boasted 600 mosques, 300 baths, 50 hospitals, nearly 100 public schools, 17 colleges and universities, and 20 public libraries. Its population of one million enjoyed a high standard of living equaled in Seville, Granada, Toledo, and cities all the way across Southern Europe from Lisbon to Palermo. Nor was this civilization a flash in the pan that existed for just a moment in history. It began with the Moorish incursions into Spain in 711 and ended *781 years later* with the fall of Islamic Granada. What a slice of history! If we go back 781 years in British history, we would just miss witnessing the signing of Magna Carta in 1215 by King John. In 1220 the first kingdom emerged in Thailand, and in North America the Aztecs began to spread across the valley of Mexico.

Such a long occupation as the Moors' inevitably leaves an indelible imprint on the lives and minds of the subjugated peoples. Ask anyone in the Balkans about the 650 years of Ottoman rule and you will notice a certain lack of enthusiasm. Yet around the Mediterranean and particularly in southern Spain, there is almost a nostalgia for the golden age of the Moorish empire. European vocabulary—especially Spanish and Portuguese—is sprinkled with words of Arabic origin (algebra, alcove, Algarve, Alicante, Alhambra); Arab music gave us the flamenco; there would be no Spanish paella without the Arabs, who planted rice in Europe, not to mention the oranges, apricots, asparagus, and spinach that grace our menus. The durum wheat, which the Moors brought with them, gave birth to Italian pasta. The Mesquita in Cordoba, the Giralda in Seville, and, above all, the Alhambra in Granada captivate Western visitors with their unrivaled architectural magnificence and delicacy. The scented gardens, fountains, palms, and fig trees of the Arab cities hint at a paradise lost, where science, art, learning, and religious tolerance went hand in hand.

If Islamic architecture, art, and good living found favor with Europeans, it was perhaps in the field of science that Islam and the West had their most fruitful interaction. Inspired by ancient Hellenistic tradition, Muslims created a society in the Middle Ages that was the scientific center of the world. Arabic was as synonymous with science as English is today, and the Arabs dominated scientific studies for over five hundred years, during which time they founded universities and formulated the theoretical basis for algebra, astronomy, and even the notion of science as an empirical inquiry. It was the infusion of this knowledge into Western Europe that eventually fueled the Renaissance and, later, the scientific revolution. From the tenth to the thirteenth centuries, Europeans were translating Arabic works into Hebrew and Latin as fast as they could. Jews also played a significant part in this transfer of knowledge. The result was a rebirth of learning that ultimately transformed Western civilization. This is a fine example of how civilizations, instead of clashing, can learn from and shape each other. No intellectual meeting has been more fruitful than that between Islamic and Western science. Europeans and Americans should be grateful for that!

Many historians are of the opinion that this intellectual marriage was one of the most significant events of history. Unfortunately, only a certain number of the major scientific works from that era have been translated from Arabic. As thousands of manuscripts have never even been read by modern scholars, much of Islam's rich intellectual history—which so convincingly belies the images caused by recent events—fails to reach us. Americans, particularly, might be favorably impressed by such a realization. A better understanding of how two cultures have mingled beneficially in the past (and for many centuries) might encourage a closer cooperation in the future.

The Crusades

But what about the Crusades and the hostilities and enmity dating from 1096? It is true that the massacres occurred on a scale unprecedented at that time, but on the occasions when leniency was granted, it was generally the Muslims who showed mercy. Although they are much touted as glorious feats of heroism for the sake of Christianity, the Crusades were an abysmal failure.

The First Crusade, a holy war waged from 1096–1099 by Christian armies from Western Europe against Islam in Palestine, was inspired by a fiery sermon of Pope Urban II in 1095. One of its leaders, Godfrey of Bouillon, established the Christian Kingdom of Jerusalem—a rare triumph in the dismal record of the Crusades. The Second Crusade (1147–1149) was led by Louis VII of France and collapsed ignominiously when their Christian men in place—the barons of Jerusalem—sided with Muslim Damascus, which the newly arrived Crusaders wished to attack. The Third Crusade (1189–1192), led by Richard the Lionheart, among others, failed dismally in its objective to recapture Jerusalem, which had been taken by the Muslim leader, Saladin. However, the Muslims generously ceded a stretch of coast between Tyre and Jaffa and allowed Christians to make pilgrimages to Jerusalem. The leaders of the Fourth Crusade (1202–1204) had originally planned to attack Egypt, which had become the center of Muslim power in the twelfth century, but they were diverted by the Venetians to Constantinople, which fell on April 13, 1204, and was subjected to three days of massacre and pillage. A horrified Pope Innocent III, who had called for the Crusade, was unable to regain control of the chaos and called off the next leg to the Holy Land.

Such was the fiasco of the medieval Crusades—true religious wars inasmuch as Crusaders had the status of pilgrims and Muslims could claim to be martyrs—but futile and unnecessary in their scope and intent. What's important here for us to learn is that the fears that engendered Christian hatred of the Muslims were a mirror image of today's Muslim resentment of "the great satan" of the West: fears of a culture labeled alien, of superior wealth and might. Study of the shambolic nature of the Crusades should lead both sides to see the utter futility of and misplaced desire for a holy war.

Ironically, all four Crusades took place in a period of history when Muslims were collaborating with and teaching advanced forms of knowledge to Christians all over Southern Europe. Even in the midst of the hostilities, Christians and Muslims were exchanging culture and growing in awareness of what they had in common. In frontier zones adherents of both religions lived side by side, worshipped at each other's shrines, served each other's masters, and took each other's side in many disputes. El Cid, the hero of the Spanish Crusades, spent most of his career, after he left Castile, in the service of Muslim emirs. Islamic beneficence and tolerance in Spain continued for nearly three hundred years after the last Crusade.

Coexistence

We find, then, that the friendly, even mutually enriching coexistence between Muslims and Westerners that we see in Europe and North America today is nothing new. It is, and was, the rule rather than the exception. Friction between Muslims and Christians and between Muslims and Jews is usually less than that observed between some Catholic and Protestant communities (Northern Ireland) or rival Muslim groups (Sunnis and Shiites). Muslim settlement in the West is an established and most likely permanent fact. Islamic extremism in these countries is rare; in Britain, for example, out of some 1,500 mosques, only a couple are known to be run by extremists. Muslims make up some 7 percent of the population in France, 4 percent in the Netherlands, 4 percent in

Germany, 3 percent in Britain, 2 percent in Spain, and 1 percent in Scandinavia and Italy. In general European Muslims are good citizens and do better at school than their Western classmates. They often suffer discrimination with commendable patience. They harbor no "Islamic conspiracy" against the West, largely because they themselves have diverse agendas. Germany's Muslims, for example, are largely Turks and have little loyalty to Palestinians. Shiite Muslims of Lebanese origin have no particular interest in the Sunni Muslims of North Africa or in the Algerian civil war. British Pakistani Muslims are more concerned with beating England at cricket than with the fall of Kandahar. The French, naturally, assume that their Muslims are only too glad to adopt a superior culture—the French! The United States, though the victim of extremism in the recent past, has historically assimilated its seven million Muslims of all races with the same ease that it has absorbed other nationalities, and there is a long queue of Islamic applicants for admittance to the U.S. Arab Americans are generally successful economically; there is no doubt which side they are on. Ten days after the strike, the American Muslim leader Imam Izak El-Pacha condemned the terrorists, stating simply that they were not believers. "As for us, we are with our country." This is likely to be the attitude of the great majority of immigrant Muslims. The 40,000 Afghan Americans in the San Francisco Bay area displayed their American flags following the September attacks and during the struggle for Kabul. Fremont, California, with its 10,000 Afghans is known as "little Kabul."

Prophets of doom (and gloom), especially Westerners, practically fell over themselves in the days following September 11 to be the first to predict a century of strife when Muslims worldwide would coordinate their terrorist attacks until the United States was brought to its knees. These calamitous prophecies were neither supported nor reiterated by Islamic authorities around the globe. Scrutiny of Muslim-Christian relations during centuries of proximity in Europe and more recently in the U.S. indicate clearly that this is not in the cards. The Crusades may have lasted over a century—in itself a mere blip in human history—and we can see what exercises in futility they were. In the 1,300 years that Islam has existed, Islamic Iberia shone like a beacon for nearly 800 of those years, as a model state unsurpassed in intelligence and tolerance since the Hellenistic heyday.

The Islamic condemnation of the September 11 strike was universal, unambivalent, and expressed in terms of shock. The staggering number of those killed and injured quickly put things into perspective. Kill a few undeserving infidels, maybe, but such calculated mass execution of innocent people (office workers) besmirched the Muslim reputation indelibly (and perhaps indefinitely). If the Muslim greeting *"Assalamu 'a laykum"* ("Peace be upon you") means anything at all, where did the Manhattan and Washington, D.C. disasters leave devout Muslims? How would Muhammad have reacted? The damage to the image of Islam was no less than that inflicted on Catholicism by the brutalities of the Spanish Inquisition. If Osama Bin Laden was responsible, he cannot be a martyr now or in the future. Islamic authorities see him as a cult leader, and, like most Western cults, this one will likely end in suicide and death. The Taliban, in their turn, are regarded by an overwhelming majority of Muslims as being fanatical and backward, with an outdated aim of igniting a clash of civilizations. With the increasingly widespread dissemination of knowledge through the Internet, a war of any duration between rival civilizations becomes increasingly improbable. Islam and Christianity have too much common heritage to lose. Ironically, such a battle might be seen as only a lively skirmish by the majority of humanity—the one billion Hindus and two billion Confucians would not necessarily feel involved!

Islamic scholars point out that they are not basically against the West (many of whose traditions were tempered by Muslims). What they *are* fearful of is the power and influence of the West inside their own Muslim societies. Oil interests loom large in this respect, though other forms of intervention also cause friction. Muslim-Christian interaction in the past has frequently been benign. The cultures shaped one another warmly in less materialistic times. There is an opportunity for Muslims, now, to shape Western culture from within, by virtue of the stable Islamic communities currently existing in Western countries. Equally important, the West has the opportunity to let them do this. In Britain, the United States, and other Western countries, there is a growing acceptance of and interest in Muslim food, art, music, dance, and architecture, and also to some extent in fashion and medicine. Some essentially Islamic values such as family closeness, loyalty, hospitality, and so forth may gain increasing support early in the twenty-first century. Islamic attractions such as the Alhambra, Petra, Jerash, Istanbul, and the Valley of the Nile are magnets for tourists. Not least, Islam continues to gain large numbers of converts in Europe and the U.S.

The Islamic revival, which was inspired by the Iranian Revolution and which continues today, is less concerned with unbelievers than it is with its own reforms. The revival is directed inward in an attempt to heal the schism within Islam itself. The Taliban, the Al Qaeda, and their ilk are by no means synonymous with this revival. They are regarded as a dying breed whose Manhattan and Washington, D.C., ventures may be a desperate last-ditch effort to gain control of Muslim direction. Extremists believe that time is on their side. More likely it is running out, especially in the Muslim world. Terrorists cannot hijack a respected religion of 1,300 years any more than the grand master of the Ku

Klux Klan could become president of the United States.

By definition, moderates outnumber extremists, and this is also true in the Arab world, where piety and devoutness are admired qualities. Furthermore, more than half the one billion Muslims in the world are not Arabs. While 300 million Southeast Asians may be vociferous in their criticism of the United States, few have the temperament to become suicide bombers. Turks, Iranians, Uzbeks, Kazakhs, and other Central Asians have their own agendas.

Islam's Own Problems

The trauma and suffering experienced by Americans and other nationalities in September 2001 should not fool the West into believing that the moment was one of Muslim triumph, with the corollary, Western demise. It is rather Islam that meets its moment of truth, after decades of difficulties and turmoil. In the 1990s, alone, problems ranged from wars in Bosnia, Kosovo, and Chechnya to revolt in East Timor, independence movements in Sumatra and Borneo, repeated hostilities in Kashmir, civil wars in Algeria and the Philippines, bombings and assassinations in Palestine and Gaza, killings in Ambon, explosive incidents in Somalia and Aden, and the destruction of Buddhist treasures in Afghanistan. Muslims seemed to be involved in all the world's current squabbles. As Islam has no core country, these problems could not be laid at the door of any unifying authority. If the West has its world policeman (the U.S.) and East Asia, its two powerful custodians of morality and order (China and Japan), the world's Muslims are torn apart by a multiplicity of interests and agendas. How can Moroccans address Filipino problems or Malaysians advise Turks? Indeed, has Islam ever spoken with one voice?

If it has, it was to reiterate anti-American sentiment. Indeed the United States is not blameless in respect to the current Arab and Islamic malaise (more on this later in this chapter). Yet it is

apparent that "the great Satan" is often made the scapegoat for
the internal schism within Islam. Inequality of distribution of
wealth and power is most visible in Saudi Arabia and the Gulf
States, but it is also endemic in North Africa, Pakistan, Indonesia, Turkey, and elsewhere. Continuing poverty and lack of recourse to democratic reform blight the chances of the majority of
Muslims to better their lot. Resentment of American and even
European prosperity is a natural consequence. Bahrain, Qatar,
Kuwait, and Yemen are beginning to experiment with democratic
elections and withdrawal of some forms of censorship, but Saudi
Arabia's autocratic regime remains in itself one of the root causes
of Islamic extremism.

Even a gradual evolution toward democracy in Muslim states
will relieve the tension between Islam and the West. Democratic
countries rarely go to war with each other. Democracy allows
oppressed or hungry peoples a voice to complain with—a route
to secure compromise, which moderates extreme conduct. The
second largest Muslim country in the world, India, with its 150
million adherents, is conspicuously absent in plans to dismantle
the United States. Indian Muslims have recourse to legal parliamentary debate and argument.

Why Has Islam Failed to Achieve Modernity?

Scholars have asked themselves why Islam failed to capitalize on
its intellectual superiority and dominant position in science at
the time of the Renaissance and to make the transition to a modern society as other Mediterranean cultures—for instance, Italy—
have done. Europeans absorbed Arab knowledge, applied it prag-
matically, and went on to develop empirical science leading to
industrial technology. Why did Islam not do the same?

Changes in the balance of power had something to do with it.
While the Crusades achieved little from the European point of

view, the growing Franco-German hegemony over most of Western Europe, allied to the increasing influence and commercial acumen of the British Empire, gradually wrested leadership in science and commerce from the Arabs' grasp. Driven out of Spain at the end of the fifteenth century, deprived of their magnificent libraries in Cordoba and Toledo, they began to lose their intellectual base (you might say their head office). Islamic knowledge, science, and philosophy were channeled in different directions, and pan-Islamic communication, strong in the tenth to the fourteenth centuries, was lost and has never been fully reestablished. The Ottomans, who took over the Arab lands in the sixteenth century, were conquerors, not thinkers, and the fruitful interplay between Islamic and Western intellects virtually disappeared.

There was a significant Islamic revival in the hundred years following 1520, but it had a strong military underpinning and was Ottoman- rather than Arab-driven . Three major Muslim states emerged: the Ottoman Empire itself, the Safavid dynasty in Persia, and the Mughal Empire in India. All three were the creation of Turkish-speaking Muslim dynasties of a military character. When Vienna was besieged in 1529, the Ottomans were indisputably the greatest Muslim power of the age. Suleiman the Magnificent, the Ottoman sultan, commanded fourteen million subjects, almost twice the population of Spain and England combined.

In spite of Ottoman power, the Islamic world of that age had one serious flaw: the schism between Sunni Muslims (adherers to the first four caliphs as the rightful successors of Muhammad) and Shiite Muslims (those who acknowledge Ali, son-in-law of Muhammad, and the Imams as the rightful successors of Muhammad). The Ottomans and the Mughal Empire adhered to the orthodox Sunni sect. The Persians, however, followed Shi'ism, which drove a wedge into the Muslim world, one that has existed to the present. Just as the Ottomans sided with the French against the Hapsburgs, the Persians took the other side, allying themselves with Austria. *Such cultural traits and divisions run through history.* We see them still, 450 years later, in the rancor between Iran (Shiite) and a Sunni-controlled government in Iraq.

The second basic weakness of sixteenth-century Muslim empires was that they were essentially land empires at a time when the maritime powers of Spain and Portugal were dominating the waters of the Mediterranean and the Indian Ocean respectively. When the British and Dutch added their sea power to the equation, Muslims were outgunned and outmaneuvered. Muscovy, too, began to raise its head, and in 1620 Cossack raiders appeared on the Black Sea and ravaged its shores. Thus the great Islamic empires of the previous centuries failed to make the transition to the modern world.

Scholars point out, however, that the decline of Islamic society was not occasioned purely by military or economic reverses. In the sixteenth century, the West effectively separated religious and state authority. This has never been achieved in Muslim states (Iran and Saudi Arabia are examples of countries where the two are currently synonymous). The relationship between religion and science is such that one precludes the other. Some Islamic scientists and historians affirm that "Islamic science" may be fruitfully informed by spiritual values that Western science ignores. The opposite view is that religious conservatism will serve to diminish the spirit of skepticism required for progressive science. Certainly Eastern science has fallen behind that of the pragmatic West. Western philosophers assert that truth is best discovered through reason, which is authentic on its own terms and needs no theological basis—Arabs would be reluctant to agree. Whatever the arguments, it seems evident that the development of modern institutions in the Islamic world will continue to be hampered until independent civil societies emerge and survive. Turkey and the Philippines currently seem nearest to the separation of religion and state. However much the West would like to foster that emergence, it will ultimately come from within—hopefully by peaceful means.

What is becoming clear is that Islamic fundamentalism (by no means universally popular among Muslims) lacks intellectual rigor and has difficulty responding adequately to the demands of twenty-first-century society. What is needed is an evolving message from the Qu'ran itself, not that of the mullahs reaching back to the phraseology of a millennium ago. Islamic intellectualism is by no means dead—it is simply suppressed in different ways and by different means. A more modern and applicable theology will emerge, probably sooner than later. Whether the lead will come from the Arab world, the East (Indonesia and Malaysia), or perhaps from Iran remains to be seen.

What the West Has to Learn

The roots of the bone-shaking crisis arising from September 11, 2001, need careful examination and analysis. Islamic clamor and criticism are persistent, but so is Western cultural myopia. How thick-skinned can we be? We have two thousand years of well-documented history behind us; all necessary knowledge is at our fingertips. Economic and military successes and failures follow each other with bewildering speed and kaleidoscopic variety. *Cultural traits, races, and religions endure for centuries—even millennia.* They are the only predictable courses.

Small, alert nationals such as the Danes, Dutch, Finns, and Swiss are very interested in the mentalities and behavior of large countries with which they have trade relations or social intercourse, and they develop a fair degree of cultural sensitivity, which serves them well. As nationals, they find they are generally popular

when they travel abroad. Unfortunately, large nations tend to neglect other cultures and to focus inwardly on the magnificence of
their own society (past or present). Britain, France, and Spain
had recent empires that engendered not a little arrogance. Russia, China, and Japan, historically isolated countries, are also inward-looking and to a large extent unaware of cross-cultural currents. The United States, unfortunately, is the least culturally sensitive of all, partly because of its isolation between two vast oceans
and partly due to its envelopment in the fog of the American
Dream. The Dream came to an abrupt (and unhappy) end on September 11, 2001. It may be continued at a later time, but for now
reality has to be dealt with.

American cultural insensitivity is more of a tragedy than it
would be for other nations, for the United States is the only superpower. The well-being of the West—and, indeed, most of the
rest of the world—depends, and will depend, on intelligent and
well-informed decisions made by the leaders of the United States.
This is where we are at this moment in history. The record so far
is not good. The American people generously employed up to
100,000 individuals in the CIA and FBI, who disposed of a budget of something between 20 to 30 billion dollars to protect them
(and many of us). They needed to develop a "feel"—dare we say
a cultural orientation—for future events, especially dangers.

American intelligence failed to predict Pearl Harbor, in spite
of the fact that more than half the Japanese fleet steamed across
much of the Pacific Ocean. The Chinese invasion of Korea caught
them by surprise, as did the Hungarian revolt and the Soviet in-
vasions of Czechoslovakia and Afghanistan. They learned very
late about the Soviet siting of missiles in Cuba, advised Kennedy
badly in the Bay of Pigs fiasco, confidently predicted victory in
Vietnam, and asserted the solidity of Communist regimes in Eastern Europe just weeks before the Berlin Wall came down. The

utter disintegration of the USSR astonished them. The Iraqi invasion of Kuwait caught them napping in an area where the protection of oil supplies is vital to U.S. interests. It took an army of 500,000 to rectify that one, though the chief villain was not caught. At least the United States was invulnerable to any major attack on its own soil, or so the country thought. In fact, the World Trade Center (WTC) had been targeted before; Russian president Vladimir Putin warned of an international terrorist plot; numerous intelligence sources predicted that an assault on mainland America was imminent. All warnings, however, foundered on the rocks of CIA and FBI smugness and complacency and on the agencies' failure to share information. What could foreigners really tell an organization that had a spy satellite system so powerful that it could identify cigarette butts on the streets of Baghdad? Did it really matter that American spymasters had precious little training in spying, spoke no language except English, and had received no cultural instruction about the people they were spying on? With a quarter of a million computers on the job, why shouldn't most case officers live comfortably in the suburbs of Virginia?

If one is critical of American cultural naïveté, one must remember that it is principally at America's own cost. But in this instance the price paid for the sloppiness of the intelligence services was terrible. Suicide terror has, in fact, a long history. At least fifty terrorists coordinated the WTC, Pentagon, and failed Washington, D.C. strike from within the United States itself. They were not detected (or at least not foiled), even though witnesses report that some of them went around boasting about a catastrophe to come and made unusual demands at flight schools and odd inquiries about crop dusting. If one does not wish to listen to one's friends, one should at least listen to one's enemies.

Cultural insensitivity at the beginning of the new century seems to know no bounds. The IMF's somewhat ill-judged prediction that the World Trade Center disaster "will have only limited impact on the international economy" makes one wonder if they are just trying to talk up the market or whether such an important institution is simply incapable of comprehending the magnitude of the culture ripples which will ensue for several decades.

Insensitivity at the government level is also rampant in the United States. If the administration persists in unilaterally rewriting the global financial system, tearing up or backing out of treaties on pollution and environmental control, supporting dictators or unpalatable regimes who are clearly detested by their own subjects and antithetical to its own stated values of democracy and individual rights, is it surprising that the American people have to ask themselves the question, "Why do they hate us so much?" Indeed one's heart can bleed for them, for they are perhaps the most generous (and innocent) people on earth, but in a world in which their governmental and business leaders wish to globalize capitalism, a unilaterally assertive stance will engender a love-hate relationship at best.

So What Is New?

Two hundred years of invulnerability at home gave the United States a holiday from history. Now they are engaged, for better or for worse. Placid Canada is the only safe frontier. Technology has replaced geographical isolation. China, Japan, Russia, and ultimately India will also be drawn increasingly into international interaction and interdependence. The largest nations will have to agree on a mutually acceptable strategy for intervention in others' affairs. Such issues, in the context of creeping globalization, will prove less prickly than they have been in the past. International aid is commonplace. In fact, sixty nations met early in 2002 to raise over four billion dollars for the rebuilding of a destroyed

Afghanistan. *Médecins sans frontières* is a positive concept. Still, many questions remain. For example, how much should a world power intervene to prevent mass slaughter or genocide, especially in the case of a neighbor? Should one not make every effort to stave off the financial or economic collapse of big countries like Argentina, Brazil, or Indonesia, where disintegration would have a domino effect on partners in commerce? How strong should the imperative be for nations to conform to treaties protecting the environment? What can nations do together about global warming, deforestation, and soil erosion? Most importantly of all in the first decade of the century, how much solidarity can be created against international terrorism?

There are some grounds for optimism regarding the last vital question. The reason for this lies in the essentially evil nature and deadly finality of the four September 11 strikes. It is too much for any rationality, Western or Islamic, to bear. It was the ultimate blow, the ne plus ultra of strikes. The World Trade Center towers were an unmistakable commercial symbol of the United States, in a sense its beating heart. A dagger was plunged into that heart. It is staggering to imagine what the corresponding attack would be on the Muslim world. To achieve equivalent symbolism, it would be on the mosque in Mecca itself. For Catholics it would be the destruction of the Vatican, for Britain the blowing up of Parliament. It is not unreasonable to believe that such disasters will not occur—we have to place so much belief in the human sense of right and wrong. The shock waves still reverberate; perhaps a viable perspective has come into being. Knocking over skyscrapers is a risky business, and Manhattan does not have a monopoly on them. Islamic Malaysia has just constructed the tallest building in the world. China hopes to go one higher and has plenty more, not only in Hong Kong.

More than one commentator has declared that September 11,

2001, was the true millennium—an analysis that contains some truth inasmuch as it is a watershed in human expectations.

Whither the West?

Robert Samuelson in his article "The Grand Illusion" in *Newsweek*, questions the continued dominance of the United States in the twenty-first century. He cites the dangers of nuclear proliferation, anti-Western terrorism, recessions and swings in financial markets, and technological breakdowns (through accident or sabotage). If the global economy sputters, he sees the American model of economic and political pluralism foundering. On the other hand, if democracy and market economies flourish, he sees the U.S. share of the world economy declining. Either way, a sad story.

But it is a mistake to write off the West. In the first place, it is not only the United States that we should focus on. If indeed the Islamic revival continues and if China fulfills its current promise, the corollary of such developments would be a more unified West. The U.S. is a product of Western civilization, with roots in Britain, Germany, France, Italy, Scandinavia, and practically every other European country. Its ultimate cultural alliance with the European Union is highly probable, if not inevitable, if Western civilization itself is threatened. We must remember what happened in two world wars when the chips were down. Next time it is likely that Germany will be on the team. The durability of a balanced West (the U.S., Europe, Canada, Australia, Latin America, New Zealand) resides not only in its military and economic strengths, formidable though these still are, but in the matured resilience of Western values. These values were forged in the crucible of the Greek city-states but have been tempered through the centuries by the Reformation and the Renaissance, by embracing democracy, by vanquishing the bogeys of Nazism and communism, and by defining the culture of Western Europe and the New World. They include openness, freedom of speech, a sense of justice, respect for the law, use of reason, religious tolerance, the seeking of fair play and impartiality, a sense of humor and proportion, an acceptance of civic responsibility, and a belief in universal human rights and human dignity. Some of these characteristics, such as openness, transparency, a reluctance to fight, and the extension of legal protection to criminals, are seen as weaknesses, even as signs of decadence.

I believe that the West, in spite of the huge forthcoming advances in Eastern and Islamic societies, will continue to acquit itself well in the twenty-first century. What it has going for it, in addition to the core values described above, is a plethora of social and semipolitical institutions—they number in the thousands—between the bedrock of the family and the authority of the state. In many societies there is a social vacuum between the home and job. In Anglo-Saxon and Scandinavian countries in particular, but also generally in Europe, clubs, societies, associations, activities, sports, courses, and hobbies of all kinds keep people busy. This is the dense fabric of Western society—active, throbbing, inventive, in every sense self-perpetuating and indomitable, with a momentum all its own.

If such social vibrancy is Western in essence, it is epitomized in the United States. As Hamish McRae wrote recently as he watched Americans rise phoenixlike from the ashes and rubble of Ground Zero, *the future starts here.*

*   *   *   *   *   *

If I may allow myself one final note of optimism vis-à-vis Islamic-driven terrorism, I will refer to an important factor that seems to be overlooked by political commentators and futurologists. Of the much-discussed one-billion-strong multitude of

Muslims in the world, *over five hundred million of them are women*. There are strong indications to suggest that the twenty-first century will be a period of rapidly rising female influence and empowerment, from which Muslim women cannot be indefinitely excluded. I am of the opinion that gender-liberation issues will be higher on these women's agenda than lending continuing support to the supposed destruction of the West, whose way of life embodies the social qualities they must ultimately seek.

Appendix A

Cultural Categorization Characteristics

Linear-Active	Multi-Active	Reactive
Talks half of the time	Talks most of the time	Listens most of the time
Does one thing at a time	Does several things at a time	Reacts to partner's action
Plans ahead step-by-step	Plans grand outline only	Looks at general principles
Polite but direct	Emotional	Polite, indirect
Partly conceals feelings	Displays feelings	Conceals feelings
Confronts with logic	Confronts emotionally	Never confronts
Dislikes losing face	Has good excuses	Must not lose face
Rarely interrupts	Often interrupts	Doesn't interrupt
Job-oriented	People oriented	Very people oriented
Sticks to facts	Feelings before facts	Statements are promises

Linear-Active	Multi-Active	Reactive
Truth before diplomacy	Flexible truth	Diplomacy over truth
Controls environment	Manipulates environment	Lives in harmony with environment
Values and follows rules	Often disregards rules	Interprets rules flexibly
Gains status by achievements	Gains status by connections and charisma	Gains status by birthright and education
Speech is for information	Speech is for opinions	Speech is to promote harmony
Works fixed hours	Likes flexible hours	Work, leisure, and life are intertwined
Values privacy	Is gregarious, inquisitive	Respectful, likes sharing
Is data-oriented	Is dialogue oriented	Likes networking
Talks at medium speed	Talks fast	Talks slowly
Thinks briefly, then speaks	Speech leads thought (thinks aloud)	Contemplates, then speaks briefly
Completes action chains	Completes human transactions	Harmonizes by doing things at appropriate times
Results oriented	Relationship-oriented	Harmony-oriented
Sticks to agenda	Roams	Often asks for "repeats"
Compromises to achieve deal	Tries to win argument	Compromises for future relations
Borrows and gives rarely	Borrows and gives freely	Borrows rarely, gives ritually
Minimizes power distance	Maximizes power distance	Observes fixed power distance
Respects officialdom	Seeks favors, pulls strings	Uses connections
Separates social and professional lives	Mixes social and professional lives	Connects social and professional lives
Deal based on products, facts, and figures	Deal based on liking the client	Deal based on harmony and appropriateness

Linear-Active	Multi-Active	Reactive
Written word important	Spoken word important	Face-to-face contact important
Contracts are binding	Contracts are ideal documents in an ideal world	Contracts are statements of intent and renegotiable
Quick responses to written communication	Responses to letters slow due to preference for spoken messages	Responses to letters slow due to need for lateral clearances
Short-term profit is desirable	Increasing the status of the organization is important	Long-term profit and increased market share are important
Likes short pauses between speech turns	Overlapping speech is acceptable	Likes long pauses between speech turns
Restrained body language	Unrestrained body language	Subtle body language
Rationalism and science dominate thinking	Religion retains strong influence	Ethics and philosophies (e.g., Confucianism) dominate thinking

Appendix B

Leadership Test

Each culture has its own concept of leadership and status. Top managers are respected and obeyed by their subordinates according to different criteria: education, achievement, birthright, wealth, and so forth.

Business leaders adopt a management style that is deemed appropriate to historical tradition and to deeply rooted national values.

   Descriptions of twenty-two such styles are given below. Identify each style with one of the listed nations. Words that would
give away the answer(s) have been replaced by dotted lines.

Arab Countries	Indonesia
Australia	Italy
Brazil	Japan
Canada	Korea
China	Netherlands
Denmark	Norway
Finland	Russia
France	Spain
Germany	Sweden
Hispanic America	United Kingdom
India	United States

1. ....leaders are often.........and people connected with royal
   families. There is consequently a lot of nepotism in......
   ....companies where sons, nephews, and brothers hold key
   positions. This applies particularly in the.........States. In
   other.........countries dictators influence business leadership;
   often the military is involved.

2. Nepotism is rife in traditional.........companies. Family members hold key positions and work in close unison. Policy is
   also dictated by the trade group, for example, fruit merchants
   and jewelers. These groups work in concert, often develop
   close personal relations (through intermarriage, etc.), and
   come to each other's support in difficult times.

3. ....top executives and middle managers are not always
   clearly distinguishable to foreigners. Managers of all levels
   mingle for decision making, and democratic procedures are
   mandatory. Though top managers can exert considerable
   pressure,.........are skillful in maintaining a decidedly con-

genial atmosphere in discussion. Horizontal communication is widespread and generally successful.

4. ....leadership symbolizes the vitality and audacity of the land of free enterprise. Management structure is pyramidical, with seniors driving and inspiring people under them..........are allowed to make individual decisions but usually within the framework of corporate restrictions. Managers are capable of teamwork and corporate spirit but value individual freedom more than company welfare. They are very mobile. If they make mistakes, they get fired.

5. ....managers are the least autocratic in the world and sit in the ring of executives consulting with everyone at that level and often with quite subordinate staff members as well. It is said..........managers wield power by appearing nonpowerful. This style, ubiquitous in..........and popular with.........., is hardly conducive to rapid decision making.

6. The class system persists to some extent in..........and in some companies' managers, though not entirely. Managers are autocratic and maintain considerable power distance between themselves and their staff. More common today, however, is the rather casual manager who sits just outside the ring of executives but is in close contact with them and well able to conduct effective supervision of their employees without interfering unduly with their daily routine.

7. ....leaders, like the French, are autocratic and charismatic. Unlike the French, they work less from logic than intuition and pride themselves on their personal influence on all their staff members. Having very powerful personalities, they are able to persuade and inspire at all levels. Nepotism is also common in many companies. Declamatory in style, ...managers often see their decisions as irreversible.

8. ....leadership is basically autocratic but shows more flexibility than Spanish, as managers mingle easily with staff and intersperse themselves at many levels. There are many "clan" and group interests in the southern half of the country, and loyalty to the leader is automatic and mandatory. In the largest cities, there is a growing tendency to select managers on merit. In the north professional competence is generally valued, though connections remain important.

9. In.........., authority is centered around the chief executive. Top managers, who have usually been groomed in one of the top business schools, are well trained, charismatic, and extremely autocratic. They often appear to consult with middle managers, technical staff, and even workers, but decisions are generally personal and orders top-down. Managers at this senior level are rarely fired when they make blunders.

10. The basic principle of..........management is that you put the most experienced, best-educated person at the top, and he or she meticulously instructs and guides his or her immediate inferior. Orders are passed down through the management structure in this manner. Though leadership is consequently hierarchical and autocratic, ...leaders do listen to suggestions "from the factory floor," as..........workers are generally well educated and inventive. In this way, consensus plays a part in..........business.

11. ....top executives have great power in conformity with Confucian hierarchy, but they actually have little involvement in the everyday affairs of the company. On appropriate occasions they initiate policies that are conveyed to middle managers and to the rank and file. Ideas often originate on the factory floor or with other lower-level sources. Signa-

tures are collected among workers and middle managers as suggestions, ideas, and inventions make their way up the company hierarchy. Many people are involved. Top executives take the final step in ratifying items that have won sufficient approval.

12. The leadership concept is undergoing profound changes in........... Efforts made by managers to promote business through official channels only are likely to founder on the rocks of bureaucracy and..........apathy. Key people, with their personal alliances, often bypass the "system" and achieve results.

13. Consensus is generally highly valued in.........., but in companies controlled by the state a leadership group (often invisible) will decide policy. In the developing expansion of capitalist-style companies, leaders with reputations of competence are emerging; also, locally elected officials (e.g., mayors) are becoming influential in the business sphere and may have only loose ties with the capital. In..........family businesses (and there are many), the senior male is the patriarch, and the usual nepotistic structure is observable.

14. Conglomerates control a lot of business in........... These were, and are, family-owned, and nepotism is very common, with all sons, brothers, nephews, and so forth holding key positions. The very size of these conglomerates has, however, necessitated the introduction of a class of professional managers. These are now ubiquitous and growing in importance. Decision making is therefore largely hybrid.

15. ....leaders are low-key (compared with Americans) but are often dynamic and action oriented. They normally sit in the ring of executives, with whom they confer democratically. A combination of professional competence and per-

sonal modesty makes them good leaders and, in international teams, good chairs.

16. ....managers, like Swedes, must sit in the ring with the "mates." From this position, once they have proven that they will not pull rank, they actually exert much more influence than their Swedish counterparts, as the semi-Americanized nature of..........business requires quick thinking and rapid decision making.

17. Leadership in most..........countries has traditionally been centered around a strong dictator, military figure, or, in some cases, dominant political parties. Nepotism is common, and staff are manipulated by a variety of persuasive methods ranging from (benign) paternalism to outright exploitation and coercion.

18. Leaders in..........have often been military officers or civilian strongmen ruling with the approval of the army. The huge size of the economy has in recent years generated a large professional class that regulates the business operations on a day-to-day basis. The volatility of the economy often necessitates state interference.

19. Leadership in..........is based on merit, competence, and achievement. Managers are vigorous and decisive, but consensus is mandatory, as there are many key players in the decision-making process. Long "..........debates" lead to action, taken at the top, but with constant reference to the ranks. Ideas from low levels are allowed to filter freely upward in the hierarchy.

20. In colonial times leadership came from the Dutch. Later, leadership was exercised principally by the military and was therefore autocratic. The indifferent nature of many..........to

the business process has, however, resulted in a lot of business management being entrusted to a resident Chinese professional class, who have the commercial know-how and international connections. Overseas Chinese shareholding in many..........companies encourages this situation.

21. ....leaders, like many British, exercise control from a position just outside and above the ring of middle managers, who are allowed to make day-to-day decisions. ....top executives have the reputation of being decisive at crunch time and do not hesitate to stand shoulder to shoulder with staff to help out in crises.

22. In democratic..........the boss is very much in the center of things, and staff enjoy access to him or her at most times. Middle managers' opinions are heard and acted upon in egalitarian fashion, but top executives rarely abandon responsibility and accountability.

Answers to "Leadership Test" can be found at
www.crossculture.com/imperative

Appendix C

National Traits

Odd One Out

In the following list of national characteristics, *one* in each case
is *atypical*. Try to identify it.

American   competitiveness, social envy, sociability,
materialism, sense of mission

Arab   morality, tolerance, patriotism, unity, tenacity

Australian   risk takers, honesty, respect for authority,
hospitality, cynicism

Austrian   class consciousness, strong sense of national identity, skilled in business, tradition, energy

Belgian	monarchical, conservatism, intransigence, pragmatism,, diligence
British	conformity, tradition, humor, diplomacy, insularity
Canadian	cultural awareness, tolerance, volatility, impartiality, tradition
Chinese	humility, thrift, gentleness, bluntness, trustworthiness
Czech	education, creativeness, aggressiveness, irony, diligence
Danish	tolerance, sense of humor, good listeners, shyness, social envy
Dutch	love of debate, laid-back style, thrift, pragmatism, industriousness
Finnish	group orientation, work ethic, reliability, stubbornness, guts
French	intelligence, kindness, humility, diplomacy, honesty
German	punctuality, drive, fidelity, tact, truthfulness
Hispanic American	humanity, volatility, compassion, teamwork, idealism
Indian	extroversion, creativity, caution in business, risk takers, eloquence
Indonesian	political restlessness, commercial ambitiousness, respect for elders, sense of shame, volatility
Italian	charisma, loyalty to family, loyalty to the Church, flexibility, extroversion
Japan	humility, intransigence, work ethic, sense of shame, tenacity

Malaysian	culturally aware, materialism, education, hierarchy, obedience
Norwegian	diligence, sense of humor, neighborliness, directness, stubbornness, compassion, melancholy, group orientation, emotion, patriotism
Portuguese	exuberance, theatricality, compassion, vision, sentiment
Russian	suspicion, impoliteness, warmth, idealism, caution
South African	cultural insensitivity, patriotism, future orientation, love of sports, hospitality
Spanish	generosity, vision, precision, sensitivity, loquacity
Swedish	thoroughness, decisiveness, honesty, justice, good taste
Swiss	love of business, daring, tenacity, neutrality, secretiveness
Thai	cheerfulness, antiroyalism, laid back, weak work ethic, pro-American
Vietnamese	tenacity, anti-Americanism, respect for the French, love of education, thrift

Answers to "National Traits" can be found at
www.crossculture.com/imperative

Appendix D

National Communication Styles

Communication Style and Nationality

Select one or two nations from among those listed on the next page for each attribute. Use each nation at least once.

patience
accepting of lies
scientific truth
white lies
fake anger
deceptive flexibility
stalling
sit-it-out tactics
high starting price

pretended naïveté

theatricality

exaggeration

understatement

saying what pleases

coded speech

ambiguous statements

rigid adherence to logic

playing devil's advocate

flattery

use of religion

rhetoric

sarcasm

silence

Arab Countries

Brazil

China

Finland

France

Germany

India

Indonesia

Italy

Japan

Netherlands

Russia

Spain

United Kingdom

United States

Answers to "National Communication Styles" can be found at
www.crossculture.com/imperative

Glossary

Akkadian   belonging to a region of ancient Mesopotamia (modern Iraq)

ASEAN (Association of Southeast Asian Nations)

Assalamu 'a laykum   "Peace be upon you." (Arabic)

australopithecine   an extinct human predecessor

biotechnology   the engineering and biological study of relationships between man and machines

cacique   an Indian chief in Latin America in colonial times

Cartesian   relating to René Descartes (1596–1650), French philosopher and mathematician

chaebol   Korean industrial or commercial conglomerate

chauvinism   very great and often unthinking admiration for one's country; proud and unreasonable belief that one's country is better than all others

Chung Kuo (the "Middle Kingdom")   What the Chinese call their country, reflecting their deep-seated certainty that China is central and all other countries are peripheral and that they are at the center of things, the place where it is all happening

313

coded speech   a particularly English way of speaking, where negative views are disguised in apparently polite terms

Confucianism   a Chinese way of thought that teaches one should
be loyal to one's family, friends, and rulers and treat others
as one would like to be treated; developed from the ideas of
Confucius (551–479 B.C.)

context-centered   dependent on the situation

core beliefs   basic concepts of a national group that have been
learned and internalized from an early age

cultural black hole (CBH)   an undiscussable core belief of such
intensity that it distorts other beliefs, views, or values

cultural habitat   a kind of "room" or "house" erected by a cultural
group containing all the beliefs, assumptions, and attitudes
of the group; by knowing and obeying the "house rules," a
visitor can overcome culture shock and achieve empathy

cultural imperialism   an attempt to impose the tenets of one's culture on others

cultural myopia   the inability to see another culture's points of view

cultural programming   the way a particular group of people or nationalities is trained from a very early age to internalize the
behavior and attitudes of the group

"cultural spectacles"   the way one's own core beliefs influence how
one views other cultures

culture   the customs, beliefs, values, art, and all the other products
of human thought made by a particular group of people at a
particular time

culture shock   the feeling of shock or of being disoriented one has
when one experiences a different and unfamiliar culture

cuneiform   wedge-shaped characters used in ancient Mesopotamian
writing

cyclic time   a concept of time as a "cycle" of recurring events, with
no beginning and no end

Cyrillic alphabet   used in Russian, Bulgarian, Serbian, and Ukrainian languages

data-oriented (culture)   a culture whose people gather information mainly through print and database sources

determinism   a doctrine that acts of the will, natural events, or social changes are determined by preceding causes

dharma   Hindu code of living, the individual's duty to conform to custom and the traditional rules of conduct for his or her particular caste, family, and profession

dialogue-oriented (culture)   a culture whose people gather information through direct contact with other people

double first   a university degree where one obtains a first class rating in two subjects

double truth/dual perception   two ways of looking at things: the immediate reality and the poetic whole

dreamtime (Aborigine)   time of creation

empathy   the ability to imagine oneself in the position of another person and so to share and understand that person's feelings

ethnocentrism   belief in the superiority of one's own ethnic group

Etruscan   an ancient language spoken in Tuscany and Umbria

Fertile Crescent   an area in the Near East arching from the Mediterranean coast in the west around the Syrian desert to Iraq in the east

GATT (General Agreement on Tariffs and Trade)

GDP (Gross Domestic Product)

Gemeinschaft   community, society, kinship group (German)

genetic code   the chemical basis of heredity

Gesellschaft   firm, company, business relationship (German)

guanxi   the linking of two people in a relationship of mutual dependence (Chinese)

hahn   Korean feeling of antipathy toward foreigners

Hegelian   relating to Georg W. F. Hegel (1770–1831), German philosopher who formulated the dialectic method

Hellenistic   referring to Greek history, culture, or art after the time
   of Alexander the Great (356–323 B.C.)

high-context (culture)   networking, dialogue-oriented culture

hiragana   Japanese native script or syllabary (48 syllables)

historicism   the belief that processes are at work in history that
   man can do little to alter

Homo sapiens   the only extant species of the genus Homo (man)

horizon (cultural)   one's worldview (limited)

ideograph   a (Chinese) character or symbol representing an idea
   or thing (alternative, "pictograph")

IMF (International Monetary Fund)

Kabuki   traditional, highly stylized form of Japanese theater where
   players use white face paint

kaisha   company, firm (Japanese)

kami   the way of the Divine, which is found in nature (Shinto/
   Japanese)

kanji   Chinese ideographic writing system

karma   the force produced by a person's actions in life that will
   influence him or her later or in future lives

katakana   Japanese native script or syllabary (48 syllables) used
   for formal documents

keiretsu   Japanese commercial conglomerate

kinematic   pertaining to motion

la dignidad del hombre   man's dignity

linear time   a concept of time as a 'line' of sequential events with
   the past behind us and the future in front

linear-active (culture)   a culture whose people are task-oriented and
   highly organized, preferring to do one thing at a time in the
   sequence shown in their appointment book

listening (culture)   a culture whose people listen well, never interrupt, and show great deference to others' opinions; they do
   not precipitate improvident action but allow ideas to mature

low-context (culture)   data-oriented culture, few oral contacts

mañana behavior   putting things off until tomorrow

médecins sans frontières   Doctors without Borders

MERCOSUR (Mercado Común del Sur, or Southern Common
       Market Agreement)   also known as the Treaty of Asunción,
       comprising Argentinia, Brazil, Paraguay, and Uruguay.

meritocracy   a social system that gives the highest positions to those
       with the most ability

mestizo   a person of mixed European and Indian ancestry

mindset alliance   empathy for another (culture), also a tactic

monochronic (culture)   a culture dominated by precision and pro-
       priety, preferring to concentrate on doing one thing at a time

monotheistic religion   worshipping only one God

multi-active (culture)   a culture whose people tend to do many
       things at once, often in an unplanned order, usually people-
       oriented, extroverted

NAFTA (North American Free Trade Agreement)

Noh   classical Japanese performance form

olvidados   "the forgotten people," persons disappearing or suf-
       fering under Latin American dictatorships

pachinko parlors   gambling establishments with pinball-like
       games

polychronic   someone who likes to do many things at once, often
       without precise planning

Por Diós y España   slogan of Spain, "for God and Spain"

power distance   a measure of the interpersonal power of influence
       between superior and subordinate as perceived by the latter,
       often determined by the national culture

PPP (Power Purchasing Parity)

pundonor   honor, dignity (Spanish)

Qu'ran (Koran)   the Muslim equivalent of the Bible

reactive (culture)   a culture whose people rarely initiate action or
       discussion, preferring first to listen to and establish the other's
       position, then react to it and formulate their own

ringi-sho   decision making through consensus (Japanese)

saudades   nostalgia, sentimentality (Portuguese)

Shogun   one of a line of military governors ruling Japan until the revolution of 1867–68

stereotyping   fixing a set of ideas about what a particular type of person or nationality is like, which is (wrongly) believed to be true in all cases

task-orientation   giving instructions or directives to colleagues or subordinates

torii gate   a simple gate at the entrance to a Shinto shrine. A Japaneses symbol for leaving the physical world and entering the spiritual world

UAE (United Arab Emirates)

uchi   home and hearth (Japanese)

values   standards or principles, ideas about the importance of certain qualities, especially those accepted by a particular group

wa   Japanese system of conciliatory relationship

web society   an interdependent society excelling in networking

Weltanschauung   worldview (German)

Weltschmerz   "world pain," i.e., depressed state (German)

yamato damashii   the spirit of Japan

Bibliography

Bradnock, Robert, and Roma Bradnock. 1995. *India Handbook, with Sri Lanka, Bhutan, and The Maldives.* Bath, UK: Trade & Travel Publications.

Chiarelli, Brunetto. 1995. "Man between Past and Future." *Mankind Quarterly.*

Clark, G. 1983. "Understanding the Japanese." Tokyo: Kinseido.

Coppens, Yves. 1994. "East Side Story: The Origin of Humankind." *Scientific American* (May).

Dahl, Oyvind. 1994. "Malagasy and other Time Concepts and Some Consequences for Communication." Centre for Intercultural Communication. Selected papers at Nordic Symposium, Stavanger, Norway.

Damon, W. 1999. "The Moral Development of Children." *Scientific American.*

Diamond, Jared. 1999. *Guns, Germs and Steel: The Fates of Human Societies.* Guilford, CT: Norton.

Engholm, Christopher. 1991. *When Business East Meets Business West: The Pacific Rim Guide to Practice & Protocol.* New York: John Wiley & Sons.

Fieg, John Paul. Revised by Elizabeth Mortlock. 1989. *A Common Core: Thais and Americans*. Yarmouth, ME: Intercultural Press.

Fisher, Glen. 1980. *International Negotiation: A Cross-Cultural Perspective*. Yarmouth, ME: Intercultural Press.

Fukuyama, Francis. 2000. *Great Disruption: Human Nature and the Reconstruction of Social Order*. New York: Touchstone Books.

———. 1996. *Trust: The Social Virtues and the Creation of Prosperity*. New York: Free Press.

———. 1993. *The End of History and the Last Man*. New York: Free Press.

Graubard, Mark. 1999. "The Biological Foundation of Culture." *Mankind Quarterly*.

Grinde, Bjorn. 2000. "Social Behaviour: Making the Best of the Human Condition." *Mankind Quarterly* XLI, no. 2.

Hall, Edward T., and Mildred Reed Hall. 1990. *Understanding Cultural Differences: Germans, French and Americans*. Yarmouth, ME: Intercultural Press.

———. 1983. *Hidden Differences: Studies in International Communication: How to Communicate with the Germans*. Hamburg: Stern Magazine/Gruner & Jahr.

Harries, Meirion, and Susie Harries. 1994. *Soldiers of the Sun: The Rise & Fall of the Imperial Japanese Army*. New York: Random House.

Harrison, Lawrence E., and Samuel P. Huntington, eds. 2001. *Culture Matters: How Values Shape Human Progress*. New York: Basic Books.

Hendry, Joy. 1993. *Wrapping Culture: Politeness, Presentation, and Power in Japan and Other Societies*. Oxford, UK: Clarendon Press.

Hofstede, Geert. 1984. *Culture's Consequences: International Differences in Work-Related Values*. Newbury Park, CA: Sage.

Holden, Nigel J. 1992. *Management, Language and Eurocommunication, 1992 and Beyond*. Manchester, UK: Institute for European Studies.

Huntington, Samuel P. 1996. *The Clash of Civilisations and the Remaking of World Order*. New York: Simon and Schuster.

Irwin, Harry. 1996. *Communicating with Asia: Understanding People & Customs*. St. Leonards NSW, Australia: Allen & Unwin.

Kulke, Hermann, and Dietmar Rothermund. 1990. *A History of India*. London: Routledge.

Kusy, Frank. 1987. *Cadogan Guides—India: Kathmandu Valley—Nepal*. Old Saybrook, CT: Globe Pequot Press.

Lewis, Richard D. 2000. *When Cultures Collide: Managing Successfully Across Cultures*. 2d edition. London: Nicholas Brealey Publishing.

———. 1998. *The Road from Wigan Pier; Memoirs of a Linguist*. Riversdown, Hampshire, UK: Transcreen Publications.

———. 1993. *Finland, Cultural Lone Wolf*. Helsinki: Otava.

Moberg, Gary P. 1988. *Animal Stress*. New York: Oxford University Press.

Morris, Desmond. 1985. *Bodywatching: A Field Guide on the Human Species*. London: Jonathan Cape.

National Geographic Desk Reference, The. 1999. Washington, DC: National Geographic Society.

Nydell, Margaret K. (Omar). 2002. *Understanding Arabs: A Guide for Westerners*. 3d ed. Yarmouth, ME: Intercultural Press.

Pearce, W. B., and K. Kang. 1987. *Acculturation and Communication Competence*. San Diego, CA: Academic Press.

Peers, Allison E. 1948. *Spain: A Companion to Spanish Studies*. London: Methuen.

Philip's Millennium Encyclopedia. 1999. London: George Philip.

Rearwin, David. *The Asia Business Book*. 1991. Yarmouth, ME: Intercultural Press.

Rees-Mogg, William. 1997. "Decline of the Past." The Times of London, January 30.

Reischauer, Edwin O. 1977. *The Japanese*. Cambridge, MA: Belknap Press.

Richerson, P. J., and R. Boyd. 1989. "The Role of Evolved Predispositions in Cultural Evolution." *Ethnology and Sociobiology*.

Richmond, Yale. In press. *From Nyet to Da: Understanding the Russians*. 3d edition. Yarmouth, ME: Intercultural Press.

Sapir, Edward. 1966. *Culture, Language and Personality: Selected Essays*. Berkeley: University of California Press.

Schneider, Susan, and Jean-Louis Bardoux. 1997. *Managing across Cultures*. Upper Saddle River, NJ: Prentice Hall.

Tan, Terry. 1992. *Culture Shock! Britain*. London: Kuperard.

Tarnas, Richard. 1991. *The Passion of the Western* Mind. New York: Random House.

Thompson, William I. 1985. *Pacific Shift*. New York: Bantam Doubleday Dell.

Trend, J. B. 1957. *Nations of the Modern World: Portugal*. London: Ernest Benn.

Whorf, Benjamin Lee. 1956. *Language, Thought and Reality*: *Selected Writing*. Cambridge, MA: Massachusetts Institute of Technology Press.

Zeldin, Theodore. 1995. *An Intimate History of Humanity*. New York: Harper Collins.

About the Author

Richard D. Lewis has been active in the fields of applied and anthropological linguistics for over thirty-five years. His work in several fields of communicative studies has involved him in the organization of courses and seminars for many of the world's leading industrial and financial companies.

In 1961 he pioneered the world's first English by Television series, produced by Suomen Television, and subsequently was script writer for the first BBC series, *Walter and Connie*, in 1962.

He has lived and worked in several European countries, where his clients included ABB, Allianz, Banco de España, Banque de France, Deutsche Bank, Ericsson, Fiat, Gillette, IBM, Mercedes Benz, Nestlé, Nokia, Saab, and Volvo.

He also spent five years in Japan, where he was tutor to Empress Michiko and other members of the Japanese Imperial Family. During this period, his services were requested by firms such as Nomura, Mitsubishi, Hitachi, Sanyo, Mitsui, and Nippon Steel.

More recently he has been heavily involved in the intercultural field, founding companies in France, Germany, Spain, Italy, and

Brazil, teaching communication skills in these countries as well as in Finland, Sweden, the United Kingdom, and the United States.

Mr. Lewis, who speaks ten European and two Asian languages, is currently chairman of Richard Lewis Communications plc, an international institute of language and cross-cultural training with offices in over a dozen countries. His recent book, *When Cultures Collide,* is regarded as the classic work on intercultural issues and was the Spring main selection of the U.S. Book of the Month Club in 1997.

Mr. Lewis was knighted by President Ahtisaari of Finland in March 1997.

Index

A

Aborigines (Australian), 2, 5, 7, 9, 236, 262, 267
Afghanistan, 17, 65, 119, 257, 282, 287, 290
Africa, xxiii, 3, 7, 9, 14–15, 43, 61, 126, 161, 200, 223, 249
Al Qaeda, 281
Albania, 255
Algeria, 43, 282
alliances with/against China—predictions:
    East and Southeast Asia, 251–53
    European Union, 254–55
    Islamic states, 253
    Pacific Rim, 255
    Russia, 253–54
American Dream, 106, 113, 119, 287
Americanization, 97, 191–92, 193, 201, 220, 221, 223
Anglo-Saxon invasion (of England), 2
Annan, Kofi, 63
apartheid, 126

Argentina, 76, 79, 86, 179, 290
Aristotle, 129, 195
Armenia, 255
ASEAN (Association of Southeast Nations), 66, 157, 164, 236, 238, 257
Asia-Pacific Economic Cooperation Group, 188
Asian model, 199, 204–05
    attitudes toward the West, 209–10
    Confucianism, 217–18, 221
    decision making, 214–15, 221
    face, 218–20, 221
    government control, 206–07
    leadership, concept of, 215–17, 221
    logic, 207–09
    mentality (the Asian mind), 205–06, 221
    mindset, 210–11
    negotiating, 211–14, 221
Asian Tigers, 192, 220, 223
Asianization, 193–95, 201, 204, 221, 222
Asoka (Emperor), 51

Augustine (Saint), 195
Australia, 7, 21, 232, 248, 262, 291
    Americanization of, 192
    cultural black hole of, 124
    cultural category of, 82, 268
    future course of vis-à-vis China, 255
    and Pacific Rim, 158, 163
australopithecines, 15
Austria, 268, 285
Azerbaijan, 254
Aztecs, 2, 9, 37, 86, 87, 88, 147, 262, 275

B

Bacon, Francis, 195
Bahrain, 43, 283
balance of power, East/West:
    ascendance of Asianization (or China), 152, 177–79, 221, 249–50, 269–70
    durability of Americanization (or Western values), 191, 221–22, 291–92
    hypotheses of some cross-culturalists, 199–200
Balkans, 59, 126, 262, 275
Baltic states, 23, 126, 257
Bangladesh, 25, 43, 44, 252, 269, 270
Belgium, 83, 191, 223, 268
belief in deity, persistence of, 29–32
Bergue, Augustin, 142
Bering Strait, 9, 88, 147
Berlin Wall, 287
Bin Laden, Osama, 280
Bin Mohamad, Datuk Seri Mahathir, 200
binocular/polyocular logic vs. monocular logic, 144–45
Boadicea, 1
Boer War, 2
Bosnia, 30, 254, 282

Boxer Rebellion, 141
Brahma-Vishnu-Shiva, 44–45
Brahmanas, 33
Brahmin caste, 45, 47
Brazil, 59, 79, 86, 179, 188, 269, 270, 290
Britain, 57, 153, 162, 174, 177, 204, 207, 232, 258, 269, 291
    Americanization of, 191, 192
    climate's effect on, 20–21
    cultural black hole of, 93, 122
    cultural category of, 67, 76, 81, 92, 268
    historical events in, 1–2, 3, 92
    as major power, 66
    Muslim (and Sikh) population in, 43, 50, 278–79, 281
    population density in, 174
Brunei, 252
Brundtland, Gro Harlem, 61–62
Buddhism, 30, 37, 53, 54, 59, 142, 153, 189, 233, 251, 253, 272
    background of, 51–52
    and business/social behavior, 52–53
Bulgaria, 59
business models, 239
    American, 191–92, 220, 291
    Asian, 199, 204–20
    Japanese, 192–93, 220
business/social behavior:
    of selected nationalities (through cultural spectacles), 93, 94–95, 96, 98–99, 100, 101–02, 103, 105, 106–07, 108–09, 110, 111–12
    of world-religion adherents, 40–42, 46–47, 49, 51, 52–53, 54–55, 59–60

C

Cambodia, xxiii, 37
Canada, 17, 177, 190 226, 227, 248, 249, 291

border with U.S., 113, 289
cultural category of, 83, 268
economic ranking of, 188, 269
and Pacific Rim, 158, 163, 166
Sikh/Overseas Chinese populations
in, 50, 190
Cartesian logic, 95, 131, 144
Catherine II, the Great, 162
Chad, 17, 43
Charles Martel, 274
Chechnya, xxvi, 30, 257, 282
Cheng Ho, 171
Chiang Kai-shek, 175
Chile, 158
China, xxv, 145, 151, 192, 193, 199,
206, 223, 289, 290, 292
civilization, longevity of, xxiv, 3, 9,
167–68, 187, 201, 236, 249
climate's effect on, 24
and collectivism, 138, 144, 154,
170, 175, 180
cultural black hole of, 121
cultural category of, 70
economic growth/ranking of, 157,
177–78, 268, 269
and globalization, 225, 227
inventions/discoveries made in,
168–70
as inward-looking, 171–73, 187,
249, 250, 269, 287
as major power, 66, 257
and Overseas Chinese, 164 (*see also*
under Hong Kong)
and Pacific Rim, 157, 163, 166
political situation in (1839–1976),
174–77
population of, 164, 168, 170–71,
174, 177, 178, 270
prospects for economic dominance
of, 177–79
reasons for decline of (1820–1952),
171–74

religion/philosophy of, 26, 30, 37,
51, 205, 206, 282
See also People's Republic of
China (PRC)
Chinese cultural traits, persistent:
collectivism, 186–87
Confucian tenets, 181
deference to age, 186
face, concept of, 182
guanxi system, 181–82
harmony, 183
hierarchy, 185
humility, 184
indirectness, 185–86
patience, 183–84
sense of nation/ethnocentrism, 188,
209, 225
virtue, 182
Chinese hegemony, preemptive considerations, 200, 221, 249–50, 269
Christianity, xxiv, 30, 37, 44, 47, 52, 61,
160, 201, 253, 272, 273, 274, 280
background of, 55–59
Churchill, Winston, 120
CIA/FBI, 287–88
Cid, El, 278
classifications of cultural types, overview of, 68–70
climate, influence of, 9, 14, 29, 158–
59, 233
on communication patterns, 18–22
effects of, 16–17, 22–26
generalizations about, 27
on human origins, 14–16
on work, 17–18
Clinton, Bill, 259
cognitive processes, basis of:
spoken language (native), 132, 133
written language (national), 132–37
See also under language
cognitive processes, East vs. West, 130–
31

changes in (national), possibility of,
    149–54
collective vs. individual, 137–44,
    153–54
and diversity of worldviews, 131–
    32
Cold War, 223
colonialism, xxiii–xxiv, 2, 79, 151, 179,
    209, 248–49, 258
Columbus, Christopher (Cristóbal
    Colón), 161, 248
communication styles:
    Asian vs. Western, 203, 221
    of selected nationalities (through
        cultural spectacles), 93, 94, 96,
        97–98, 99–100, 101, 103, 104,
        106, 108, 109–10, 111
Communism, 120, 175, 179, 233, 246,
    250, 291
    Communist Party, 59, 176, 177, 188
Confucianism, 26, 30, 52, 54, 79, 180,
    181, 185, 196, 200, 205, 206, 216,
    217–18
Confucius, 130, 170, 175, 184, 200,
    205, 216, 217, 247, 251
Congo, 17, 249
Constantine I (Emperor), 56
Copernicus, 195
Coppens, Yves, 14, 16
core beliefs of selected nationalities
    (through cultural spectacles), 92–93,
    94, 95–96, 97, 99, 101, 102–03, 104,
    106, 107, 109, 111, 243
corporations/multinationals:
    ABB, 193, 239
    AT&T, 193
    Coca-Cola, 230, 231
    DaimlerChrysler, 263
    Deutsche Telekom, 239
    Ericsson, 239
    General Electric, 230
    Hewlett-Packard, 239

    IBM, 230
    Levi Strauss, 193
    McDonald's, 193, 231
    Microsoft, 228
    Motorola, 193, 239
    Nestlé, 193, 239
    Nokia, 227, 239
    Samsung, 205
    Sonera, 239
    Sony, 205
    Unilever, 230, 239
    Virgin Group, 228
Cortés, Hernán, 86
Costa Rica, 17
Crimean War, 2
Croatia, 254, 257
Crusades, 6, 30, 31, 36, 277–78, 280,
    283
Cuba, 188, 287
cultural adaptation, 67, 68
    macrolevel divergence, 239, 240
    microlevel convergence, 240
    See also cultural diversity, manage-
        ment of
cultural black holes (CBHs), 93, 244
    by country, 121–25
    compared with cosmic black holes,
        116–17
    defined, 117
    examples of, 117–21
    state-induced, 126
cultural categories, 66, 67–70, 92, 130
    comparisons among, 76–85
    fusion of (case study, Mexico), 86–
        90
    linear-active, 67, 69, 70–71, 129–
        31, 137, 144–47, 151–52, 166,
        220, 266–69
    multi-active, 69, 70, 71–72, 130–
        31, 137, 146–47, 151–52, 166,
        220, 226, 266–69

reactive, 67, 69, 70, 73–75, 130–
    31, 137, 144–47, 151–52, 166,
    220, 226, 266–69
cultural diversity, management of, 236,
    262
    at national core-value level, 240–
        44
    at practical (business) level, 237–
        40
    See also cultural adaptation
cultural diversity, sources of, 7–12,
    130–32
cultural ecologies (historical civiliza-
    tions):
    Atlantic, 158, 161–62, 166
    Mediterranean, 158, 160–61
    Pacific (probably), 158, 162–66
    riverine, ancient, 158, 159–60
"cultural imperialism," 199, 204, 265
cultural integration, West/East (and rest
    of world), 149–54, 266–69
cultural myopia, 91–92, 112–14, 286
cultural programming (conditioning),
    national versions of, 6, 13–14, 29,
    91, 118, 235–36
Cultural Revolution, 176
cultural spectacles, self-assessments:
    Americans, 106–07
    Chinese, 180
    English, 92–94
    French, 95–97
    Germans, 99–101
    Italians, 102–04
    Japanese, 109–11
cultural spectacles, views of the other:
    Americans by Japanese, 107–09
    Americans by others, 241
    English by French, 94–95
    French by English, 97–99
    Germans by Italians, 101–02
    Germans by others, 242
    Italians by Germans, 104–06

Japanese by Americans, 111–12
culture-bound behavior. *See under* de-
    terminism
culture shock, 262, 263
culture survival vs. culture collapse, 236
cuneiform writing (Akkadian), 33
Cyril (Bishop), 34
Cyrillic alphabet, 34
Czech Republic (Czechoslovakia), 232,
    257, 287

D

Damon, W., 153
Darwin, Charles, xxii, 31, 162, 195
"Davos Culture," 199
democracies, Western-style and Asian/
    African, 258
Deng Xiaoping, 175, 177
Denmark, 192, 268
Descartes, René, 162, 195
determinism, xxii
    cultural (and national identity),
        xxiv–xxvi, 13–14, 130
    economic, xxi, xxii–xxiv
    genetic, xxi, xxii
Diamond, Jared, 35
Diaspora, 48

E

Eastern Orthodox Churches, 36, 37, 56,
    57, 59
economic statistics/rankings, 104, 157,
    177, 188–89, 268, 269
Economist, The, 58
Ecuador, 17
Egypt, 2, 25, 43, 48, 173
Eightfold Path (Buddhism), 52
Einstein, Albert, 125
El-Pacha, Izak (Imam), 279
Elizabeth I (Queen), xxiv
empathy, how to achieve, 264–66

with selected nationalities, 93–94,
   95, 97, 99, 100–01, 102, 104,
   105–06, 107, 109, 111, 112
empires, past:
   Belgian, 223, 249
   British, 95, 223, 248–49, 284, 287
   Chinese, 249
   Dutch, 223, 248–49
   French, 223, 248–49, 287
   German, 249
   Islamic Arab-Turkish, 246, 249
   Italian, 249
   Mongol, 173, 246, 249, 250
   Mughal, 284
   Ottoman, 275, 284
   Portuguese, 248–49, 285
   Roman, 33, 34, 56, 102, 160, 167,
      249, 272–73
   Spanish, 248–49, 285, 287
Eritrea/Ethiopia, 24, 249
Estonia, 257
Etruscan (language), 33
European Union (EU), 66, 68, 94, 236,
   238, 253, 254–55, 257, 268, 291

F

face, concept of, xxv, 87, 121, 143, 151,
   182, 207, 209, 218–20, 225
Falkland Islands, 119
feminine values, 127, 152, 153, 194–
   95, 197, 198, 200, 222, 267, 293
   and commonalities with Asian val-
      ues, 199, 221
Ferdinand (King), 161, 248
Fertile Crescent, 2, 3, 9, 35, 273
Fiji, 67
Finland, 17, 19, 26, 59, 81, 123, 153,
   218, 227, 268
Five Pillars of Islam, 38
Foch, Ferdinand (Marshal), 247, 248
Four Noble Truths (Buddhism), 52

France, xxiv, 59, 66, 95, 153, 161, 177,
   232, 254, 269, 291
   Americanization of, 192, 223
   climate's effect on, 16–17, 19
   cultural black hole of, 122, 123
   cultural category of, 67, 82, 92, 268
   Muslim population in, 43, 278
Franklin, Benjamin, 162
Frederick II, the Great, 162
French Revolution, 31
Freud, Sigmund, 195
Fukuyama, Francis, 258
future trends, guide for forecasting,
   245–46
   cultural traits as, 246–47
   list of famous predictions, 248

G

Galileo, 195
Gama, Vasco da, 161
Gandhi, Indira, 51
Gandhi, Mohandas K. (Mahatma), 47
Gates, Bill, 200
GATT (General Agreement on Tariffs
   and Trade), 97, 238
generational change vs. cultural change,
   151, 220, 222, 234
Genghis Khan, 24
geography, 9, 14, 27, 187, 233, 289
Georgia, 255
Germany, 66, 105, 153, 224, 254
   Americanization of, 191, 192, 223
   climate's effect on, 20
   cultural black hole of, 125
   cultural category of, 67, 71, 130,
      268
   economic ranking of, 157, 269
   Muslim population in, 279
   and World Wars I and II, 233, 291
global business competitiveness,
   rankings in (2002), 58–59

globalization (of business), xxvi, 12, 17,
    30, 67–68, 76, 149, 200, 220, 238,
    289
  concepts of, 153
  defined, 224
  different interpretations of, 225,
    226–27
  and information technology, 163,
    224, 227–28
  values of, 225
globalization (of culture). *See* standardization of culture
globalized ethics vs. national/state religions, 60–63
Govind Singh (Guru), 50
Great Leap Forward, 176
Greece, 19, 23, 82, 192, 207
  ancient, xxiv, 160, 167, 196, 276,
    291
Grenada, 119
Grove, Andy, 162
Guatemala, 17
Guizot, Francois, 179
Gulf Arabs/States, 37–38, 40, 284
Gulf War, 30
Gutenberg, Johannes, 162

H

Haiti, 119
Hall, Edward T., xxiv, 69
Harrison, Lawrence, xxiv
Hawking, Stephen, 116, 126
Hegelian logic, 131
hieroglyphic inscriptions, 33
Hinduism, 30, 37, 49, 51, 52, 53, 59,
    118, 233, 251, 272
  background of, 44–46
  and business/social behavior, 46–47
hiragana script, 134, 135
Hirohito (Emperor), 35
history, 9, 14, 27, 29, 65, 167, 233, 245,

    247, 262
  masculine bias of, 195–97
  partial version of, 1–3
  rewriting of, xxiv–xxv, 119–20
Hofstede, Geert, xxiv, 69, 194
hominids, 14–15
Homo erectus, 7
Homo sapiens, xxii, 7
Hong Kong, xxiii, 175, 290
  Asian Tiger/economic success of,
    66, 192, 225
  devolution to PRC, with Overseas
    Chinese, 164, 174, 188–89, 190,
    250
  linear-active influence on wealth
    creation in, 79, 152, 268
  and negotiating, 211, 212
Hopi view of time, 147–49
Hoyle, Fred, 116
Human Development Index (U.N.), 268
Hume, David, 195
Hungarian revolt, 287
Huntington, Samuel, xxiv, 69, 199, 200,
    201, 249
Hussein, Saddam, 224

I

ideographic writing (pictographs), 133–
    35, 169, 268
IMF (International Monetary Fund),
    289
India, xxvi, 49, 126, 149, 161, 192, 200,
    215, 216, 219, 225, 248, 250, 257,
    289
  climate's effect on, 25
  cultural category of, 83
  culture, longevity of, xxiv, 201,
    236, 251
  democracy, version of, 258
  and economic growth, 269, 270
  films made in, 232

future course of vis-à-vis China,
251–52
Hinduism/Buddhism in, 37, 44, 45,
51, 251
Muslim adherents in, 43, 283, 284
Indian Mutiny, 50
Indonesia, 192, 193, 283, 286, 290
climate's effect on, 17, 21
and colonialism, xxiii, 249
conflict in, xxvi, 30, 188, 206, 257,
282
freer form of Islam in, 37, 43
future course of vis-à-vis China,
252–53
and Overseas Chinese, 164, 189
and Pacific Rim, 163
population growth of, 269, 270
Industrial Revolution, 122, 162, 201,
227, 270
Innocent III (Pope), 277
intellectual property rights, 136, 180
International Conference on Population
and Development (U.N.) (1994), 61
International Institute for Management
Development, 58
international teams (cross-cultural business), 149–50, 151, 229, 263, 264
Interpol, 238
Inuit culture, 26, 234, 236, 262
Iran, 34, 36, 43, 65, 80, 253, 285, 286
Iranian Revolution, 281
Iraq, 43, 65, 188, 253, 285
Ireland, 30, 57, 59, 192, 268, 278
Iron Curtain, 225
Islam, 30, 43, 47, 52, 55, 59, 61, 118,
153, 189, 233, 249, 272, 280
business behavior in, 41–42
contrasted with West, 39
failure of to achieve modernity,
283–86
historical background of, 272–73

internal problems of, 37, 281, 282–
83
and Moorish legacy in Europe,
160–61, 274–76
social behavior in, 40–41
tenets of faith/Arab values, 37–38,
43
Islamic extremism/fundamentalism,
278, 281–82, 283, 286
Islamic Granada (Iberia), 161, 273, 275,
280
Israel, 37, 47, 114, 255
Israeli-Palestinian conflict, xxvi, 30,
257, 262
IT (Information Technology) Revolution, 162, 186, 187, 199, 201, 224,
227–28, 247
Italy, 19, 56, 59, 82, 104, 218, 232, 269,
279, 283, 291
Americanization of, 192, 223
cultural black hole of, 123
cultural category of, 67, 268
Muslim population in, 279
and the Renaissance, 161, 274
view of "truth," 131, 207

J

Jainism, 49, 52
Japan, xxiv, 14, 21, 66, 110, 112, 138,
145, 174, 178, 199, 209, 215, 225,
232, 252, 257, 289
business model of, 192–93
Confucian behavior in, 26, 205, 206
cultural black hole of, 121, 182, 219
cultural category of, 67, 70, 268
economic miracle/ranking of, 177,
179, 193, 223, 246, 269, 270
future course of vis-à-vis China,
251
globalization strategy of, 226
isolation of prior to 1853, 109, 111,
171–72, 251

and negotiating, 211, 212
and Pacific Rim, 157, 163, 164, 166
parliamentary democracy of, 109, 258
population size/ranking of, 163, 174
and relationship with China, 200, 250
religions of, 30, 37, 51, 54, 142, 251, 282
and World War II, 3, 233, 251, 287
writing system of, 133–35, 174, 251
Jefferson, Thomas, 162
John (King), 275
Jordan, 43
Joyce, James, 233
Judaism, 37, 47–48, 55, 160, 196, 272, 273, 274

K

kanji writing system, 133–35
Kant, Immanuel, 195
karma, 45, 46, 51, 215
Kashmir, xxvi, 282
katakana script, 137
Kazakhstan, 254
Kemal Ataturk, 34–35, 233
Kennedy, John F., 37, 287
Khomeini, Ruholla Mussaui (Ayatollah), 36
King James Version, 34
Kluckhohn, Florence, 69
Korea, 21, 121, 133, 154, 174, 182, 216, 226, 250, 257, 287
    Asian Tiger/economic success of, 192, 225, 269, 270
    Confucian tenets/behavior in, 26, 205, 206
    cultural category of, 67, 70
    future course of vis-à-vis China, 252

Korean War, 65, 119, 223
North Korea, 206, 250
and Pacific Rim, 157, 163, 164
religion of, 30, 51
South Korea, 179, 192, 206
Kosovo, xxvi, 30, 255, 257, 282
Kublai Khan, 169
Küng, Hans, 62–63
Kuwait, 43, 65, 119, 224, 283, 288
Kyrgyzstan, 254

L

Landor, Henry Savage, 141
language, 9, 14, 29, 233
    as determiner of thought patterns, 132–33
    as factor in religions, 32–34
    and social practices, mutual reinforcement of, 138–44
languages associated with world religions:
    Arabic, 33
    Avestan, 33
    Chinese, 33
    Gothic, 33
    Hebrew, 33
    Latin/Greek, 33, 34
    Sanskrit, 34, 252
    Urdu, 34
Lao-tzu, 130
Laos, xxiii
Lapp culture, 262
Lascaux/Altamira caves, 5
leadership, hierarchy vs. meritocracy, 215–17
Lebanon, 43
Lee Kuan Yew, 79
legal action/procedures as contrary to Confucianism, 143, 152, 206–07
Libya, 43
Lincoln, Abraham, xxiv

linear-active cultures. *See under* cultural categories
Lions Clubs, 238
Locke, John, 162, 195
logic and reasoning:
    (East) Asian vs. Western, 144–46, 207–09, 219
    multi-active, 146–47
Louis VII (King), 277
Louis XIV (King), 161–62
Luther, Martin, 34, 195
Luxembourg, 59, 268

M

Macedonia, 255, 257
Madagascar, 148
Mafia, 104, 259
Magellan, Ferdinand, 161
Magna Carta, 201, 275
Malaysia, xxiii, 50, 192, 200, 206, 227, 253, 286, 290
    chief religion of, 43, 252
    and Overseas Chinese, 164, 189
Malraux, André, 95
Malta, 23
Manchuria, 21
Manchurian Incident, 174
Mandela, Nelson, 126
Mao Zedong, 175, 176, 177
Maori culture, 179, 236
Marcos, Ferdinand, 258
Marshall Plan, 63, 191, 223
Marx, Karl, 31, 162, 195
masculine values, 194–95, 197, 200
Mauritania, 43
Mayflower, 2
McRae, Hamish, 292
Meiji era, 251
MERCOSUR (Common Market of the South), 66, 238, 257
Mesoamerica, 35

Mesopotamia, 2
Methodius (Bishop), 34
Mexico, 130, 158, 163, 177, 269, 270, 275
    cultural black hole of, 124–25
    Mexican mindset, case study, 86–90, 147
Michiko (Empress), 63
"Middle Kingdom" (*Chung Kuo*), 121, 171, 172–73, 175
"Middle Way," 52, 153
Milton, John, 162
mindset, Asian vs. Western, 210–11
Mongolia, 21, 24
Morocco, 43
Morris, Ivan, 142
Muhammad, 31, 273, 280
multi-active cultures. *See under* cultural categories
Muslim populations in the West, 43, 278–79
Myanmar (formerly Burma), xxiii, 51

N

NAFTA (North American Free Trade Agreement), 66, 236, 238, 257
Namibia, 257
Nanak (Guru), 50
Napoleon, xxiv, 96
national conflicts vs. cultural conflicts, 65–67
national identity, concept of, xxv–xxvi
nation-states, survival of (prediction), 257, 261
Native American tribes, 2, 7, 9, 147, 236, 262
NATO (North American Treaty Organization), 236
Nazism, 120, 126, 291
negotiating, Asian vs. Western, 211–14
Nepal, 44, 51

Netherlands, 14, 36, 57, 59, 67, 82, 153, 174, 191, 192, 268, 278
New Zealand, 21, 158, 236, 248–49, 255, 268, 291
Newton, Isaac, 195
Nietzsche, Friedrich, 30, 31, 195
Nigeria, 269, 270
Nisbett, Richard, 135, 136
Nixon, Richard, 259
Norman Conquest, 1, 2, 92
Norway, xxv, 22, 82, 268

O

oceans and seas:
    Atlantic, 15, 20, 159, 161
    Black Sea, 17, 249, 285
    Indian, 171, 285
    Mediterranean Sea, 19, 20, 160, 285
    Pacific, 159, 163, 164, 166, 249, 287
Old Testament, 31, 274
Oman, 43
Opium War, 172, 174
organizational patterns, Asian vs. Western, 204, 221
Overseas Chinese, 152, 164, 188–90, 250

P

Pacific Rim, 157–58, 162–66, 255
Pakistan, xxvi, 43, 44, 219, 225, 252, 253, 269, 270, 283
Palestine, 43, 48, 273, 282
Panama, 119
Papua New Guinea, 262
Parliament of the World's Religions (1993), 63
Paul (the Apostle), 55, 195
Pearl Harbor, 287
People's Republic of China (PRC), 164, 189, 190, 212, 257. *See also* China
Perry, Matthew (Commodore), 140
Philippines, 21, 43, 70, 163, 164, 189, 192, 227, 252, 282, 286
Plato, 129, 195
Poland, 20, 232
Polo, Marco, 169
Polynesia, 7, 35, 207
population figures/rankings, 78, 152, 163, 166, 269
    China, 168, 170–71, 174, 177
    Islamic countries, 43
    Jains, 49
    Muslims in the West, 43, 278–79
    Overseas Chinese, 188–89
    Sikhs, 50
Portugal, 20, 23, 56, 76
predictions about the future:
    alliances with/against China, 251–55
    Asia and Latin America, 269–70
    Chinese dominance, 249–50, 268–69
    list of famous, 248
    role of U.S., 258–59
    survival of nation-states, 257
    triumph (or not) of Western-style democracy, 258
Protestantism, 31, 36, 37, 56–59, 197, 291
    view of society, 60
Putin, Vladimir, 288
Pyramids, 160

Q

Qatar, 43, 283
Qur'an (Koran), 37, 273, 286

R

reactive cultures. *See under* cultural categories

Rees-Mogg, William, 200
religions, world. *See* specific faith
religious beliefs, factors in the influence
     of, 9
     existence of a core country, 39
     historical events, 36
     institution of established/state reli-
          gions, 35–36, 233
     language, 32–34
     political link, 34–35
Renaissance, xxiv, 129, 161, 201, 270,
     274, 276, 283, 291
Richard I, the Lionheart, 277
Rift Valley, 15
rivers:
     Amazon, 262
     Euphrates, 158, 159, 273
     Indus, 158, 159
     Nile, 158, 159
     Tigris, 158, 159, 273
     Yangtze, 24, 168, 176, 188
     Yellow, 158, 159, 168
Roman Catholicism, 31, 36, 37, 56–57,
     233, 249, 280
     view of society, 60
Roman invasion (of Britain), 1, 2
Rotary Clubs, 238
Russia (Russian Federation), 17, 65,
     163, 166, 176, 177, 179, 207, 225,
     250, 257, 262, 287, 289
     cultural black hole of, 123–24
     cultural category of, 67, 82
     and Eastern Orthodox Church, 36,
          37, 59
     future course of vis-à-vis China,
          253–54
     Siberia, 24, 158, 253
     See also Soviet Union (former)
Russian Revolution (1917), 179
Russo-Finnish War, 257
Rwanda, 7

S

Safavid dynasty, 284
Saladin, 277
Samuelson, Robert, 291
Sankara, 51
Saudi Arabia, 17, 36, 37, 43, 283, 285
Schengen Agreement, 238
Sen, Amartya, 63
September 11, 2001, 29, 30, 113, 118,
     146, 271–72, 274, 279, 280, 282,
     287, 290
     and future of the West, 291–92
     lesson of, 286–91
Serbia, xxvi, 59, 254
Seven Wonders of the Ancient World,
     160
Shiism, 37, 278, 279, 284–85
Shinto, 53–55, 272
Sicily, xxv, 19, 23, 87, 219
Siddhartha Gautama (the Buddha), 49,
     51
Sikhism, 50–51
Singapore, xxiii, 14, 17, 50, 205, 206,
     211, 212
     Asian Tiger/economic success of,
          59, 66, 179, 192, 225
     linear-active influence on wealth
          creation in, 79, 152, 268
     as Overseas Chinese, 164, 189, 250
Slovakia, 257
Slovenia, 257
social practices/behavior. *See* business/
     social behavior
Somalia, 24, 282
Soviet Union (former), 31, 120, 224,
     250, 254, 288. *See also* Russia (Rus-
     sian Federation)
Spain, xxiv, 19, 36, 56, 86, 124, 192,
     218, 279
     cultural category of, 76, 82
     economic ranking of, 59, 269

and Moorish empire, 161, 275, 284
    regional diversity of, 24
Spanish Inquisition, 280
Special Economic Zones (SEZs) (main-
    land China), 164
Sri Lanka, 44, 51
Stalin, Joseph, 123, 176
standardization of culture, 12
    and cultural diversity, 229–30
    and cultural (national) values, 240–
        44
    and education systems, 232
    and factors affecting rate of change,
        233
    generational change vs. cultural
        change, 234
    and IT Revolution, 224
    and the media, 230–32
    and persistence of national cultures,
        234–36
Stone Age, 153
Stonehenge, 1
Sudan, 43
Sukarno, 189
Suleiman I, the Magnificent, 284
Sun Tzu, 214
Sunnism, 37, 278, 279, 284–85
Sweden, xxv, 81, 122, 130, 138, 153,
    192, 194, 227, 268
Switzerland, 204, 268
Syria, 43, 114

T

Taiwan, 79, 145, 205, 206, 227, 250, 257
    Asian Tiger/economic success of,
        66, 179, 192, 225
    as Overseas Chinese, 164, 189, 190
Taliban, 280, 281
Talmud, 48
Tamerlane, 24
Tang Dynasty, 170

Tarnas, Richard, 195, 196, 197, 198
Tasmania, 7
Teilhard de Chardin, Pierre, 62
Thailand, 37, 51, 149, 154, 192, 206,
    209, 212, 227, 257, 275
    future course of vis-à-vis China,
        252
    and Overseas Chinese, 164, 189
Thatcher, Margaret, 119, 248
Thirty Years War, 2
Tibet, 37, 51, 79, 250
time, concepts of:
    as cyclical, 87, 149, 151
    Asian, 147
    Hopi, 147–49
    Mexican, 89–90
Tito (Marshal) (Josip Broz), 59
Tokugawa, Ieyasu (Shogun), 140
Tonnies, Ferdinand, 69
Torah, 48
Trompenaars, Fons, 69
Truman, Harry, 120
truth/reality, Asian vs. Western views
    of, 131–32
Tunisia, 43
Turkey, 23, 34, 37, 43, 80, 253, 254,
    255, 283, 286
Turkmenistan, 254

U

United Arab Emirates (UAE), 43
United Kingdom (UK). See Britain
United Nations, 63, 187
United States, 9, 14, 17, 21, 31, 50, 65,
    66, 86, 113, 162, 167, 178, 200, 204,
    226, 236, 254, 270, 283
    "Americanization" as lifestyle of,
        192, 220
    cultural black hole of, 119, 123
    cultural category of, 82, 268
    as culturally insensitive, 287, 289
    democracy, version of, 258–59

economic ranking of, 59, 171, 177, 268, 269
and illusion of isolation, 187, 287
as masculine society, 194
media/films of, 231–32
Muslim population in, 43, 279, 281
and Overseas Chinese, 189, 190
on Pacific Rim (California), 157, 158, 163, 164, 166
as product and epitome of Western civilization, 291–92
Protestant-ethic way of life, 26, 57–58, 106
as sole superpower/world police-man, 30, 107, 224, 259, 282, 287
WTC as symbol of, 290
universal traits (innate, age-old), xxii, 3–7, 153, 154, 266, 270
as congruent with Asian values, 153, 154
Urban II (Pope), 277
Uzbekistan, 254

V

values, Asian vs. Western, 202, 221
imminent fusion of, 198–201
need for integration of, 266–69
and Western moral crisis, 153–54, 197–98, 210, 266–67
Vardhamana (Mahavira), 49
Vedism/Vedic scripts, 44, 45
Vietnam, xxiii, 133, 154, 163, 182, 192, 206, 212, 250
cultural category of, 79
future course of vis-à-vis China, 252

religion of, 30, 51
Vietnam War, 65, 76, 119, 223, 257, 287
Viking incursions (into Britain), 2
von Weizsäcker, Richard, 63

W

Washington, George, xxiv
Watson, Thomas, 227, 247, 248
Whorf, Benjamin Lee, 147
World Trade Center (WTC), 288, 290
World Trade Organization, 187
World War I, 2, 50, 65, 117, 141, 225, 253, 291
World War II, 2, 3, 55, 63, 65, 120, 179, 193, 225, 233, 251, 253, 291
writing systems, impact of:
on cognitive processes, 132–35
on verbal vs. spatial/visual skills, 135–37
Wulfila (Bishop), 33

Y

Yayoi culture, 54
Yemen, 43, 283
Yugoslavia, 30, 65, 82

Z

Zen, 153, 208
Zhou Enlai, 176
Zionist movement, 48, 118
Zoroastrianism, 33